Combat Medic
World War II

John Kerner, M.D.

iBooks
Habent Sua Fata Libelli

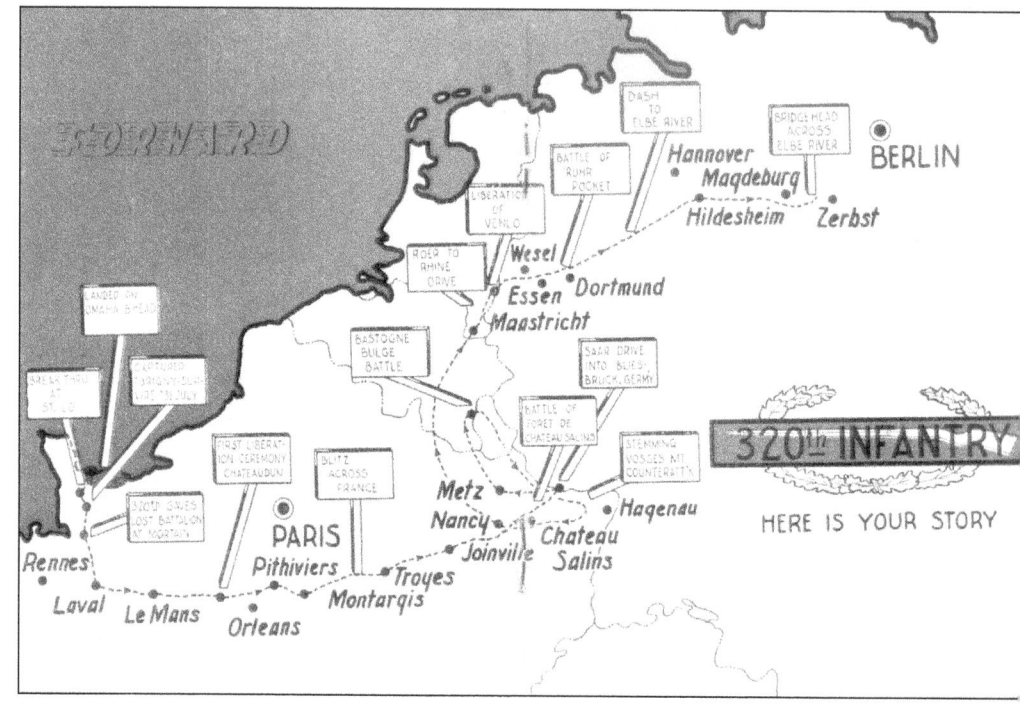

Combat Medic
World War II

John Kerner, M.D.

iBooks
1230 Park Avenue
New York, New York 10128
Tel: 212-427-7139
bricktower@aol.com • www.BrickTowerPress.com

All rights reserved under the
International and Pan-American Copyright Conventions.
Printed in the United States by J. Boylston & Company, Publishers, New York.
No part of this publication may be reproduced, stored in a retrieval system, or transmitted in any form or by any means, electronic, or otherwise, without the prior written permission of the copyright holder.
The iBooks colophon is a trademark of
J. Boylston & Company, Publishers.

Library of Congress Cataloging-in-Publication Data

Kerner, John.
Combat Medic, World War II
p. cm.

1. Biography. 2. Medical—History. 3. Women's Health. 4. World War II Nonfiction, I. Title.

ISBN-13: 978-1-59687-456-5, Trade Paper

Copyright © 2002 by John Kerner, M.D.
Cover design by Ryan Kerner
Second Printing, September 2012

for Gwen

Table of Contents

Acknowledgments viii
Prologue. ix
Chapter 1   Called Up 1
Chapter 2   Training 7
Chapter 3   On Leave 17
Chapter 4   The Voyage Over 21
Chapter 5   Bodmin 31
Chapter 6   Invasion 41
Chapter 7   Organization. 53
Chapter 8   Battalion Surgeon 57
Chapter 9   Childbirth 71
Chapter 10   The Men of The Second Battalion 77
Chapter 11   Mortain 87
Chapter 12   Letter to Dorothy 93
Chapter 13   Le Mans 95
Chapter 14   Chateaudun 99
Chapter 15   Travel Across France 107
Chapter 16   Nancy 115
Chapter 17   Lorraine 127
Chapter 18   Bastogne 135
Chapter 19   Roer 147
Chapter 20   Paris 161
Chapter 21   Rhine 173
Chapter 22   To Meet The Russians 181
Chapter 23   Occupation 191
Chapter 24   Agi 209
Chapter 25   Norfolk 223
Chapter 26   Lucky Strike 239
Chapter 27   Home 253
Afterthoughts 265

Acknowledgments

During World War II, I wrote a large number of letters to various members of my family. Fortunately they were saved. Some fifty years later, for the first time, I began to read the letters and found that they might well provide a framework for either a novel or a memoir. I was encouraged in my writing by a professor of history at UC Santa Cruz. After I had written some, my patient Karen Wood convinced me to continue the work as a memoir. She became my first editor. Much like other authors of memoirs, I at first thought these efforts would appeal mostly to family and friends. However, when I sent copies to authors and agents, I was surprised to find that they thought this was a story suitable for publication. A particular stimulus was the positive reaction of my teacher Professor Barth Marshall.

I am indebted to Tom Rosenberg who recommended that I talk with Don Ellis of the Creative Arts Book Company. Mr. Ellis was interested and proceeded to expedite the project of preparing this memoir for publication. There were many people whose advice was most helpful: My cousin Frances Brodsky, my friends Doctor Al Ackerman, Carole Becker, Merla Zellerbach, and of course, my wife Gwen. However, I am most indebted to Paul Samuelson whose editing skills helped educate me and to the production staff at Creative Arts, who put this work together.

Prologue

In the 1930s, there was great competition to get into medical schools in California. There were only three first class programs: UC, Stanford, and USC. Those were still depression years and the cost of graduate education was a significant factor. The University of California's program was by far the least expensive and certainly one of the best in the country. To get into the class of fifty there were three considerations: first, over-all grades; second, grades in required courses; and third, the score in the medical aptitude test. Those who wanted to get to medical school concentrated on their studies and left little time for recreation. During vacations, they often worked to help pay for their education. Even when accepted, there was great competition, for a significant percent of the students were dropped from the school even though the country needed doctors for the war effort. This whole process resulted in superbly educated students in things medical but students not prepared for the stresses that were to face them in World War II.

When I was called to duty on very short notice, I at first thought that I would be assigned to a hospital somewhere. After all, I was a top student. I ended up in combat and even more incongruously in charge of soldiers for whose actions and lives I was responsible. Along the way, I had to mature in ways for which I had had no real preparation. The only good part was that I met some wonderful women. I hardly recognized myself when I returned home. While we were being shot at in Europe, life at home had continued with the only problem being rationing. The most difficult adjustment for me was that people at home had no concept of what fighting men had gone through.

This book is a memoir of those times constructed with many of my letters which were saved, and with vivid memories. Because of the time lapse, there may be a few errors, but essentially the events are true.

Combat Medic

Chapter 1

Called Up

December 24, 1943

I was called up for active duty by the U.S. Army on December 24, 1943. It was a cold, gray day, and I was scrubbing for surgery in the old U.C. Hospital up on Parnassus Avenue in San Francisco. The sinks were the large, deep sort used in scrub rooms everywhere, but in one respect, they were unique, for above them were huge windows facing northward to the Bay and the Golden Gate.

The professor was talking about the patient upon whom we were about to operate, a woman in her late forties who had been having uncontrollable vaginal bleeding due to fibroids of her uterus. She was to have her uterus removed, and the professor was discussing the wisdom of also removing the ovaries to reduce the risk of ovarian cancer in the future, versus the advantage of keeping the ovaries for a source of estrogen. (Estrogen supplementation was just beginning to be used at that time.)

The professor, Dr. Traut, was a martinet, but he was the best teacher I had ever had and a skilled surgeon. (He played a major role in developing the Pap smear test that was to make possible early detection of cervical cancer and to save of thousands of women's lives.) He was a big, blond man, and we called him Dr.

Traut or Sir and hardly ever spoke to him unless he asked us to. During this procedure, I was watching a long convoy of merchant ships and destroyers making its way toward the War in the Pacific.

My best friend, Skip Jarvis, came into the operating room. Skip was one year ahead of me in the residency program. The professor had marked him as the man he most wanted to keep along with me as second choice, when the rest went to the military. Our house staff at that time consisted of three interns, three first year residents, two second year, and one senior. The university had permitted one or two deferrals per department. When Skip volunteered later for the Marines, Dr. Traut never forgave him and would not take him back after the war.

That Skip came unbidden into the operating room was in itself quite unusual: no one not authorized by the professor was to be found in Dr. Traut's operating rooms. Skip told the professor that I had received what appeared to be an important telegram. I asked if it could be read to me, and the professor told Skip to go ahead.

Skip read: PROCEED DECEMBER TWENTY SIX CARLISLE BARRACKS PENNSYLVANIA REPORT COMMANDANT MEDICAL FIELD SERVICE SCHOOL FOR TEMPORARY DUTY APPROXIMATELY SIX WEEKS THENCE DENVER COLORADO REPORT COMMANDING OFFICER GENERAL FITZSIMMONS GENERAL HOSPITAL FOR TEMPORARY DUTY PENDING FURTHER ORDERS FORMAL ORDERS AWAIT YOU AT DUTY STATION THIS TELEGRAM AUTHORITY.

Other members of my class had already been called up, but, although I was a reserve officer, I thought that I had been deferred to maintain the teaching program at U.C. In any event, there it was. The professor said, "You have things to do, John. Go do them. Jarvis, take John's place."

Completely unprepared for these orders, I had to get ready to go in forty-eight hours, and the next day was Christmas. Fortunately for me, my friend Sam Ziegler was in town from the

Pacific, where he was stationed with an Army group in China. I had known Sam since childhood. He was a neat, orderly young man who, much to the surprise of his friends, volunteered shortly after Pearl Harbor. Somehow, he had ended up in Mainland China working with a group of Americans who were trying to coordinate American efforts with the Chinese against the Japanese. He was sent back to San Francisco on a mission which he did not want to discuss, after which he was to return to the war theater.

Sam was the only person I knew who knew anything about Army procedures, and he told me what to do. First, I called a transportation officer in the Presidio, who got me on a train to Pennsylvania with no trouble, despite the holiday rush. Then I borrowed the O. B. car—the professor didn't know that we still had it. It had been used for home deliveries which were stopped during the war. I picked up Sam, and we went to the Presidio PX for service uniforms. I was outfitted with G.I. clothes: underwear, socks, shirts, ties, G.I. shirts, pants, and, shoes—the same clothes that enlisted men wore. This expedition turned out to be one of the most useful I had ever made.

Sam and I then went downtown to Hastings, where I was fitted with dress uniforms, a "green" shirt, "green" jacket and slacks. That was the color of dress army uniforms, really a greenish khaki. I also got "pink" slacks. These really were a light tan. They said all of these would be ready by 4:00 P. M., and even though this was the day before Christmas, they were ready. I had just finished spending more money than I had spent on any day of my life.

Now came the hard part. I had to let my family and Chris in on the news. I had been growing closer to Chris, but I was not sure that I loved her. She was attractive, bright, and great fun to be with. Her family background was French, and she was secretary to one of the senior faculty members, Ned Overstreet, and I had just convinced her to leave her job and to go back to college to finish and get a degree. Young residents in training in gynecology and obstetrics at that time were told not to consider marriage until they were finished with their training. I was trying to be sure to follow the "party line." The professor was strict.

My family was another matter. My father was a self-made man who had gone to work at an early age for a Massachusetts company called E. P. Charlton. This company merged with Woolworth, which my father helped to develop before going on to start his own variety stores. He worked hard and rarely questioned what his children were doing. As a result, we were quite strong as individuals. My mother was an attractive woman who, finding all of her children out of the house, decided that she should be in business. At that time she was just starting in as an interior decorator, and eventually, she built a national reputation. My sister Dorothy the brightest of the three children, was four years older than I, and had four children—Julie, Renee and Jeanne, twins, and the youngest, Nick. As a student in medical school I often baby-sat for these kids. I was very fond of them. My sister's husband, Henry, though born in San Francisco, came from a French family. We all enjoyed his sophistication, which was matched by that of my sister. My brother Bob was seven years younger than I and a remarkably good student who had entered college at an early age.

I, too, had been an excellent student, and made Phi Beta Kappa at U.C. Berkeley in my junior year. In the 1930s, there was only one state medical school with only fifty to a class, but I was admitted without much worry. U.C was much less expensive than Stanford, my other choice, and money was short at that time. In my last year of medical school, I worked in the hospital much more often than did the other members of my class.

I had a difficult time deciding on what to plan after graduation, because the War had started. However, when Dr. Traut offered me a position, I could not refuse. His reputation was formidable, and he was just starting as chairman. So of course, I planned to continue my training with the thought that eventually I would go into the Army as a qualified specialist. How wrong I was! My family, of course, had thought exactly as I did. Because I had not been called when others in my class were called, we all felt that I would continue my training.

That Christmas was a strange one.

In the morning before joining my family, I stopped off at Chris's in full uniform, which I was wearing for the first time. I am sure it was a bit of a shock. Her father was a retired Army officer, so I know he approved. But her mother worried about what might be in store. After some time alone, Chris and I agreed that we would keep our friendship alive. Our parting kiss was intense.

My sister Dorothy had a very comfortable old San Francisco home which she and her husband had remodeled to hold their growing family, and where we all gathered for holidays. When I arrived in my uniform, everyone was there, including Bob, who had come in from Berkeley where he was in the V-2 Naval Program and was training to become an officer.

My mother and father were trying to look unworried. We opened our presents and tried to act holidayish, but it was difficult. Our lives had been settled and comfortable: never before had we faced uncertainty of the kind that now had entered our lives and for which we were completely unprepared. The forty-eight hour notice added to the shock. Still, there were no tears. We all expected that I would be assigned to a hospital somewhere doing what I had been trained to do—perhaps caring for WACs, nurses, and Army wives. The only serious problem appeared to be that I would be away from home for the first time and of course, that my training would be interrupted. None of us had the vaguest intimation of the future.

Chapter 2

Training

January–March, 1944

The next three months were like nothing I had experienced in my life. A good friend, Bob Holmes, was leaving at the same time I was for Army Camp at Carlisle, Pennsylvania. We met at the train and boarded the City of San Francisco, with a stop in Chicago.

The next morning in the lounge car, we met an old classmate from Berkeley. He had been a star in our physics class when our section leader and professor was Orlando Lawrence, a pioneer in nuclear physics. Doctor Lawrence had told us that an atomic bomb was possible and of frightening potential. I knew that Enrico Fermi was in Chicago at the time, beginning work on the top secret Manhattan Project. Since this former classmate was in mufti, I jokingly said, "Are you going to Chicago to work on a bomb?" I thought nothing much of that question, but that evening, an FBI man stopped by our room and asked me a number of questions, I thought, because I was a new officer. I never guessed until a year and a half later when the bomb was dropped that my question about "the bomb" that was only meant to be funny was his real concern.

In Chicago, for the first time in my life, I was treated regally. Bob and I were given a free room in the Drake Hotel for the day and the best table in the elegant Pump Room. In New York, we boarded a train to Harrisburg, Pennsylvania, and shared a cab to Camp Carlisle outside of town, where no one seemed to know or care that we arrived late. It was Christmas weekend, and cold. All the stores on the post were closed, and I was one of the few who was comfortable; for I had brought all kinds of warm Army clothes with me. I owed Sam for that.

We were assigned to a barracks. Even though we were officers, we were directed by sergeants who were to be our instructors. The day after we arrived, we began a program of lectures and marches. These were done in rain, snow, and slush. Most of the men in my class had only their dress uniforms. I had G.I. clothes including long underwear, galoshes, high shoes, and wool socks.

Later on, during our first day, we got a whole set of shots. In medical school, we had all sorts of inoculations, and I always got terrible reactions to typhoid shots. We were not excused from marching, even if we were feverish from the shots, which I was. I wrote to my sister about these shots. The first day we got three shots. The first one was not too bad just multiple punctures. The second, typhoid, hurt only a little. Then up pops tetanus. (No wonder so many children hate the pediatricians that dispense it.) Your arm felt like someone had hit it with a sledge hammer, although after an hour or so, my arm seemed to quiet a bit and I could move it a little.

Then, the secondary reaction starts. Since I had had typhoid shots before, my reaction was quite marked. I had chills, fever, and intense muscle ache. A grain of codeine and ten grains of aspirin didn't phase the ache or the fever. It wasn't long until the top of my head felt like it might come off. All of these reactions occurred during the night. On the following morning, I was just able to move my arms to get dressed. Outside there was fresh snow. I did have high shoes, but no boots yet. Most of the men did not even have high shoes. The snow soon turned to slush in a heavy rain. There we were, sick and wishing we could die. However, that ended, as do most nightmares, and I soon felt better. The second typhoid shot wasn't bad. The tetanus shots were the worst.

On our first day out, we had to march as a unit over rough terrain and then stand in the cold for two hours and hear a lecture, which was mostly how to find your way in rough terrain. We were miserable from the cold and hardly paid any attention to the lecturer. We then marched at a very fast pace—almost running—back to camp. They were trying to toughen us up, and we covered eight miles in one and a half hours. That pace in all those heavy clothes was something for a bunch of medical students. I made it about five pounds lighter. Some thirty men fell by the wayside.

The following night we were dropped in pairs in the mountains, given a chart and compass, and told to find our way to an assembly point. The chart would say, for example, "go 850 yards, then go 400 yards northwest to point #2". The object of this exercise was to end up at a given point where there was coffee and doughnuts. We had been watching demonstrations and climbing over mountains all day; so we were dead tired and sore before the night work began. My partner was Mississippi, who joined me in all my travels and travail from the time I hit camp. He had gone to medical school in Louisiana. It took me quite awhile to understand what he was saying, as though we spoke different languages. We made it to the assembly spot early. This was a triumph and we were proud of ourselves.

Soon, others began to straggle in and we all waited, drinking coffee and eating doughnuts in clear mountain air with bright stars and an orange moon with stringy clouds drifting across it. We sang. It was quite strange that the songs were not what one might expect. The ribald was as rare as the contemporary. The men were sentimental, and they sang mostly the songs of the last war. They all knew "Genevieve Sweet Genevieve" better than they knew "Pistol Packing Mama." They sang "Down by the Old Mill Stream," "Home on the Range," "Red River Valley," and "Say Hello to Broadway."

At that time, no one saw any glamour in what they were doing. They were all giving up too much. Most of these men had wives, many had families. I was happy that I wasn't married. The worry was intense, although no one had yet heard a shot. What we got was not, "if you go over," but "when you go over." We were continually told how to arrange our affairs for moving out.

Early on, I began to learn the language of the Army. I just did not use profanity until this time. I wrote Dorothy about the standard terms: "Snafu," which stood for Situation Normal, All Fucked Up and "Fubar," the superlative, Fucked Up Beyond All Recognition.

In spite of all of this, our first weekend was free. Mississippi had a car, and we went to Harrisburg about twenty miles away. Harrisburg, the capitol of Pennsylvania, is dull, puritan, and unexciting. We got a good hotel room looking over the valley, had a few drinks and a tremendous dinner in a warm comfortable restaurant in the lower level of the hotel. There I was introduced to blue point oysters, which were a specialty of the house and were delicious. Then we retired to our room at about twelve. We slept until eleven thirty the next morning, had a sumptuous breakfast in bed, read, and fell back asleep until 4:30. We then took long luxurious baths and showers. I made train reservations for my next stop, which was to be Fitzsimmons General Hospital in Denver.

On our second weekend, we went to New York City. We got there too late to get to a show and had to return early Sunday, so we went to the Radio City Music Hall. The girls were beautiful and the dancing—particularly the chorus—was the best we had ever seen. We did enjoy it, but in retrospect, we were too young and inexperienced to do all that we could have. We really did not know about night clubs or where to find non-professional women.

At Camp, we alternated rather tough basic training, which included sloshing around in the mud and innumerable lectures, with trips to New York. But the lectures were remarkable. They were given by excellent speakers, and it was our first exposure to first class visual aids. For me, it turned out that this was the most useful part of my training. These speakers introduced us to projected slides. They used public address systems. Sometimes, they used working models. They spoke clearly and did not read their presentations. At most they spoke from notes. Years later I was able to use those same techniques to teach house staff and fellow physicians.

Finally, we got around to examinations, which were written and covered all the material we had been given, such as Army organization, tactics, hygiene and map reading. We had all been good students, and we worked hard in preparation. Our fate was sealed even then. I knew that I was to go to Denver, but I thought that assignment would be brief. There was a notice on the bulletin board announcing that if anyone was interested in psychiatry, he could get special training and assignment. I ignored this opportunity, since I expected to win a spot in some sort of hospital. I lived to regret that course of action.

At that time, I began to enjoy the perks. In New York, we were treated in a remarkably friendly way. I noticed that all servicemen and officers who seemed to be heading toward combat received much more consideration than we had in San Francisco; it was certainly in contrast with the harshness of life at Carlisle. Prices of hotels, restaurants, and theaters were discounted significantly. There were many free services and often free tickets. Trains from camp were met by pleasant little old ladies with sandwiches, doughnuts, and coffee. I had the largest income of my life.

Still, I would have been willing to trade all of that for being active in medicine. I was a highly trained young doctor, but my specialty was obstetrics and gynecology, a specialty not in high demand in the service. I believed that because I had been a high achiever that the Army would want to put my abilities to their best use. However, along with the risks involved in military service, there was glamour and a feeling of being part of history. I also was in the best physical shape of my life. During my training at the University Hospital in San Francisco, I and most of my classmates had little time for exercise beyond running up and down the stairs. So, we were pale and flabby. All the marching and climbing at Carlisle had toughened us up.

In February, I was posted to Fitzsimmons General Hospital for a six week assignment. The place seemed like heaven. At first, I was assigned to general medicine where I befriended a patient who was a pilot with mild tuberculosis. He had a car and lots of gas coupons and gave me the use of both for as long as I wanted them. Shortly after that, at my request, I met the chief of obstetrics and gynecology. He knew my chief, Herbert Traut, and he was impressed with my record. He even assigned me to his unit for the time being, but made it clear that because I was not a member of the American College of Surgeons, he would not keep me. Fitzsimmons was the hospital that was responsible for the care of women in the various services who needed hospital care. I was given my own surgery schedule, which was quite a treat, since up to that point, I had done minimal surgery on my own. I thought that by doing outstanding work I might impress the colonel and be able to stay, but that was not to be.

In the meantime, there I was in a modern hospital with excellent living conditions, a car, and innumerable women. There were nurses, patients, and civilian workers. There were dances, and Denver was right there. Heaven!

There was one experience that I recall vividly. I was dating a very attractive nurse who was also good fun. There was a patient who was enamored of this woman and who was also a Golden Glove champion. We were coming home from a dance one evening when this soldier jumped out from some bushes and began to attack me. I had taken boxing in college and did the best I could to defend myself, but this guy could have killed me. The nurse started screaming, which brought a number of people who broke up the fight.

This wonderful life ended suddenly. Along with some friends, I found myself assigned to the 10th Mountain Division. It was based at about 14,000 feet, at Camp Hale, near Colorado

Springs, and getting to this base was an adventure in itself. Since I had the car, I decided to drive there, taking with me seven friends, three of whom had been in my medical school class, and four I had known from Army Reserve Camp about eighteen months earlier.

The weather was literally freezing. We drove through a puddle at one point, and the water that splashed on the windshield immediately froze. There was no way to remove the ice in that cold; so I drove the rest of the way to camp with my head out the window to see. Fortunately, we did not have much farther to go, and I was dressed warmly. On the other hand, one of my friends who was riding with me developed frostbite of his earlobes just walking from the car to the office. Temperatures in the area would go as low as forty degrees below zero.

We signed in, and soon found out that this was a crack division, considered one of the best. It appeared that my friends and I would probably be battalion surgeons, which is the lowest doctor's classification in the Army. Essentially, it's being a glorified first-aid man, usually with a command of about twelve aid men.

We were given splendid equipment. There were parkas with wolf fur around the face. We had long underwear. There were pile vests, very heavy socks, ski boots, felt "bunny" boots, waterproof boots, mountain sleeping bags, the best skis available, and well made backpacks.

We had just found quarters when we were told that we were going out for five weeks of maneuvers and had a couple of days to get ready. The troops, both officers and men, had been carefully chosen and included some superb skiers. We found them pleasant socially, and we were surprised that we were included. Of those of us who came from Denver together, I was the only one who had skiing experience. We were all expected to learn the drill and be part of the team.

Base camp at Camp Hale was at 11,000 feet, and when we left to go on maneuvers, we went even higher. The temperature got as low as forty below zero. We were required either to walk, use skis, or use snow shoes. I selected skis, which are not easy when you must carry a sixty pound pack. Others carried even more. We were not permitted to use tents and slept in the snow in our mountain bags spread on insulation pads. The mountain bags were made in three layers—a wool liner inside of a down layer with a waterproof cover. We called them "mummy bags" because of their tapering shape.

These bags were designed for combat. If we pulled the zipper up hard, the whole bag would open so that we could get out fast. Initially, we did not know about that. The first night out, one man in our group, trying to get warm, tugged on his zipper, and his bag opened. He then could not close it and almost froze before finally someone was able to help him. It is quite funny in retrospect; however, he was a very sad soldier. When we got in the bag, we took off some clothes, but we kept them and our shoes in the bag. If we did not do that, our gear would be frozen solid by morning.

I guess the most difficult part of life in these temperatures was elimination. Any part of your anatomy, if exposed for long, could get frost-bitten. Latrines provided some slight shelter, but not much. I learned more rapidly than most how to contend with the cold. There was one important trick, and that was to change socks often. The perspiration in our boots would freeze if we were not careful. I carried many more pairs of socks than anyone. I also put on "bunny boots" of thick felt at night. On super cold nights, I put on three pair of heavy socks and covered them, Russian style, with loose canvas covers. Those who were not as careful as I often got frost-bite. Yet, even though I was able to ski a lot, this was not a pleasant life. We had been a select group of medical students, and the idea of ending up as battalion surgeons, even in an elite division, held no appeal. Most of all, we were overwhelmed by the work and by what we were expected to do.

The maneuvers were scheduled for five weeks, but there were a good number of casualties. The hospital got busy, and three of us were assigned there. The casualties were mostly from frostbite, and, with a Canadian officer there to supervise, I became expert in dealing with that treatment problem. Our procedure was to warm the body and expose the frost-bitten area usually the feet. Believing that it might be dangerous to warm only the frost-bitten area, we increased circulation by warming the rest of the body. The work was hard and long.

I soon found that the seven of us were to be reassigned to a division that was preparing to go overseas. In the Army, it is always interesting to note how rumors get around with absolute regularity. Some turn out to be true as this one did.

Our reaction to this reassignment was interesting. The 10th Mountain Division was as elite as any division in the United States Army. But the training program was miserable. Trying to survive in the snow at 14,000 feet with no shelter was beyond a group of young doctors who had spent the last nine years studying in their rooms, labs, or libraries, and working on hospital wards. Everything considered, we were pleased to get out. In our naive fashion, we thought that the people who would be fighting in Europe were already there, and we would have relatively easy safe duty. Interestingly, we seven who were chosen were the last to have joined the 10th but we had not yet been admitted to the level of the "elite." The veterans of the 10th Mountain Division were proud of their unit. They were tough and handled the vicissitudes in good fashion. They did not think too much of us recent arrivals. When we left to go back to Denver, we were not allowed to take any of the first-rate equipment with us.

Chapter 3

On Leave

April, 1944

Everything was changing and beginning to seem unreal.

We left the snowbound Rockies for a week's home leave before heading east to join the 35th Infantry Division. Leaner and in better condition than ever before in my life, I was physically almost a different person. I had money for the first time and a more elevated status than as an intern.

Social horizons widened, as well. The seven of us who had come together to Colorado and had known each other from ROTC, Army camp, or medical school had been assigned to separate units and had spent little time together. I found that, like my friends, I had to learn to get along with all kinds of people from many different backgrounds. There was a lot to learn for a "nice, young Jewish doctor."

There was another change. Other people seemed different, or at least, I had begun to look at them in a different way than I had in the past. Up to now, my main concern had been becoming a doctor, and the other people in my life—family, friends, classmates, and professors—were a wonderful source of support. Relaxation with friends was a pleasant relief from the intense pressure that was a part of life for medical students and junior house officers.

Now when I looked at other people, those close to me, as well as strangers, I often wondered if they realized what life was like for young men and women involved in the war. Most people seemed completely unaware of the hardship and difficulty of military training. So, to a certain extent, my training had produced a degree of alienation from others which was new for me. Of course, I had no concept of what was in the future and no idea of how tough the future would be.

On my brief leave in San Francisco, with Chris away at school, I dated some of my old girl friends, but they did not interest me too much, and, although they were attracted by the glamour of the uniform, they were not too interested in me. San Francisco looked and felt strange.

On my last night home, I drove to Coit Tower. It was a clear night, and there was a bright moon. Though there had been blackouts in San Francisco, on this night the lights in the City were on, and I could recognize the landmarks of my life: the Mark Hopkins Hotel, the towers of the Bay and Golden Gate bridges, the Shell Building, the Telephone Building, and the Bay. I filled my mind with that view and left wondering if I would ever be back.

Dave Roth and I traveled together to Cincinnati and arrived at Camp Butner late. We had missed a connection, not knowing that the times in the railroad station of Cincinnati and the city itself were not the same. We were sure that we would be in serious trouble when we signed in, but no one seemed at all concerned. For the next couple of weeks, we tried to adjust to an entirely new life.

I was assigned to a collecting company. Such a company was a part of each infantry regiment. There were three regiments in the division. The evacuation plan for wounded formulated in World War I: Medics from the infantry battalions should locate the wounded. The medics were to do as much as they could immediately. The wounded were then to be taken by litter or with assistance to the battalion aid station, which would be reasonably close by. The aid station was to start more complete first aid and try to get the wounded evacuated to the collecting station usually about five hundred yards farther to the rear. This was to be done by carrying the wounded on litters or with other assistance. Our function at the collecting company, after collecting the wounded from the battalion aid stations (there were three to each regiment) was to provide more advanced first aid that might include better dressings, splints, plasma transfusion, and pain relief. Then the wounded were to be evacuated by ambulance to the division clearing station. All of the activities in training were based on World War I ideas and procedures, and most of those ideas proved to be useless. We were trained to do a great deal of walking and carrying of litters. We were to discover the ingenious soldiers would figure much better ways when they were in combat.

Abruptly, we were told to pack. We were to ship out very shortly from New Jersey. There was a lottery for a night's leave to New York. Dave and I won. We were told when to be back, and we knew that the penalties were severe if we did not return on time.

We treated ourselves to dinner at Fontainbleau—martinis, paté, onion soup, steak, camembert, and wine. We were just finishing dinner when a friend from San Francisco walked in. What a contrast! He had an Army job in New York, which, compared to our combat assignment, seemed soft and enviable.

After dinner, we went to Carmen Jones, and it was special— everything the critics had said, and more. There was a night club scene all in purple and another in blues. The prize fight (the bull fight in Bizet's version) was cast in the brightest of blacks and reds. We loved it, and wondered when we would again see anything as polished and thrilling.

From the theater we went to Cafe Society Uptown, a well known night club, to see Jimmy Savo, who was very funny; Hazel Scott, a beautiful black woman with great style who played the piano and sang, and Mildred Baily, with her wonderful and sweet singing voice. From there we went to smaller clubs like Leon and Eddy's, and finally to the Copacabana, where we were given a front row table for a performance by Jimmy Durante. I guess that was a high point of the evening, and Dave and I spent the rest of the war enjoying some of his lines.

When the show ended, it was early morning, and we were hungry. We asked a cab driver where to go, and he suggested Louis the Waiter's. When we were seated, the owner, who had recently been profiled in the *New Yorker*, came over and suggested that we have lox, bagels, and cream cheese. Hard as it is to believe, we did not know what that was! But we said we would each have one. He said, "You'll eat six." He was right.

Afterwards, we wandered into a couple of more clubs and then down Fifth Avenue. We returned to camp at five in the morning, having had a wonderful evening but wondering, as we often did now, if we would ever return.

Chapter 4

The Voyage Over

May 12, 1944

We left the United States May 12, 1944.

Our ship was the H. B. Alexander, a large vessel seized from Germany during World War I into which we were jammed like sardines. With five other officers, I was assigned to a stateroom designed to accommodate two. We felt lucky that we had an outside room, though the portholes had to be closed at night. The enlisted men were much more crowded with their bunks in tight layers. Early the next morning, we moved out, and a convoy formed around us. Our ship was the flagship and the largest in the convoy, so we were assured of some comfort. However, it also was the best target. There were thirty or forty others, including a number of freighters which also probably had troops aboard.

Camp Kilmer in New Jersey was a dreary sort of place, but we had been there only briefly, and at least it was close to New York. Because there had not been much to do there, I spent a great deal of time on the rifle range and qualified as an expert marksman. That never did me any special good, but at least I was familiar with firearms.

When we loaded, we each carried a good deal of equipment, but we were permitted to send a footlocker separately. The Army required that we always have enough clothes and equipment with us so that we could function if all the rest of our belongings were lost. I had a muzette bag, a small bag carried with a shoulder strap. It held clothing for a couple of days and emergency rations. I also carried a val-pak, which was a folding suitcase that held a uniform, other clothing, and my 201 file containing important information about me. We traveled from Kilmer to the ship, first by train and then by a ferry that crossed the East River, with the lights of lower Manhattan in the background against the sky. As we disembarked from the ferry and marched up the gangplank, a band was playing. Otherwise, our progress was without much fanfare.

Interestingly, the trip to Europe seemed relatively luxurious. All my friends were aboard, including Holmes and Hollister, from medical school. The food was good. There were four to a table in what had been the main dining room. We had a waiter. There were two meals a day with unlimited food at each meal and multiple choices. We had few duties on board, so there was a good deal of card playing and reading books from the well-stocked library. We slept during the day and played cards at night; because the rooms were hot with the port holes closed, and there was no air conditioning in this old ship.

Duties were light. From time to time, we had various drills, mostly to train us about where we should go in case of attack. I did occasional duty as "Officer of the Day" or as "Surgeon." Officer of the Day stayed with the enlisted men and did his best to keep order. Surgeon worked from the clinic and did sick call. Most of the illness was simple. Typically, it was motion sickness with a few respiratory infections and occasional gastrointestinal problems.

There were ships as far as the eye could see. In the center were transports like ours. Beyond them were freighters, and patrolling around the convoy were assorted warships, most of which looked to us to be destroyers. On two occasions on our trip freighters were hit with torpedoes. We could see plumes of dark smoke, and then we could hear the crunch of depth bombs. Those sights and sounds put a certain amount of fear into us, who had never been in combat. We were reminded emphatically that there was a real war going on.

During the voyage, I honed my skills at various card games. We had hours and hours with nothing special to do; so, card games for money became our principal pastime. I had played a great deal of poker in my life, and I was good at it. I started to play gambling games in high school. My parents and those of my close friends did not mind, since we played for very small sums and at home. We took turns playing at each others homes, and the mothers provided refreshments at the end of the evening. We learned, and we became skilled.

The group aboard ship seemed more interested in hearts and bridge than in poker. I did not know much about those games, but I had always loved cards, and I quickly learned. By the end of the voyage, I had accumulated more money than I had ever had in my pocket.

I found all of this life incredible. In a few months, I had traveled farther than I had in my whole life. I had had experiences in New York beyond anything I had ever done. My approach to women was gradually changing. Instead of "nice Jewish girls" who experimented tentatively with sexuality, we met with more worldly, but less educated women. But how naive were we!

The trip to England was quite long and not unpleasant. Because we were trying to avoid submarines, we did a zigzag course; so, it took us two weeks to cross the Atlantic. We went north along the coast of Ireland to Liverpool, where we landed at night.

The city had been bombed repeatedly, and there were fires burning; though they seemed under control. There was blackout, of course. We saw some British soldiers and tossed them oranges and cigarettes. They had not seen oranges in years. American cigarettes were still quite rare. They threw us English coins. It was late at night, but to our surprise, there were Red Cross girls handing out coffee and doughnuts, cigarettes, gum, and lifesavers. We enjoyed seeing the girls more than their gifts. It had been weeks since we had seen a girl.

The organization was remarkable. With amazing efficiency, we were loaded onto trains and moved out. Our destination was Bodmin in Cornwall, though when we got on the train, we did not know where we were going. My first trip in a European train was intriguing, and it brought to mind stories I had read. We traveled in one of those compartments that held six people. The train moved through blacked out areas of monumental ruin. This was not Merrie England.

As we moved away from Liverpool, the countryside spread out on a clear warm day. We opened the windows and were overwhelmed by the beauty of the landscape. We rarely see such lush green in California. The fields in that part of the country were divided by well tended hedges, whose patterns extended as far as the eye could see. The fields were often populated with fat cattle. Every so often, we came on a home or a cluster of homes, all of bright red and rough brick and gray slate or red tile roofs. Every home had a garden, with trees, and the villages we saw were neat and clean.

Bodmin was wonderful. The railroad station was surrounded by rhododendrons. My group was taken to a school house just outside of town on a hill looking down on Bodmin. We set up a temporary camp in the building. There were cots, some bathing facilities, and a mess area of sorts. There was no sign of war there, except for us.

I had never traveled overseas, except for visits to Panama and Cuba when I was about ten. As soon as I got the chance, I wandered down to town. Visiting the shops was a particular joy. I loved using their money, and I had quite a bit of it. I bought Sadler's Boot Polish for 8d.—about thirteen cents. Prices were low. There was a three piece set of candelabra, old Sheffield with its silver beginning to wear through; the cost for the three pieces, including the center piece with three arms, was fifteen pounds or sixty dollars. Although I did not buy these pieces, not knowing how to get them home, I noted these wonderful buys because of my mother's interest in decorating. I also admired—for eight dollars—

a lovely silver punch ladle with the upper portion of the handle in dark wood.

It was spring, and the countryside in Cornwall was magnificent. There were rolling fields in the area, and in them, well fed cows who produced the wonderful cream we loved on the local strawberries. The area in and around Bodmin was more green than any area I had ever seen. There were lilac trees and purple rhododendrons splashed all about. It was easy to see why the people loved England. The homes were small and often poor, but their windows were all crystal clear and their yards well maintained. When you were able to look in the doors, you found their furnishings clean and well-cared for, though often shabby.

Road marches were a daily event. I enjoyed seeing the countryside, but usually I was miserable with terrible hay fever. At the time, there was no special medicine for that condition; so there I was, sneezing with my eyes and nose running. I liked the exercise, but tried to avoid the marches when possible. My comrades thought I was "gold bricking."

There were woods with hawthorn and splendid rhododendrons growing wild, most of them bright purple. The trees were chestnuts, bays, and also oaks, which somehow, had been spared when most of the oaks in Britain were felled to build the Royal Navy fleet. These forests were like parks, with ferns growing on their floors, no dense underbrush, and no dead trees. All seemed well cared for. Farther away were houses of hewn stone and whitewashed brick, the most available local material.

Even in these small towns, there was often a gaping space with part of a home or church standing as a memorial to the old blitz. We saw few vehicles except those of the Army. On the rails were "goods wagons," freight cars about a third the size of those seen at home, but in proportion to everything else around us. Our headquarters was in an old stone and slate roofed poorhouse overlooking Bodmin, and our temporary residence was the schoolhouse, although within a few days we moved to a small hotel in the town.

Our hotel, on the main street of Bodmin, was at least two hundred years old. It had been used for troops for some time. The last occupants had been moved closer to the staging area for the invasion. We preferred this old hotel to tents. There were makeshift showers, and small stoves for heat. I shared a relatively large room with another medical officer. We had two large windows, no carpet, and minimal furnishings. With all of that, it was better than we had expected, in part because each of the officers was assigned a "bat-man," an Army private who, for a small amount of money, in addition to his regular pay, was sort of a valet. He cleaned the room, kept our shoes shined, and performed other tasks. Certainly, this was a very new procedure for me, and I must say, I did not mind it at all. The food, however, was disappointing and quite unsatisfactory after the excellent fare on the ship. It was classic British with an accent on bread, cheese, and dried fish (kippers). and of course, tea.

Our hotel opened directly onto the main street, which was long, narrow, and winding, with shops and larger homes facing it. The shops were charming, but there stocks had been depleted by war. One of the churches had been almost completely destroyed by a bomb from the old blitz. The few cars were small. We had never seen such low powered vehicles, though they certainly were what was needed. They fit the narrow roads and used hardly any petrol. Besides, the British rarely traveled long distances.

It took a while to meet any of the local citizens, but the children tagged after us Yanks with insatiable curiosity. Theirs was equaled by mine. I was intrigued by such things as the label on our lavatory, W. C. in gold letters; the shoulder of a road was a "verge"; the sign requiring a left turn said, "Deny yourself a turn to the right." The small steam engine with little noise and no smoke traveled on a roadbed flanked by great hedges of rhododendrons in full bloom, and giant rose vines grew over the fronts of old stone houses.

Increasingly, our mission weighed on our minds. I often went for supplies to neighboring cities like Plymouth, because we always had in mind what we might need in France, although we just could not be sure what it would be like. In the process of getting materials from various depots, I stayed in real hotels and got to talk with people who treated us in a most friendly fashion knowing that we were on our way to France. Notably, in the hotels, the male workers were either boys of about eleven or men of about seventy-five.

The high point of the visit to Plymouth was staying in a fine hotel, the Grand. Old and lovely, it faced the Hoe and was considered the best in Plymouth. We had booked a large room for the three of us. It had the most comfortable beds I have ever slept in, and I would dream about this luxury in months to come. We had hot and cold running water in the room, another luxury for us, although the W. C. was down the hall. Each floor was on three separate levels and connected by broad elegant stairways. There was an excellent officers club, though we found few other Americans there. They were massing for the invasion.

The contrast between this luxury and the devastation in this beautiful city was overwhelming. Huge areas had been destroyed by German bombs. There were immense gaps where buildings had stood. Yet, the British, in their usual industrious way, had cleaned, though they could not rebuild, having neither manpower nor materials.

On our first trip to Plymouth, I met a young woman whose father owned a pub in which we had some drinks. She took me on a tour of the city, and we went dancing. She was the first woman whom I had a chance to talk with since leaving home. Our relationship was pleasant but superficial. I do not recall holding her more than when dancing, and I do not think we ever kissed. The women in England had lost so many of their men that they seemed to fear getting at all close to a man whom they might later mourn.

In spite of occasional trips to Plymouth and Exeter, life for the most part, was tedious. Breakfast was early in the morning, with food supplied by the British, and to us, rather poor. Kippers combined with bread, canned butter, and jam with a very poor excuse for coffee made a sorry breakfast. Fortunately, it was not too long before we began to get American supplies of eggs and spam with, more important, some decent coffee.

After breakfast, there were often road marches. Though I liked to walk, even with a pack, the terrible hay fever, caused by spring pollens made these marches torture for me. After the marches, we returned for lunch, which was often sandwiches usually made with spam, though we occasionally got turkey.

After lunch, we often had training sessions. I occasionally would teach a class in first aid or hygiene and we were advised to teach World War I techniques. For example, the dressing for wounds was a large pad with tapes attached to the corners. The dressing was to be held in place by tying the tapes together. I learned that the dressings would be much more effective held in place with Ace bandages, which were elastic. The elastic bandages also were much better to control blood loss because of the pressure they applied. My inclination was to teach a more modern care of wounds, supplemented by a judicious use of splints. We were also required to teach the use of sulfanilamide. It was one of the few antibacterial agents available. It came in small packets, and it was to be sprinkled in wounds to avoid infection. I was not sure that this was a good idea; since the sulfa would act as a foreign body. I followed instructions. After these classes would follow some sort of exercise, such as practice in climbing and descending rope nets placed over the sides of mock ships. We also spent inordinate amounts of time practicing loading and unloading our vehicles. Of course, the idea was that when we reached our destination, we would know where everything was. However, doing this sort of thing over and over again got to be almost unbearable. Besides, we felt that it would be difficult to know what our situation would be even if we ever should get ashore in France.

We spent considerable time getting our vehicles ready to land. Because of the likelihood that we would have to land in shallow water, it was necessary to make the engines waterproof and to extend the exhaust pipes vertically about six feet so that they would clear water. We also practiced endlessly getting in and out of various types of landing craft. For the most part, it was planned that we would land from LSTs (Landing Ship Tanks), fairly large flat bottomed craft which would hold three or four vehicles with trailers. LSTs had quarters for officers (cramped, but with showers) and less commodious areas for enlisted men. In their bows were ramps designed to be let down so that the vehicles could emerge, ideally, on shore.

There were also small landing craft for the infantry and aid men (Higgins Boats), also equipped with ramps which were to drop in shallow water so that the men could go ashore. These smaller craft were to be carried on the larger ships and put in the water off shore. To get into these smaller craft, the men would have to climb down the heavy rope nets on which we had practiced. This work was not easy, because both the mother ship and the small craft were moving, and the men were loaded down with equipment. We medical officers also had to practice this maneuver. There were practice beaches which were supposed to be similar to those in northern France where we were to land. This whole business of training to land under fire caused more than a little anxiety. We hoped we would not be the first to go.

Fortunately, my life was about to change a bit, and that would take my mind off of the anxiety caused by thoughts of the invasion.

Chapter 5

Bodmin

May, 1944

    In general, it has always been difficult for soldiers, even officers, to meet educated people. Most of us who were able to meet young women met them in shops or, as was my experience in Plymouth, in a pub. There was one exception: the Red Cross Canteen. The women who worked there were those who did not need jobs. I went there from time to time, not only for the coffee and doughnuts, but more for the conversation. I got to know a lovely woman who probably was a bit older than I was. In fact, most of the women working at Red Cross Canteens in England were older. The young woman of whom I speak, Ann, was a member of a family who owned a nice old hotel just outside of Bodmin. She was blond with blue eyes, attractive, but not beautiful. She looked good in her Red Cross uniform, and she wore a wedding ring.

    Periodically, there were dances, separate ones for officers and for enlisted men. One evening there was a dance in a large room in the local hospital. The room was beautiful with vaulted ceilings. The orchestra was much better than usual. Usually the music was provided by non-professional local older men and women who as volunteers formed an orchestra. This orchestra was from an army band; and it was good, knowing the latest popular songs from home and playing them well. There even was a rather good male vocalist.

At these dances, the women were mostly from the various services Wrens (like our Waves), ATS, Red Cross, and some civilians. I was enjoying myself, meeting various attractive and bright young women, when I noted Ann serving non alcoholic drinks. I asked her to dance.

She was fresh and bright and obviously well-educated. In a way we were already friends since we had talked at her canteen. When the dance was over, I walked her home to the hotel. She asked me in, since it was still relatively early.

The hotel was nationally famous, though small, and had been run by Ann's family for generations. It was built on the ruins of an old abbey set on a hill looking out on vistas of unbelievable beauty—green fields, old trees loaded with fresh spring leaves and lovely arbors of roses.

The oval main room was not large. The furniture was old English, and it was all beautifully kept. I did not know a great deal about soldiering, but I did know about furniture, my mother having been a well-known decorator. The carefully inlaid rosewood secretary contained lovely old china. There was a fine Ironstone inkwell on the desk portion, and on the shelves above, behind glass doors, was a set of dishes with a delightful butterfly pattern.

In front of the large window, to the right taking advantage of the splendid view, was a simple old desk with a long drawer across the full width and three smaller drawers on each side as part of the support structure. The fittings were of brass. Its chair had carved wooden arms and the back and seat were upholstered in green velvet, which was a bit threadbare. Opposite the window was a magnificent old English commode of burled oak. Over the commode was a group of pictures including two large crayons of Ann's grandparents, flanked by exquisite miniatures of the family. Balancing the secretary at the entrance to the room was a cabinet containing beautiful glassware that appeared to be Waterford.

The seating was conducive to conversation. On either side of the desk were window seats covered in chintz, slightly worn, but a colorful combination of green and white. In the center of the room was a large sofa covered in the same material. On one side of the sofa was a wing chair. On the other side was a bench which easily accommodated two people. In front of the sofa was a large coffee table on which was an English Spode tea set. There were also Spode ashtrays and a glass container of daffodils. The draperies, pulled back on each side of the window, were of double-thick muslin to be drawn across for blackout after dark. The carpet, slightly worn, was white and oval to conform to the shape of the room.

On the far end of the room was a small fireplace with brass fire tools. The fireplace was flanked by two Sheraton side chairs, one with a small table next to it and the other with a newspaper rack beside it. Two lamps made from old apothecary jars were on the commode and a standing lamp with a ratchet device so that it could be raised or lowered was placed near the wing chair. There was a small lamp on the desk. In the center of the ceiling was a large cut-glass chandelier with holders for candles.

The room reminded me of home. I described it in a long letter to my mother.

Ann introduced me to some of the hotel guests, and the conversation was stimulating. Because of the war, none of them had been to the United States, and they were interested in just about everything that went on there. Their principal knowledge had come from films, and they were certainly happy that gangsters were not as important as our films portrayed them to be. What especially interested them was that, though I was a doctor of medicine, I had spent a major portion of my college years studying English literature. They all had classical educations.

Two of the guests had come to town in anticipation of a circuit court which was to be held soon. They were both older men and had been trained in the law. One of them had served in World War I. He was interested in our preparations for the invasion, but I was forbidden to discuss that subject. We were very much afraid of spies. I knew that in spite of our obvious preparations for the invasion (the countryside was loaded with trucks, tanks, and the other machinery of war), details of our plans were top secret.

So, the conversation went on to the differences between British and American educational systems. At that time, American universities tended to prepare their graduates for careers more than did those in Britain. While my conversations with my friends tended to be about our medical training or our social lives, these people liked to talk about politics, literature, and of course, the war. Would it end with the invasion? Would an invasion against "fortress Europe" be possible?

I was tired of talking about the war, but it was wonderful to discuss art and literature. These people were particularly surprised at my knowledge of furniture, china, and interior decoration in general. I think we all wondered if we would ever get back to a situation where those things were of greater interest than war. This was one of the best nights since I left home.

Ann was an interesting woman. She was married to a British Army officer who had been stationed in India and Burma for over two years and had left shortly after Ann and he were married. They had no children. She talked fondly of him. Their separation was obviously difficult, and it was unlikely that he would get leave soon.

She was about my height with hair done in a simple bob, and she wore practically no makeup. She was a bit reserved, but she had a sense of humor and sometimes teased me in a friendly way about some of my Yankisms. Her figure was well-proportioned, though not startling (I especially liked her ankles). Often she wore the uniform of the Red Cross. At home, she wore quite simple clothes, but she looked good. I thought she might be a little older than I was, but I never had the nerve to ask her. She was the best dancer I had met in England.

When I left, she gave me a gentle kiss and invited me to dinner two nights later. I looked forward to that.

The next day things began to change. Our division was reviewed by General Eisenhower, Winston Churchill, and George Patton. As they went down the ranks, we were amazed to see this group of leaders. Churchill sort of slouched along, Eisenhower was neatly dressed in a rather simple uniform with four stars, Patton was more elegant with jodhpurs and boots and three stars. Churchill and Eisenhower spoke to about every third man. Patton was not permitted to say a word, it seemed. (We did not know that he had been in some trouble.)

General Eisenhower came to me, and said, "Where are you from soldier?"

I replied, "San Francisco, sir."

He said, "I was stationed at the Presidio there. I enjoyed the city very much. Good luck."

"Thank you, sir."

It was exciting to be addressed in this way, and I never would forget it. However, I wondered if we were to be the first wave ashore, having been honored by this top ranking group. I hoped not.

Later in the day, we practiced climbing down the side of a ship on a rope net, and loading and unloading on landing craft of various types, and reviewing our previous training. On the following day, we rechecked our equipment for, it seemed, the twentieth time.

On the morning of the next day, we all received an announcement from SUPREME HEADQUARTERS ALLIED EXPEDITIONARY FORCE, with a SHAEF symbol, and the following:

Soldiers, Sailors and Airmen of the Allied Expeditionary Force. You are about to embark upon the Great Crusade, toward which we have striven these many months. The eyes of the world are upon you. The hopes and prayers of liberty-loving people everywhere march with you. In company with our brave Allies and brothers-in-arms on other Fronts, you will bring about the destruction of the German war machine, the elimination of Nazi tyranny over the oppressed peoples of Europe, and security for ourselves in a free world. Your task will not be an easy one. Your enemy is well-trained, well-equipped and battle-hardened. He will fight savagely. But this is 1944! Much has happened since the Nazi triumphs of 1940-41. The United Nations have inflicted upon the Germans great defeats, in open battle, man-to-man. Our air offensive has seriously reduced their strength in the air and their capacity to wage war on the ground. Our Home Fronts have given us an overwhelming superiority in weapons and munitions of war, and placed at our disposal great reserves of trained fighting men. The tide has turned! The free men of the world are marching together to Victory! I have confidence in your courage, devotion to duty, and skill in battle. We will accept nothing less than full Victory! Good Luck! And let us all beseech the blessing of Almighty God upon this great and noble undertaking. Signed: Dwight D. Eisenhower.

The invasion of the European Continent had begun and we were not to be in the first wave. Though I wanted to do my part, I reluctantly admitted that I was relieved that we were not to be the first to face the Germans. We waited anxiously by the radio.

Yet, the business of the community continued as if nothing was happening. The circuit judge came to town. He is the King's representative and was treated accordingly. He left the city hall in flowing red robes, preceded by the town mace bearers carrying their ancient gold maces. The mayor followed in an ermine-trimmed robe and wearing the gold chain of office. There was a beautiful coach, attended by footmen and police officers. This splendid procession went first to the church and then to the courthouse, where court would be in session for four days. At first, I was taken aback that more attention was not being paid to the invasion, however, after long years of war, I believe that the English maintained their sanity by showing themselves what they were fighting for. I felt they had a right to do it their way. They has suffered through so much.

During that day we intensified our preparations. The vehicles had been waterproofed. We had practiced getting out of landing craft, and we had practiced climbing on rope nets that could be tossed over the side of larger craft, if necessary. We went over our packing lists for what seemed like the hundredth time.

The next day, when we heard that no gas had been used against landing troops, I took an illegal action. I unpacked some of my heavy gas decontamination equipment, and replaced it with as much liquor as I could buy in the town at the officers' mess and elsewhere. This move proved to be one of the best decisions I ever made.

On the next day, I went to dinner at Ann's hotel. I liked Ann and looked forward to being with her. We knew that my unit would be leaving soon. I am sure that it reminded Ann of the time, years before, when her husband had left. We knew that the Allies had landed, but we also knew that progress had been slower than had been hoped for. At the dinner table Ann and the other guests tried to be upbeat, and there was much talk about what the world would be like after the war. After dinner, the other guests left. Ann and I sat near a small fire in that lovely room and talked. Suddenly, she said, "Come upstairs with me."

Of course I did not know what to expect. She took me to her bedroom, a beautiful room reminding me of something my mother might have done. The furnishings were covered in rose-colored chintz, slightly worn, but colorful. There was a four poster bed with a canopy, a graceful chaise near a window, and a fine old desk. Leaded windows with small glass panes overlooked the landscape.

Ann smiled at me, and we kissed for the first time. Now I was in a situation unlike any I had ever been in before. My sexual experience had been limited to relatively difficult situations like the back seat of an automobile, and most had been little more than intense necking. Further, in spite of my medical education, my sexual knowledge was minimal. I knew one thing, I liked Ann and I felt at ease with her. On the other hand, I knew she was married, and I had every reason to believe that she loved her husband.

At first kissing was warm and friendly, but it became more passionate. I was getting more and more excited. Ann broke from the embrace. She went to a commode, took out a pair of pajamas, and tossed them on the bed. Then, she went into the bathroom. I put on the pajamas, opened the bed, and waited. There was not much light in the room, as the English were always conserving. I left only one very small lamp lit.

Ann appeared at the bathroom door in a simple white night gown. Without a word, we got into bed. She flipped off her gown, and I got my first glimpse of her lovely breasts. My pajamas were soon off, and we were in an embrace. I entered her, I guess roughly, and ejaculated almost immediately. I was so embarrassed. She said soothing words and touched me gently, and to my surprise and joy, I rapidly became erect again. Now there was gentle love making. My insertion was with care and ease. This time, for the first time, I was involved with female orgasm, which was almost frightening. I joined in what was certainly the most exciting event of my young sexual experience. She said, "Thank you dear John. We both needed that." We both dozed off, exhausted in each others arms.

I was awakened by the roar of motors. Outside, four-by-fours, the heavy Army trucks, were on the move. Something big was going on. I rapidly dressed, kissed Ann, and rushed out.

I have often wondered exactly what went on there. We certainly liked each other, and we enjoyed each other's company. However, I do not think it was love. She missed her husband, and she knew that I was off to a hazardous future. We both felt the need to be close to someone. We both knew that we would probably not see each other again. The invasion was starting, and I would be leaving very soon. Why not do this for both of us? I was surprised by what happened, but Ann knew much more than I did. She had lived with war for years. This brief affair was her idea, but I was a willing participant. The English knew that the mortality rate in the Army was extremely high. They had lost so many men in the two wars of the twentieth century. Certainly, I will never forget that night. The evening, in retrospect, captured all the craziness and ambivalence of the times.

When I reached my quarters, I found intense activity. The vehicles were mostly loaded. My batman had packed my personal things, and they were in my three-quarter ton truck. The trailer was loaded, and I checked to see that the liquor was there. We took off before dawn.

We were moving slowly, and when we passed the hotel, I rushed over to the door and left all of the special things I could lay my hands on. My father often sent canned food, so I had some of that. There was some coffee, a rare commodity at that time. More important, I had time to scribble a note to Ann. "Ann dear, I will never forget last night. I wish you the best. I send my love.– John." We left Bodmin. I was sad, yet also excited and anxious. This was the time we had waited for.

Chapter 6

Invasion

June–July, 1944

We traveled eastward and reached a large staging area surrounded by strong wire fences. Our temporary quarters were tents. We were permitted to write letters, but not to give information about where we were or what we were doing. We thought we were near Southampton.

I wrote home that "I have no regrets about my lot so far. This is an adventure I would have been sorry to miss. It would be foolish to feel that this is all without danger, but there is danger everywhere, and it is a doctor's duty to do his best where he is needed. At this time, I am impressed with our army, and its aims are those of all of us. I do love you all, and I shall do my best to see that I get back to see you soon, bringing as many others with me as possible." Obviously, I was trying to reassure my mother, and perhaps myself.

The next day, we loaded onto landing craft. My vehicle was put on an LST. I had a small cabin. There were even hot showers, that were not available in the marshaling area. I wrote a letter which I was not sure would get back. At the time, we were

SUPREME HEADQUARTERS
ALLIED EXPEDITIONARY FORCE

6 June 44

Soldiers, Sailors and Airmen of the Allied Expeditionary Force!

You are about to embark upon the Great Crusade, toward which we have striven these many months. The eyes of the world are upon you. The hopes and prayers of liberty-loving people everywhere march with you. In company with our brave Allies and brothers-in-arms on other Fronts, you will bring about the destruction of the German war machine, the elimination of Nazi tyranny over the oppressed peoples of Europe, and security for ourselves in a free world.

Your task will not be an easy one. Your enemy is well trained, well equipped and battle-hardened. He will fight savagely.

But this is the year 1944! Much has happened since the Nazi triumphs of 1940-41. The United Nations have inflicted upon the Germans great defeats, in open battle, man-to-man. Our air offensive has seriously reduced their strength in the air and their capacity to wage war on the ground. Our Home Fronts have given us an overwhelming superiority in weapons and munitions of war, and placed at our disposal great reserves of trained fighting men. The tide has turned! The free men of the world are marching together to Victory!

I have full confidence in your courage, devotion to duty and skill in battle. We will accept nothing less than full Victory!

Good Luck! And let us all beseech the blessing of Almighty God upon this great and noble undertaking.

Dwight Eisenhower

Please save — Johnny

uncertain as to what to expect. We knew that we had placed troops ashore on June sixth, but we also knew that progress had been slow. We suspected that faster progress had been expected, and we were not sure whether we might be forced back into the sea as at Dunkirk. On the other hand, we had seen the masses of equipment, and we knew of the extensive preparations. Though some days had passed since D-Day, we were frightened.

As we approached the beach, we could hear the firing of the heavy guns on the destroyers which had come in close to shore and looked almost as though they could be grounded. Later, I heard that they had been an invaluable source of artillery support of our invasion force. In fact, we now had forward observers ashore, survivors of the initial landing who had moved inland, though only a short way. As we looked toward the beach, we saw occasional explosions of enemy artillery shells.

We landed directly on Omaha Beach.

It was terribly torn up, and not all the dead had been removed. Badly shot up landing craft, tanks, and other equipment were strewn about, and our attempts at creating piers had obviously failed. On the other hand, engineers had somehow built a road of sorts leading off of the beach. They had laid metal strips, like they used for making airfields, over much of the sand, and with bulldozers they had made a road where the ground was more firm. We knew that the faster we got out of the exposed area provided by the beach the better. The cliff was probably only a few hundred yards away, but that seemed quite a distance to travel for shelter.

We were instructed to get off of the beach as fast as possible. The MPs were magnificent. They directed traffic in spite of the incoming shells. They ignored the danger to themselves and tried in every way to get us off the beach and to some sort of shelter where we could organize. We could see the cliffs that had caused so much trouble on the first day. They probably were not very high, but to us they loomed in a menacing way against the sky. It must have been terrible for the men who had to fight their way across the beach and then force their way up these cliffs. Even now, occasionally, a shell landed on the beach, but I saw no casualties as we rushed for the exit road.

My unit, the 110th Medical Battalion, assembled just beyond the beach in a field surrounded by huge hedgerows, and we parked our vehicles close behind one of them. The hedgerows of Normandy were the product of hundreds of years of farming in the area. As the years went by, the hedges grew more and more dense. Soil collected around their roots, and more of the plants grew. This natural process resulted in a very sturdy wall, a kind of fortification. In our training no one mentioned the hedgerows, but they would prove to be a major problem in the invasion of France. I recognized at once that putting the vehicles and myself behind one of those hedges would offer significant protection. However, it provided equal protection for the Germans who knew how to use them for defensive purposes.

We had arrived at this point without any casualties in our unit. We were learning to recognize the snap of bullets going by and the sound of our heavy shells going overhead. To me, they sounded like freight trains. When German 88 shells came in, we heard the whistle and the explosion simultaneously. But the weapon more than any other that harassed us in the hedgerows was the mortar. We could hear those shells before they landed, so we tried to find some cover. We had been exposed to some of the sounds of battle in our training, but these were real, and we did not know the safest course of action. The first night, I tried to dig a foxhole, but the ground was too hard for me. At last, I found an abandoned German foxhole. It was deep, had straight sides, and room for me to lie full length.

As I was settling in, my friend Dave Roth looked over the edge of the hole, and he said, "What are you eating?" "Caviar," was my response. Somehow or other, mail had arrived, and I'd received a small package of food from home. Dave never forgot that.

The next morning, we were uncertain what to do. I cut my hand trying to shave a chocolate bar into hot water to make hot chocolate. We had no special way to organize food, but we did have

K-rations, which usually contained a can of some high calorie mixture (at breakfast, eggs), some crackers, powdered fruit juice, which would be mixed with water, sometimes coffee, and usually some kind of candy.

We prepared to move out with the objective of setting up a collecting station for the casualties that would result from the action planned which, we gathered, was to be the capture of St. Lo. The absence of information was most frustrating, and we had the horrible feeling that no one knew quite what to do. We did know that our division was to take part in a major offensive, and that it was important for us to be prepared to receive wounded. Our company commander finally was able to get a map showing our plan of action and using it, he chose a good location.

Our collecting company was set up in an old quarry that was perfect for this purpose. The wall of the quarry was toward the enemy. We put up a moderate-sized tent near the wall, where it was safe from almost all fire. There was an access road toward the left rear of the quarry through which ambulances and jeeps could come and go. There were a few well dug foxholes, made by Germans when this was a defensive position for them, and I rapidly acquired one.

We had discovered during our short stay, that we and our equipment were not fired upon because of our red crosses. That being so, we made the crosses even larger on ourselves and on our vehicles.

Our main tent was set up with a light lock, so that no light would show at night. I put a litter in my foxhole and placed my bedroll on it. Others tried to find sheltered areas near the sheer rock wall. Within a day or so, we were ready. I had time to write, and surprisingly mail kept coming for me. My requests home were mostly for food. K-rations were so boring, and it would be some time before we could set up a kitchen. From the time we landed, a steady light rain fell, which didn't do much for our morale.

As we waited for our first battle, I reflected in a long letter to my sister that I was pleased that my younger brother was still in school rather than being involved in all of this.

My unit, a platoon of the collecting company, consisted of a superb group of enlisted men who were older than most soldiers because they had been in the National Guard. However, that they were old friends was to prove a real problem. They had a great sense of humor which was to be life-saving for many. They loved the stories that I had to tell. Most of these men were married and many had children. In this situation, officers and men came much closer together. We knew our lives would be interrelated until all of this was over. I rapidly began to be called "the chaplain" rather than Lieutenant or Sir. When people have troubles in the army, the proper response was "Tell it to the chaplain." I kidded the men a good deal, and I held relatively informal "chaplain's meetings." If there was anything an enlisted man wanted (except a trip home), I tried to get it for him. Though I had little control over it, I got full credit whenever mail arrived.

Well, we were at last ready for our first major battle. The First Infantry Division and the Twenty-ninth had landed on D-Day and had been decimated. Our job was to fill in the gap caused by the loss of so many men. Our plan being to take St. Lo on our first day, we attacked at dawn. The result was disaster. The Germans were ready. Though they had many fewer men, they were seasoned and knew the ground. The casualties began to pour in.

In most cases, wounded were given first aid by battalion aid men who then got the injured soldier to the battalion aid station by helping him, carrying him, using a litter, or if possible, by jeep. If the aid man had not done so, sulfanilamide was dusted in the wound, basic bandages were placed, and when necessary, plasma was started and morphine administered. We had been taught to carry the wounded from the aid station to the collecting station by litter. That was backbreaking and dangerous. We moved ambulances to the aid stations where they picked up the wounded and delivered them to our collecting station, that was further from the fighting and permitted more deliberate care—improved wound dressings, splints, plasma, and efforts to provide comfort, mostly in the form of morphine and cigarettes. The wounded men left our station by ambulance for the division clearing station. (Soon field hospitals were to be established.) This run was relatively safe; because the front was a thousand to fifteen hundred yards forward.

This experience was especially difficult and frightening for me because, not only were the wounds horrible, but ours had previously been a National Guard division, and the men had known each other—in some cases quite well—before being called up. The guard was a sort of club for these boys from Kansas and Nebraska. Seeing their friends with horrible wounds was devastating for them. Unlike the emergency room work I had done during my medical training, in which we did our best for the patients, but our relationship with them was relatively impersonal, this situation involved a cohesive group of men who had been friends. Intense personal feeling fueled the already pressing need to perform. Then, too, they must have been aware that, "If it can happen to my friend, why can't it happen to me?"

I had never seen anything like these wounds. We would see a large hole in a man's chest with bits around and hear the sound of air going in and out. We saw a section of the abdominal wall blown away with bowel protruding. Limbs might be all or partially absent.

That first day, I learned a great deal. I had never before used a morphine syrette, a little tube containing a quarter grain of morphine, which is a substantial dose. When I tried to use my first syrette, the morphine would not come out. A private pointed out to me that there was a little peg in the end which had to be pushed to open the channel into the morphine. This was one indication of how little prepared I was for all of this.

I also learned that the best way to deal with wounds of extremities was to splint them with "wire-ladder" splints, a supply of which I had picked up in Plymouth. These splints were made of wire and could roll up. The sides of the splint consisted of slightly

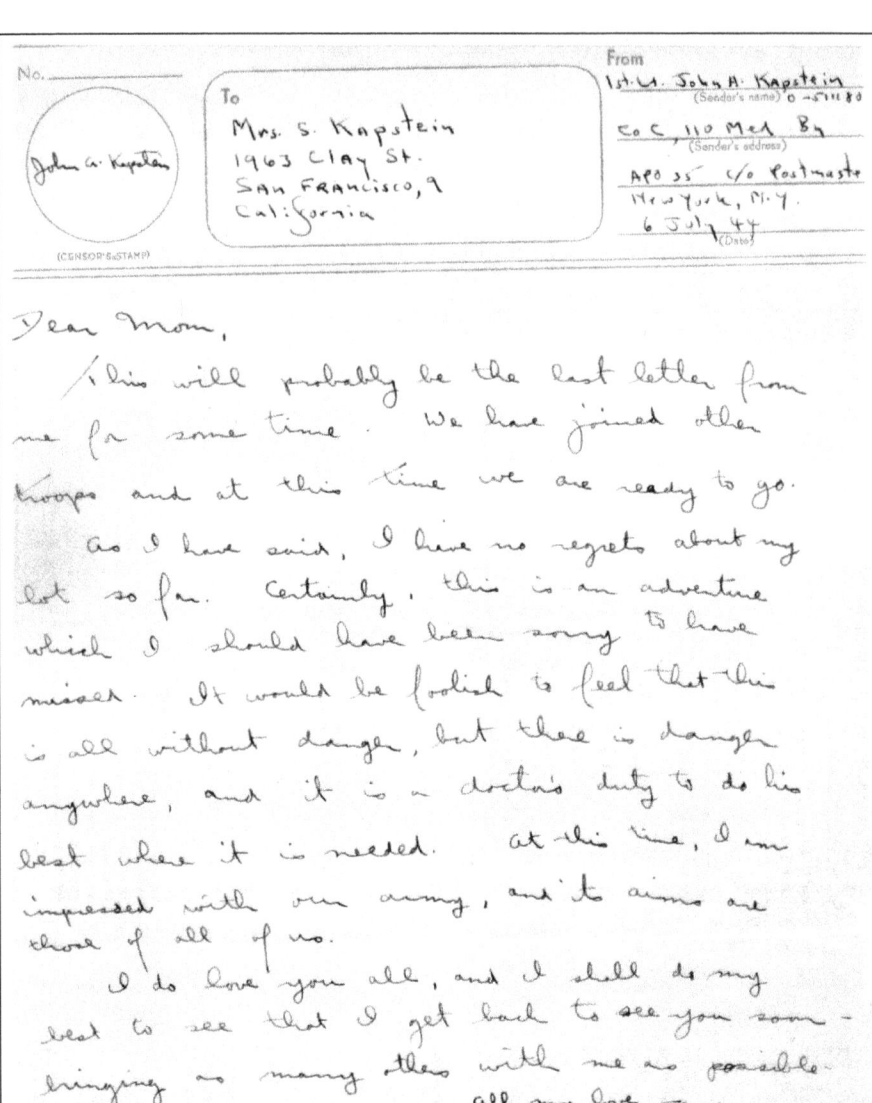

Dear Mom,

This will probably be the last letter from me for some time. We have joined other troops and at this time we are ready to go.

As I have said, I have no regrets about my lot so far. Certainly, this is an adventure which I should have been sorry to have missed. It would be foolish to feel that this is all without danger, but there is danger anywhere, and it is a doctor's duty to do his best where it is needed. At this time, I am impressed with our army, and its aims are those of all of us.

I do love you all, and I shall do my best to see that I get back to see you soon - bringing as many others with me as possible.

All my love,
Your ever lovin' son,
Johnny

heavier wire, and the cross pieces were like the steps in a ladder. They were lightweight, easily carried, and effective. I developed a fondness for elastic bandages, of which I had also obtained a supply in Plymouth. Later, when I moved closer to combat, I always had the men loaded down with splints and elastic bandages, plus, of course, the standard combat dressings, which were mostly from World War I. These dressing that I described before, were quite large, but were compressed into a small package which made it possible to carry a good number. They had long tapes on each corner, but those tapes were not as effective as my elastic bandages, or, as often was necessary, as plain old adhesive tape. Although transportation and equipment had evolved considerably since World War I, I think that the decisions about emergency medical care had been made by people who had served in that earlier war. Rapidly, we learned that we would have to be innovative to deal with the kinds of problems we were to face.

I learned always to have a package of morphine syrettes in my pocket, as well as a pack of cigarettes and a lighter. Cigarettes were often the first request of a wounded soldier. I wore a cartridge belt, which I kept loaded with chunks of chocolate supplied by my father. Somehow the large Hershey or Nestle bars which he sent got through. I also fed this chocolate to the tired men working on the wounded.

At the end of this first horrible day, I proved my good judgment in England: The Scotch which I had bought and put in an area where gas contamination materials should have been was a good gamble. A couple of bottles of Scotch that first night had a very salubrious effect. I doled it out carefully, knowing we had a great deal more to go through.

Our location was approximately a thousand yards from the front, fairly close for a collecting station. By the book, we should have been at least another five hundred yards farther to the rear. Yet, as close as we were, most of the first casualties we saw had been to the battalion aid stations and had received some sort of treatment. It was awhile before casualties occurred near enough to us for us to see them first. My first such experience was a man from a tank destroyer who had three compound comonuted fractures (with the skin broken and bone protruding) below the knee. With him was another man wounded almost as severely. I carefully dressed and splinted these legs and was pleased to hear later that they were saved by the amazing orthopedic team which was part of our first field hospital.

When I finally got to my bed, to my surprise, I slept. Occasional flares lit the sky to almost daylight. Heavy shells fired by our ships offshore and by our heavy artillery went over our heads sounding like freight trains. Incoming, we could hear the snap of bullets and the crunch of German 88s. Occasionally, we heard the whistle of descending mortar shells, and we were to hear much more of them in the future. But the spot which we had chosen for the collecting company was perfect from a military point of view, and only rarely did a shell hit near us.

The battle for St. Lo lasted many days. Although the plan had been to take the city in a single day, we did not finally do so until July 19. On the first day, we made little if any progress. We knew that our division had sustained tremendous casualties. This lack of progress and the huge number of wounded that we had seen, taught us that much of our training was ineffectual. Now, we had to learn from experience.

The hedgerows were the greatest problem for our commanders. At the base of them were narrow trenches of varying depths. With little modification, these provided excellent foxholes, machine gun and mortar emplacements, and screening for snipers. The rows were only a few hundred yards apart, and behind each one was the dreaded unknown. The hidden enemy, with weapons designed for this kind of fighting, was in a strong position. Our commanders had to devise ways to get through this maze.

We also had to contend with booby traps and strategically placed mines. The largest was the Teller mine, a thick disk with a protrusion on top which, when compressed, caused the mine to explode. The Germans placed these along roads and in other areas where tanks and other vehicles might pass. The largest part of the mine was buried, so that only the trigger was exposed. These devices could blow the wheels off vehicles and the tracks off tanks. In the process, they often tore the legs and genitals off riders in the vehicles. I learned to put sandbags on the floor of my truck. The booby traps were wires placed so that if a soldier hit one of them, an explosive would detonate. Also, there were antipersonnel mines that when activated by pressure would pop into the air and explode. Our men had to learn how to avoid these vicious devices.

We medics, too, were now to learn from experience. In good American fashion, we modified the Army's system of medical care for the wounded, just as our commanders had to learn how to contend with the German defense plan.

Chapter 7

Organization

July, 1944

At the time of the invasion of Normandy, we had been at war for over two years. Yet, our medical organization and our plan for care of the wounded were based on practices and methods developed in World War I. This state of affairs was absurd in view of the changes in warfare. That was classic army. Early in this war, the Germans introduced the concept of blitzkrieg (lightning war) and demonstrated that rapid encirclement of the enemy resulted in major military success. The Nazis advanced rapidly, using tanks supported by aircraft and moving their best troops in armored personnel carriers. This plan of action proved to be more effective than the slow, methodical advances often advocated by Field Marshal Montgomery and was the exact opposite of the trench warfare of World War I. That form of warfare was doomed to end in stalemate and great loss of life in trying to break through enemy lines. When American forces landed in Normandy, most of our training had been geared to this more stationary kind of combat. Patton was the one Allied general who understood the new style of warfare. The Germans knew about Patton, and they feared him more than any other Allied general.

An infantry division basically consisted of three infantry regiments. Our regiments were the 134th, the 137th, and the

320th. Each regiment consisted of three battalions, and each battalion had three companies. Of course, there were associated various other units like field artillery, medical battalion, and engineers. An infantry company was the farthest forward toward the enemy, and therefore sustained the highest number of casualties, though of course, there were casualties to the rear from shell fire and occasionally from bombs.

It soon became obvious that the old plan for evacuation of wounded was both dangerous and inefficient. The combat aid men and the battalion surgeons changed the system, and superior officers, who, for the most part, stayed away from the fighting, deferred to the people closer to combat.

The battalion aid men found it was very difficult to carry wounded for any distance, particularly under fire. But each battalion had two jeeps, and the profile of a jeep is lower than that of a man standing. So, the aid men began loading the wounded onto jeeps and evacuating them from the immediate area of combat as soon as possible. They put Red Cross flags on the jeeps and painted red crosses on their helmets and jackets, since, in Normandy, at least, the red cross was respected and not fired upon.

Our division was made up mostly of farm boys who were used to working with tools and fixing damaged tractors, trucks, and plows. They knew how to do simple welding, and they could do wonders with bailing wire. They soon devised racks to fit over the hoods and back ends of jeeps so that they could carry up to four wounded at a time to the battalion aid station. They also replaced litter bearers with ambulances to transport wounded to the collecting station. The wounded could then be rushed to the collecting station for slightly more sophisticated care before being sent on to the rear. These new methods brought a wounded man to the collecting company in about thirty minutes, instead of in an hour or two as was usual with the old plan based on the use of hand-carried litters.

These new and efficient ways of providing emergency medical care were initiated by men in the lower ranks, not by those in the upper echelons who had been content to reapply methods developed in World War I without regard to their effectiveness. The loss of life in that war was in part a result of this delay in providing care for the wounded. Of course, in World War II, we had methods of treatment not available in the earlier war, particularly the use of plasma, which made it possible to overcome shock.

The innovations of these soldiers resulted in the saving of untold numbers of lives. If a man reached one of our aid stations alive, he had a ninety percent chance of surviving his injuries. Yet still, loss of life, was staggering.

Just as the ingenuity of our aid men saved lives, so did that of forward combat troops. For example, our tanks could not climb over the hedgerows without exposing their under sides to direct fire. The tankers came up with the idea of attaching a large metal pointed beam to the front of their tanks. This point broke through the hedgerow, and the tanks came through firing. They also devised a rotating flail which could be attached to the front of a tank to explode mines in front of advancing troops. We must give great credit to the innovative spirit of our fighting men, who were not bound to "the book."

At one point during combat, General Patton wanted us to wear ties. It turned out that none of us had ties. Even if we did, I do not believe we would have worn them. There was no way to punish us. There was no worse duty than with forward units of combat infantry. Patton was to learn too. He and his staff were impressed with the way we had improved the evacuation process. On the other hand, whenever I saw Patton, he was in full uniform with a glistening helmet with his stars in front and with pearl-handled pistols on his hips. His staff also was dressed in a more formal manner. On the other hand, our commanding officers were more likely to be wearing clothes similar to that worn by the front line men. At my level, we did not wear our officers' insignia for fear of being sniper targets. Though our officers bars were on our helmets, we painted over them with G.I. paint so that they could be seen only up fairly up close.

Chapter 8

Battalion Surgeon

July, 1944

Our collecting company daily became more established in the quarry. After our first devastating attack trying to reach St. Lo, life quieted down, and our commanders were waiting for more support and wished to regroup.

This lull gave me time to go to the rear where I could follow up on some of the more severely wounded whom I had treated. I found the evacuation hospital to be doing a remarkable job. The surgeons there said that my technique for caring for extremity wounds probably saved many limbs. My splints kept the wounded limbs immobilized so that motion of jagged bones would not cut through vital structures. The elastic bandages helped control bleeding and keep extremities firmly in place against the splints.

I also had a chance to check on some friends who had been wounded, and I was able to write to their families. Letters from doctors and other medical staff were often the first news that the families heard beyond notification by the Army that their loved one had been wounded. I did regret not being able to work in the hospital situation.

While visiting the rear, I was able to get a hot shower, clean clothes, and a real meal. I returned to the company to find orders which were a bit disturbing: I was to take command of a battalion aid station. One of the medical officers there had been wounded, and the other had collapsed emotionally. Our commanding officer assured me that, when possible, he would get me back to the collecting company.

The battalion aid station, the most forward medical installation, is usually staffed with two medical officers, a few techs, and twenty aid men whose job was to pick up the wounded and give them first-aid, while trying to prevent them from being wounded again and endeavoring to keep themselves from being hit so that they could continue to be of help getting the wounded to the aid station, often a tough job. These men were assigned to the three rifle companies and the heavy weapons company that made up the battalion

A jeep from the aid station came to pick me up. I loaded in my bedroll and the things I thought I would need, leaving behind a good deal of my stuff with my men from the company to look after. When my men gathered around to bid me good luck, they all seemed happy that it was not they who had to go so far forward, where there was no protection such as the quarry provided. I was frightened.

When I arrived at the battalion aid station, things were in disarray. The station, only four hundred yards from the front lines, had just suffered a mortar attack. Already, three medical officers had left. One had been wounded and two were victims of "combat fatigue." I do believe that the station had been mistaken for a command post, for the red cross had been respected rather well up to then. There had been no serious injuries, but some of the equipment had been badly damaged. The jeeps and major supplies had been placed behind a large hedgerow, so they had not been damaged.

I found the medical officer curled in a ball in the corner of a dugout. He was in tears. This was disturbing for me because I had known him in medical school, where he had been a jovial asset. I helped to get him to an ambulance. He was taken to the rear where he remained for the rest of the war. (He later became a first rate ophthalmologist.)

This situation was not only new and stressful, but it required knowledge that I did not have. The most important duty of the commanding officer was to find a good place for the aid station. It had to be close enough to the extreme front lines to provide almost immediate help to wounded. At the same time, it had to have some shelter to protect the aid men and their patients, and access to an evacuation route. The commanding officer also had to direct the care of the most severely wounded. That I knew. I had to rely on the enlisted men to help me get oriented.

I started to heat my C-ration on a small gas stove, and almost immediately it was knocked off by a shell fragment. At least I had not been hit. I had hardly arrived there when a messenger from battalion arrived to say that I should take some men to treat a group of civilians who had just been hit by a German shell. I loaded a jeep with supplies and took off with my new driver and all the aid men I could pile onto the vehicle. The driver, "Gangster," was the oldest man in the unit. He had the beginnings of a beard, which was mostly gray. He was not a large man and he was not very military, but he did his job. Prior to the war, he had been a driver for a rum runner in New Jersey and he could get a jeep around fast.

The men had placed sandbags beneath my feet so that if we hit a mine, I might have some protection. We were alert at all times for traces of digging in the road. Our jeep had a prominent red cross flag. On the way, we came across a G.I. who had stepped on a mine. His lower leg was shattered beyond repair. It was necessary for me to amputate the most damaged portion immediately. We evacuated him in the ambulance that we had traveling with us.

We arrived at a large structure with a central courtyard. Civilians from the countryside had assembled there for safety. Because of the activity, the Germans might have thought this was a command center. They had dropped a major shell directly into the courtyard. There were dead and dying and wounded all over. I told the men to ignore the dead and to stop major bleeding when they could. I headed for the most severely injured that I could find. I also sent the battalion guide to get as many ambulances as were available.

The first object of my attention was a young girl of about five to six years. She was about the same age as my nieces at home. She was unconscious, but she had a flicker of a heartbeat. She was not breathing. I gave her mouth to mouth resuscitation and noticed there was some blood coming from her mouth. Probably the explosion had caused major internal injuries, though there were no external wounds. She started to breathe, though irregularly. With some difficulty, because her veins had collapsed, I started some plasma. I had pumped some in when she died. There was nothing I could do to revive her. I felt terrible, but I had more to do.

Nearby, was an older man who had had a major portion of his leg below the knee badly damaged. Surprisingly, the wounds did not bleed much, but the man was obviously in shock. An aid man had placed a tourniquet. I took the tourniquet off to see how much bleeding there would be, knowing that if I left it on, the man would lose his leg. I then made a splint with the wire ladder material I carried, put on pressure dressings, and started some plasma. Pumping the plasma obviously helped. I used a bulb from a blood pressure set and attached it to the air intake tube. Getting blood pressure up quickly was much to be desired with severe shock. The man was going to be all right. Whether his leg could be saved was another question.

We went from person to person. The courtyard was slippery from blood. The aid men were impressive. They knew what to do and moved quickly. Before long, ambulances began to arrive, along with some men from the collecting company. I felt good seeing the men I knew. I told them who to take first and suggested they bypass the collecting company station and head for the field hospital.

We stayed until the last living person was removed. There must have been twenty, with about as many dead. We were exhausted. We made sure that survivors who had not been injured in the blast could manage the dead. They were grateful to us but, of course, distraught over the loss of family and friends. We headed back to our aid station for some food. I broke out a bottle of Scotch, which was again a life saver after a very depressing day.

It is difficult to believe how unsophisticated I was, or for that matter, how naive were most graduates of medical schools at that time. I had never seen anyone who had been killed until the beach. We had seen cadavers and people who had died from disease or of other natural causes. However, seeing someone who has been killed is a grim experience. Somehow, the courtyard was worse than the beach in my mind. That courtyard splashed with blood and full of bodies stays in my mind to this day. There was a man with a cap and mustache still sitting in a chair. One of his legs had been blown off. He evidenced no sign of life. The young girl brought to mind my three nieces of her approximate age. The horror of that association continues.

There was a major change in my feelings about the war. My fury and hatred towards the Germans grew, and I wanted to help to destroy them.

The next day, we were to continue our advance toward St. Lo. That advance was preceded by a tremendous barrage from our artillery, which was now in place. We heard the now familiar freight train sound of heavy shells going over our heads. Now more experienced, our battalion cautiously moved forward, trying to take advantage of the heavy hedgerows. Tanks had been brought in to clear paths through mine fields. These were the tanks with long chains attached that flailed in front of them to explode the mines. These tanks were also targets, but the drivers risked their lives so that our men could move forward.

A sergeant more experienced than I helped me to pick a spot for our new aid station. It was a small field surrounded by hedgerows. There were trees and narrow openings at two corners. We enlarged those openings sufficiently to permit a jeep to pass. The ambulance drivers were afraid to enter this area. Men from the rear seemed always to fear being close to the front. Eventually, the ambulance drivers adjusted, but they always spent as little time forward as possible.

Soon after dawn, we began to receive casualties, many of whom were severely wounded. The aid men assigned to the station and I checked the dressings on the less severely wounded and gave them tetanus shots. We painted red Ts on their foreheads to let those in the rear know the shots had been given. We gave out a good deal of morphine and cigarettes, and we got these men out fast. We used the needle on the end of the syrette, a little tube like a tooth paste tube, to fasten the device to the wounded man's clothing to show we had given morphine. Our major objective was to get them to the rear before they were wounded again.

I assigned myself to the more severely wounded, making every effort to control major bleeding and starting plasma often. That was not always easy. I learned to use the femoral vein, which is deep in the groin, but larger than those in the extremities. It is not that easy to hit under those conditions.

Suddenly, there was a whistling sound followed very shortly by an explosion toward the rear of our field. It was my first experience with a mortar directed at us. Then there was a series of explosions much closer. Following my instinct, I dove for cover behind the forward hedgerow, as did most of the men who could move, and was soon covered with dirt and rock from the explosions. I suspect that because of the activity in our aid station, the Germans thought our station was a command post. They still seemed to respect our red crosses in the open. That this attack was made in error did not help us.

Then our heavy mortars seemed to get the range and began returning fire. Then it was quiet. I looked around. Everyone was covered with dirt. But there, standing, was one of my privates holding a bottle of plasma in his hand as the line went into a man lying on a litter near him.

That sight changed my life. I was embarrassed by not having attended to the wounded during the barrage by the example the private had set. Somewhere deep in my mind, I decided that such a thing would never happen again.

I made rounds. Some of the wounded had sustained new wounds. It was impossible to clean them adequately. We used up all our water trying to irrigate. We used up most of our bandages. We loaded the wounded onto jeeps as fast as possible and even persuaded an ambulance driver to come closer to our station where we could load wounded more easily. We instructed our drivers to return with more of everything. The amazing thing was that no one had been killed. Only one aid man was injured enough to require evacuation.

At this point one of the men said to me, "Lieutenant, you have blood all over your pants." I thought it was from one of the wounded, but then I noted a tear in my pants and then a superficial slash in my thigh. I did not remember being hit, and it was only then that I began to have some pain. I gave myself a tetanus shot. It was easy to clean this wound and to put a small bandage on it.

When the wounded had been evacuated, we gathered around to talk. A sergeant pointed out to me that if I filled in a wounded report on myself, I would be eligible for a Purple Heart. I said that it would be impossible for me to do that. After seeing the horrible wounds for which soldiers got Purple Hearts, I would be insulting them to accept one. Later on, it turned out that each medal was worth five points, the equivalent of five months in combat or ten months elsewhere. Even so, I could not have accepted such a decoration.

There was always a sense of exultation at having survived. One of the aid men had found some Calvados. I am still convinced, as I was then, that the desire for alcohol fueled our advance. It was the first thing the men searched for when they reached a farm. We began the first of many nights soothed by that rather raw, wonderful apple brandy.

We had had little to eat all day. We lived mostly on K-rations, boxes smaller than a Cracker Jack box containing a small tin of high fat food such as a mixture of eggs and minced ham, a

Aid Station Crew Second Battalion, 320th Infantry

A shelter behind a hedgerow, Normandy

fruit bar, some hard candy, powdered coffee or fruit juice, which contained our daily ration of vitamin C, and a small package of high calorie crackers. Most of us went for the fruit bars and coffee. Unfortunately, we rarely drank the fruit juice and therefore ended up with various degrees of scurvy. Even us physicians were not as nutrition conscious back then.

Even with all of our troubles, the mail came through, including the one-pound bars of Hershey or Nestle chocolate that my father regularly sent me. Also, there were D-rations that were simply bars of fortified chocolate with enough calories to last a day. They were not nearly as tasty as the Hershey, but if necessary, they could be used for trading. I supplemented my diet by making applesauce in my canteen cup from apples that grew on the trees left standing in Normandy. That was probably my source of vitamin C. When we were lucky, we were able to get C-rations. These were two cans. One would contain something like pork and beans. The other would contain large round cookies or crackers, candy, coffee or dehydrated fruit juice. If anything decent was available, the local infantry saw that we got it whether it was food, Calvados, clean clothes, or a new jeep. While the medics had gotten little attention during maneuvers, they were now appreciated tremendously.

A day later, we moved and, having learned how to use the hedgerow squares, set up a similar aid station. We were no sooner organized, then we began to receive a small barrage of mortar shells. We were warned briefly by the characteristic whistle of the shells coming in and backed up against the row for cover. Fortunately, this time there were, as yet, no wounded. In the midst of all of this, a private crawled to where I was and handed me a bunch of letters! It was amazing that mail was felt to be more important than just about anything. Among the letters was one from my good friend Jim. It contained a four leaf clover which, I have carried ever since.

We moved our station almost daily. On one of my first days in the battalion, I was out looking for a spot to set up, when a recon car in front of us hit a mine. As I rushed to help the men who were

George Kleinsteiber "Gangster" Napleon's Chateau.
My jeep.

Station Section C Co., Normandy

wounded, I noted signs of a number of Teller mines in the area. The telltale sign was dirt that had been dug up and replaced. Usually, these mines were planted near the edge of the road where the right wheels would hit: officers usually rode on the right sides of vehicles. Only enlisted men were supposed to drive. My driver and I carefully marked the mined areas with bandages. The engineers would be coming to clear them.

At this point, we were fighting side by side with the British. They were unbelievably courageous. I especially remember a man who had just lost a leg and might lose his other. He had been a gunner in a light tank that had taken a direct hit from an 88. Somehow his fellows had removed him from the tank without his having bled to death. Because there were no other medics around, we went to work. While we controlled the bleeding from the stump of his left leg, which had been severed above the knee, one of my men gave him a shot of morphine and a cigarette. I then cleaned the wound with water and placed a pressure dressing using some ace bandages. We splinted the other leg with a wire-ladder splint which we had unrolled and controlled bleeding with G.I. dressings and ace bandages. One of my other men started some I.V. plasma, which he hung from the side of our jeep. The British soldier never cried out in pain and courteously thanked us for what we were doing.

There was a never ending demand on us. We heard the cry "Medic!" day and night. I began taking benzedrine to stay awake. There was so much to do. In theory there were supposed to be two medical officers in each aid station, but I never had one join me. It was no place for a doctor to be, most thought.

One day, just before we finally got to St. Lo, I collapsed from exhaustion. I awakened not knowing where I was. The men had placed me on a litter, covered me with a blanket, and put me in the safest area they could find close to a hedgerow. They reported this event to the battalion commander who later took it into account in his assessment of my performance, which included being awarded the Bronze Star.

ONE	TO: Mrs. Henry Klein	FROM 1st.Lt.John A. Kapatei
John a. Kapolei	14 Sixth Avenue San Francisco, 9 California	O-511180 Co.C, 110 Med Bn. APO 35, c/o Postmaster New York, N.Y.
(CENSOR'S STAMP)	SEE INSTRUCTION NO. 2	(Sender's complete address above)

28 August 44

Dear Dotty,

Now that things are relatively in hand, and while I have a bit of time, I think this is a good time to tell you a little about the war. We landed on the now famed Omaha beach. Though the invasion was fairly old at that time, the debris still was much in evidence. We were rushed off our LST inland to an assembly area. In another day, we moved inland, and on the following morning, we replaced a division that had pushed as far as it could from the beach. The first night inland, before we replaced the division, I slept in a foxhole for the first time. Artillery was going off all around us, and at that time we had not learned to distinguish the sound of our artillery from the explosion of the enemy shells; so it was a pretty frightening night -- though all the noise was our artillery. Our first position was the gravel quary of which I told you long ago. It was fairly close to the front for a collecting station, about a thousand yards. I'll never forget the first morning when the casualties began coming in. In the early battle experience, the men though t that conditions were much worse than they really were. Most of the men we saw then had been already treated in the aid stations. It was sometime before casualties occurred near enough to us for us to be the first to see them: They were from a tank destroyer. One had three compound communted fractures below the knee, another had a severe wound below the knee. I was happy to learn that these legs were preserved in miracles of orthopaedic surgery. All this was in the battle of St.Lo. Finally, as you know, our troops broke out into Brittany. It was at that time, that we moved to the beautiful apple orchard. When we took off again, it was toward the Vire river. We had been advancing for two days when I received orders to take over the second battalion aid station and its job of battalion surgeon. The station had had three medical officers leave already. One had been wounded, two had become victims of combat fatigue the day I was sent up. The aid station was about four-hundred yards from the front lines. All of the men were pretty scared especially since most had seen their commanding officers leave that day. I started to heat my C-ration on a little gasoline stove (of which we have three for thirty men) only to have it knocked off by a shell fragment as my initiation to my new position. On the following day, I moved my station up with the troops. The first casualties were from mines one of which demanded medically for a rough field amputation which I did. I soon found that I would see much worse. And so we proceeded. A day or so later was the day that a German shell landed in a crowded group of civilians. There had been a tank destroyer fairly near them, and a German hiding behind our lines signalled for fire. It was the most horrible sight I've ever seen. It was at this place that that lovely little French girl died while I was working desperately on her. But worse was coming. As we advanced on the river, we came down an open hillside facing a much higher hill held by the Germans. My station had hardly been set up, in the shelter of a hedgerow when the Jerries began

HAVE YOU FILLED IN COMPLETE ADDRESS AT TOP?

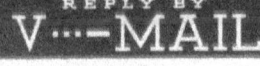

HAVE YOU FILLED IN COMPLETE ADDRESS AT TOP?

There were two important developments in my life that were related to the fact that there was a Chaplain attached to my battalion aid station. He was a good man, but the conditions were beyond him. So, after the mortar attack on my station, he decided to leave. I did not see him again until after the war. However, he left behind a portable typewriter. Though I had regularly written letters home, I found it much easier and faster with the typewriter. So, whenever there was a break in action, I wrote letters. It was probably a form of therapy, though I did not recognize that aspect at that time. A large number of the letters I wrote were saved and returned to me after the war. There were over two hundred of them. I did not reread these letters until recently. A history professor at U.C. Santa Cruz encouraged me to write up the material in those letters. He felt it would fill some of the gaps in our knowledge regarding those times. This narrative is a product of that discussion.

There was a second use of the typewriter: "Kappy's News." Shortly after I joined the infantry battalion, my men found an old beaten-up radio. Ingenious as they were, they got the radio going with bits of wire and a battery that was designed for mine sweepers. The BBC daily broadcast the news at a very slow rate so that it could be picked up all over Europe and any other interested party. I was one of those. I typed the daily news as I heard it, and posted it on a tree or any other convenient spot. I also would include any local information that I had obtained. Men from all over the battalion came to read my newsletter; since there was no other reliable source. Later we began to receive the Army newspaper, the *Stars and Stripes*. That publication often did not have as much current news as mine did, and we did not see it often.

Chapter 9

Childbirth

July 15, 1944

As we approached St. Lo, the fighting grew more intense. However, I had begun to learn the ropes. I now knew that it was important to put my aid station in a sheltered area as close as possible to the front lines to make it easier for my aid men to get wounded back to the station. Usually, I set it up behind a large hedgerow, which protected it at least from direct fire. Our main worry was mortar fire, because mortar shells made a high arc and dropped almost directly downward. Finally, I tried to set up the station near an evacuation route so that I could put wounded on jeeps or ambulances to get them back farther from the combat area.

What we did was relatively simple, but at the same time, awful. The aid men tried to control hemorrhaging and to cover wounds. When the wounded man got to our aid station, if he had any significant wound, we started an I.V. of plasma, which came packed in square boxes each bottle with an I.V. line attached. It was not easy to start I.V.s since wounded men were often in shock, and shock usually causes veins to collapse.

I was particularly good at starting I.V.s, in part because in medical school I had done blood tests on draft candidates, many of whom were narcotic addicts whose veins had been quite ruined by the injection of drugs. In addition, I had been trained mostly on women patients, and women's veins are smaller than men's. Then, too, as I mentioned before, I was good at hitting the femoral vein. None of the men had training in that. So, when any of my men had trouble starting plasma, I was called upon.

It is necessary to hang plasma bottles above the patient so that gravity will cause the bottle to drain. We had to use various makeshift supports. Often we put a bayonet on a rifle, pushed the bayonet into the ground, and attached the plasma to the butt of the rifle. Occasionally, I would pump to make the plasma flow more rapidly as we tried to overcome shock.

On our next move, I set up my aid station in back of a partially ruined stone barn, making a crude shelter out of two pup tents. This measure was necessary to keep us and the wounded out of the rain, which seemed ever present, and it also provided an area that could be blacked out at night. It was a sturdy barn and quite a large one. In this location, though close to the front, we were sheltered from direct fire, and were unlikely to be hit by mortar shells. There also was a road leading to the rear. It was not much of a road, being unpaved, but it led to our collecting station about a thousand yards farther to the rear.

It was important for the shelter to be light proof because German planes came over at night. They had a steady low beating sound and attracted a great deal of antiaircraft fire, though I never saw one of these German planes fall. They usually did not risk flying during the day since we had air superiority. At night they dropped flares that lit the sky like daylight so that they could find bombing targets.

At dusk, on our first night in this new location, two Frenchmen came into our station carrying a ladder. On it, lying on a quilt, was a young woman with a distended abdomen and obviously in active labor. She was in great distress, because of fear and her labor pains. From the nature of her pain, there was no question that the labor was far advanced.

First I listened to the baby's heart with a stethoscope. We took the young woman into our shelter for further examination. I could barely get into the tent with an aid man, the ladder, and the patient. I put a blanket on the ground, and we moved her onto it from the ladder. It was then necessary to remove our patient's underclothing and she seemed embarrassed. By good fortune, the aid man spoke a little French, so he helped in giving the girl instructions.

I covered her with one of our blankets and looked at her perineum. With contractions her labia separated and, to my surprise, I found that the baby was presenting a footling breech. I could see its buttocks and one foot. Under the best of conditions, breech deliveries, particularly of first babies, are of major concern to obstetricians. The largest part of the baby, the head and shoulders,comes last. In normal deliveries, with the head first, the birth passage is dilated by the head so that the rest of the baby usually follows without a problem. With a breech, because of the lack of complete dilation of the birth canal, the baby's head sometimes gets caught, which delays delivery, with possible damage due to asphyxiation or skeletal injury. The next best part of the baby to dilate the birth canal is the baby's bottom, but in this case the presenting foot complicated matters. Caesarean section was out of the question, and also there was not time enough to get this woman to a hospital.

I had to get more help. Inside the tent were two aid men, the patient, and me. We took up all the available space. One of the aid men held a lamp, and one supported the girl's legs in a fashion I directed. We cleaned her perineum with soap and water. The man who understood a little French instructed her at my direction. By this time, with each contraction some of the breech and a foot protruded through the introitus, the entrance to the vagina.

I had been trained to do an episiotomy in this situation. An episiotomy is an incision at the entrance of the vagina toward the rear. It is performed to make more room for delivery of the after-coming head. This incision is usually done with scissors. My aid men and I always carried a pair of heavy bandage scissors that are angled, with the tip of one blade having a blunt projection to slide under bandages that need cutting. We carried them to cut off the clothes of wounded men to get to wounds. I had my pair, but of course they were not sterile. I cleaned them with alcohol. We did not have suture material and other necessary instruments immediately available so it would be difficult to do a good repair. Therefore, I decided to try to deliver the baby without episiotomy and to keep the scissors at hand. I would only make the incision if absolutely necessary.

Naturally, I did not have obstetrical forceps, which are often used on the after-coming head. I washed my hands as best I could. I did not have sterile gloves. I massaged the posterior part of the vagina to make more room. Things were moving rapidly, but I hoped for the best.

I delivered the baby using a maneuver I had learned as an obstetrical intern. It is important to let the baby deliver spontaneously until the scapula (the large flat bone on the rear of the shoulder) is in sight. Then it is easy to deliver the legs across the belly. The shoulders are turned so that they are anterior and posterior. The posterior arm is delivered wiping it across the baby's chest, then the anterior arm. The baby is then rotated so that its head is anterior posterior, with the chin in the sacrum. The head is delivered keeping it flexed. You can do this by placing a hand so that one finger is in the mouth and two on the ridge above the mouth. You lift the baby so that you can see the mouth and clear it. Then with further extension of the baby the head is delivered. Gentle pressure on the lower abdomen helps. The total delivery time was no more than three or four minutes though it seemed like an eternity.

The method worked to perfection. Somehow, under my direction, the man holding the light was able to apply proper pressure. The other man was busy supporting the girl's legs and keeping them spread apart to make delivery possible.

The baby, a girl, was fine. We tied the cord with some narrow dressing and I cut the cord with the bandage scissors. A small dressing was placed over the stump of the cord and held in place with a roll bandage wrapped around the baby. We gave it to the mother. The baby was crying lustily, music to our ears. I encouraged the mother to try to nurse right then, because nursing encourages the uterus to contract. We did not have drugs for this purpose, such as pitocin or ergotrate. Contraction of the uterus would cut down blood loss and help with the delivery of the placenta. The mother understood about nursing, and having given up her modesty, exposed her breast, and the baby started sucking immediately.

There had been no sedation, and the baby was wide awake. Miraculously, there had been only a very small tear during the delivery, and it did not bleed significantly. I delivered the placenta with a simple maneuver which involved some gentle pressure on the top of the uterus and gentle traction on the cord. Fortunately, this process went simply and well. Perhaps the mother's nursing helped.

The men had never seen an obstetrical delivery before, but they worked well with me. Just before the mother had been brought to our station, the ambulance assigned to us from the collecting company had left with two badly wounded men, and it returned at this point. Occasionally we heard the tearing sound of German hand-held rapid fire weapons. Our men called them "burp" guns. There was some responding fire from our side, mostly small arms with the occasional thump thump of our fifty caliber machine guns. In spite of that, we loaded mother and baby into the ambulance. We also loaded the two men who came with her. I encouraged the mother to keep on trying to nurse the baby to prevent postpartum hemorrhage. She understood that. They left, without saying thank you. I guess they were all too frightened.

The young woman was fortunate to have been taken to my aid station because I am sure there was no one within many miles who had the remotest idea how to deliver a baby presenting as a breech. At that point, there was a vital change in the attitude of the aid men. They respectfully congratulated me. They realized that, even though I knew little of military matters, I could make good medical decisions and act on them. The next morning, we got a report that the mother and baby were doing well, and I received some bottles of Calvados from some of the locals.

It is interesting to note that those civilians were the first we had seen since those wounded and killed in the courtyard two weeks before. I will never know how they knew where my aid station was. The whole event somehow got to be known, and it was written up in the *Stars and Stripes*. That was the only baby I delivered in my entire time in the Army. I often wonder about that young mother and her daughter, about how their lives turned out.

Chapter 10

The Men Of
The Second Battalion

July, 1944

The men of the battalion aid station of the 2nd Battalion of the 320th were of a different mold. They were from Kansas and Nebraska. Many were from farms, and some were from less affluent areas of cities like Omaha. Some were married. Some had girl friends. Many had known each other well before their service, and had gone to National Guard meetings and to summer camp together. Interestingly, the aid men had been chosen, not because of their medical background, but because they seemed least likely to make fighting men. Many had been school teachers. Some were art teachers. The farm workers were chosen who seemed to be less interested in combat. All of them were younger than I was, except for my driver.

My jeep driver, George Steinbriner was the one who had been a driver for rum runners in New Jersey. I do not know how he got to the Division. He was much older than the average soldier. He was often unshaven. He could drive like crazy, and he just did not seem to have fear. I kept Volkman close to the aid station. He was a gentle person who had a knack for emergency medical care. With no formal medical training, he was the best among the men in starting I.V. plasma, often difficult in the collapsed veins of wounded in shock. Clark was another who remained cool under the most trying circumstances. Banks, my staff sergeant, was my teacher. He was older than most. He had learned rapidly, and was the man responsible for converting our jeeps to litter carriers. He helped me to learn the ropes in finding good places for the aid station.

On the first day of the offensive, the division was told to take the city of St. Lo. On that day, it was repulsed with devastating losses inflicted by Germans in effective positions. The division did little better the next day. It took eleven days to go the relatively short distance of about fifteen miles to St. Lo. During that time, we all grew up.

I could never get over the bravery of the aid men ministering to the wounded in the field. When I joined this group, they had had two days of huge demands on them. They were often under fire, although the German infantry respected the red crosses they had painted on our helmets and field jackets.

Our division was inexperienced and just had not learned how to function in modern combat situations. Leadership errors, such as going down the wrong road, led to carnage among our troops. A company of our battalion was sent down a road that seemed to be the right way to approach a German strong point, but the map was wrong, and the company found itself exposed. The Germans knew how to take advantage of even our most minor errors. They were experienced in ways of war, and they knew how to use their advanced weaponry, the most effective of which was the 88 mm. gun, a small artillery piece which could be fired with the accuracy of a rifle. The 88 was used against tanks, as an antipersonnel weapon, and even as an antiaircraft gun.

The Germans, besides using hedgerows as defensive fortifications, had created strong points. Typical was the church of St. Gilles. It was sturdily built of sandstone, and its walls were eighteen inches thick. At the top of the church was a machine gun nest. The rest of the structure bristled with firepower. Labor battalions had further strengthened the area with concrete walls three feet thick. This church blocked the road to St. Lo, and many men fell before it. Heavy artillery could not close it down. Finally, some brave men in tank destroyers drove up to the church and fired directly into it.

It turned out that the tank destroyers were among the most effective weapons. They were really mobile armored artillery. It was they that finally helped the infantry to get through the hedgerows. They would keep the German machine gunners bottled up while our infantry surrounded them.

Certainly, for me there was so much to learn and to teach. Immediately on arriving and seeing the nature and the number of casualties, I sent for as many elastic bandages, wire splints, bandage scissors, and field dressings as could be delivered. They came almost immediately. I learned that the request of combat medics could be more powerful than that of many field officers.

It was necessary for me to teach my aid men methods and techniques different from those in which they had been trained. For example, they had been taught to put sulfanilamide in wounds. Even though it had been developed by my surgery professor, Howard Naffziger, its use for our purposes seemed to be a poor idea. My reasoning was that the sulfanilamide powder acted as a foreign body and interfered with healing. If this medication had been in a liquid form, it would have been better. I instructed the aid men to irrigate the wounds with water, or better, with dilute soap and water whenever possible. We did use the sulfa powder but only in moderation. At that time, the only antibiotics were sulfa drugs and we were just beginning to learn how to use them safely. The next step—though this was the first step in cases of hemorrhage—was to put on a dressing and to apply pressure with an elastic bandage. If the wound was of an extremity, I instructed the aid men to place a splint if there was time. These techniques had already been tried by me in the collecting company, but the conditions there were more leisurely. If an aid man and his patient were under fire, it was best to get the wounded man out of harms way, even if the wound treatment was not perfect.

I had little experience in leadership and, certainly, none in selecting a proper position for an aid station, which had to be set up as close to the fighting as possible, yet to offer some sort of protection from direct fire—such as the station in which I delivered the baby—and to have access both to the headquarters of the battalion and to the collecting company. Because of rain and the need to work at night, I usually tried to construct some sort of shelter unless I could find a very sturdy farmhouse out of the line of fire. I was worried about the possibility of tetanus in barns; so I usually kept out of them and set stations beside them. Scouting for these sites was frightening for me. I had to head for the most intense fire, being careful to avoid the mines which the Germans had placed along roads and often in fields. My map reading ability was poor at first, and often I would get lost. Once a G.I. rose from the side of the road to warn me that if I went another hundred yards, I would be inside the German lines.

But even greater than my fear of being wounded, which I had learned to accept, was my fear of being captured. Often at night, I could hear German conversation. It literally made my blood run cold. I knew about the German treatment of Jews, and I did not know, were they to capture me, if they would respect the Geneva Conventions. It was mandatory that I learn quickly to read maps, and I did.

Within a couple of days, I had learned the abilities of my men. There were twenty-two of them. It became obvious to me that Banks had the respect of the men and that he was cool under fire. He and I made a good command team. We usually scouted for new station sites together. Two of our aid men were attached to each combat company. Three companies were combat infantry and one had heavy weapons. The rest of the men made up the aid station team.

As I was learning this new job, we received huge numbers of casualties. We worked steadily. Our main job continued to be to fight shock, which meant that we had to give plasma and control hemorrhage. Having done that, we improved the dressings that the aid men had put on when they first picked up the wounded. If an aid man and his patient were under heavy fire, the most important thing was to get the wounded man to a sheltered area. The aid men would place a dressing and try to control hemorrhage, but because they were anxious to get the wounded out of danger, their control of bleeding and their splinting were often inadequate. It was difficult to keep wounds clean. At the station, we would give morphine if it had not already been given. A red M on the soldier's forehead meant that he had been given morphine. If heavy fire prevented an aid man from writing this message, he would just stick the empty morphine syrette to the soldier's clothing.

The dose of morphine was one quarter grain, which is a significant amount. When we were uncertain whether a wounded soldier had been given morphine, we gave him an injection, which could have been a second dose. We dispensed cigarettes freely. We usually placed wounded on litters so that they could be transported quickly to jeeps or ambulances. Often we did not have enough litters, so we put the wounded on blankets or even on the ground. There were often piles of bloody clothes near the station. Whether owing to bravery or shock, the wounded soldiers hardly ever cried out.

When we finally entered St. Lo, that city was a pile of rubble. We had suffered major losses of men, but the survivors here were a different group. We were seasoned combat soldiers. Yet, in St. Lo, we had a full dose of how horrible war can be. We were almost overwhelmed with what we had to do. Fortunately, there was little fighting after dark, although the Germans threw in occasional mortar and 88 shells.

Learning how to use the hedgerows and to overcome the German defenses took time and cost many lives. Fortunately, I did not lose a single aid man at that time, though a few had sustained wounds. Of my wounded aid men, only two had to be evacuated; two, after being bandaged, chose to stay with us. That was quite

This was my wonderful little stove

3 3/4" long x 2 3/4" wide

surprising; for I thought, they would accept any excuse to get to the rear. Our little unit had developed an esprit de corps. Obviously I was pleased and reported the bravery of these men to my superior, who later put them in for decorations.

By the time we reached St. Lo, I was exhausted and had put a dent in my supply of benzedrine, which I used at times to keep myself going. I also made coffee at every opportunity. I had a small gas stove in my jeep, on which I was able to heat water. We had learned how to survive and how to work together, and that knowledge was to stand us in good stead as we approached our next challenge.

There are vivid memories of that time, some humorous. One day, some of our men came upon a screened structure which had a horrible odor. They decided to set it afire before it could contaminate our troops. A French farmer had placed his cheese in this structure to let it ripen. It will be impossible to forget the unripe apples from which I made apple sauce. I remember abandoned equipment and packs everywhere. Local calvados could be as powerful as alcoholic drinks get. (I often carried a canteen of it.) I cannot forget a dead G.I. standing behind a hedgerow; our constant fear of booby traps and mines; bees swarming around the jam that came with some of our rations (and I became allergic to their stings); and coming upon both dead German and American soldiers.

Through all of this, there was a valuable piece of equipment that I somehow acquired from the Germans shortly after I became a battalion surgeon. It was a remarkable pocket sized stove, a metal box 3-3/4 by 2-3/4 inches and an inch thick. The top unfolded, becoming two upright metal supports upon which one could place anything that needed to be warmed. The little stove came with tablets that burned, giving off very little light. It was possible to heat a ration or a canteen cup over its fire to make coffee or, as I often did, applesauce. When I had used up all the tablets, I got a small jar lid, put ethyl alcohol in it, and set it afire. It, too, warmed my meal with very little flame and no conspicuous light. It was truly an ingenious design and inexpensive to make. Our Army had nothing like it. I was so grateful for this gem that I have kept it to this day. We did have a couple of Coleman stoves that burned fuel, such as gasoline, but they were much bulkier than mine. These were usually used to make coffee for the aid men and the wounded and to boil water.

As we progressed across France, I continued to learn from the Germans, who were much more experienced at war than we were. The little stove was only one example. They were skilled at camouflage and in setting up strong protective screens. Their discipline was obvious.

Letter from Normandy

Dear Dorothy,

We had been advancing for two days when I received orders to take over the second battalion aid station and its job of battalion surgeon. The station had had three medical officers leave already. One had been wounded two had become victims of combat fatigue the day I was sent up. The station was about four hundred yards from the front lines. All of the men were pretty scared, especially since most had seen their commanding officers leave that day. I started to heat my C ration on a little gasoline stove (of which we have three for thirty men) only to have it knocked off by a shell fragment as my initiation to my new position. On the following day, I moved my station up with the troops. The first casualties were from mines, one of which injured men and demanded medically a field amputation which I did with my heavy bandage scissors. I soon found out that I would see much worse. So, we proceeded. A day or so later was the day that a German shell landed in a crowded group of civilians. There had been a tank destroyer fairly near them and a German hiding behind our lines signaled for fire.

It was the most horrible sight I've ever seen. It was at this place that that lovely little French girl died while I was desperately working on her. But worse was coming. As we advanced on the river we came down an open hillside facing a much higher hill held by Germans. My station had barely been set up in the shelter of a hedgerow when the Jerries began to shell the neighboring CP. Heavy shells whistled over our heads and were landing all about us. Casualties began to come in carried by my litter bearers. You can't desert a wounded man, so with only slight cover, we worked on them while the shells kept landing. Spent fragments hit me in the knee without so much as breaking my skin. I hardly noticed it as I was putting a plasma needle into the vein at the time. Our artillery soon opened up, and we were able to cross the river. That morning, I had gone out looking for a spot for an aid station. The roads were not cleared of mines, but war demands that you take some chances. A recon car in front of us hit a mine. The men in it were not badly hurt. As I treated the wounded, I could see the telltale evidence of other teller mines in the early morning light. My driver and I took time to mark them to protect others who advanced ahead of the hardworking engineers. We finally pulled up to our objective. The British were nearby in Vire. I treated some British soldiers who certainly had guts, especially one who had lost a leg and stood in danger of losing the other.

We moved from there to another location. While moving, I had the experience of having a shell come over my head and land about fifty yards in front of me. The fragments went forward, so none of my men got hurt. Needless to say we hugged ditches closely for a while. From the time I left the collecting company, I dug no more than a couple of fox holes. There just wasn't time. I just looked for natural cover when the going got hot. At Mortain, my driver and I were the first to get through to the surrounded troops. Many of those had been wounded and not really treated for many days. They were still being shelled when we got there. This was the first time that our red crosses had been deliberately shot at. We were facing SS troops. We got the wounded out when the rest of our outfit got through, however before that we used gallons of plasma and most of the bandages we had. When all was secure, we moved out until we were stopped by a barrage of mortar shells, many of which were very close. We took cover. It is hard to believe, but at that point, a soldier came with some mail. In one letter was a four-leaf clover from Jimmy (Schwabacher). It was from their ranch. (I still have it.)

All my love to you and your swell kids. I think the worrying times are over, or I wouldn't have talked so much.*

Love, Johnny

* (How wrong I was.)

Chapter 11

Mortain

July, 1944

We did not stop in St. Lo. The city and the surrounding area were devastated. We were now to be part of the Third Army, and our assignment was to break out of Normandy, head across France, and take as many prisoners as possible. This increase in mobility put a strain on my aid group, which had been planned, World War I fashion, to be infantry. We needed more transport. I had two jeeps and trailers. We loaded as many aid men onto the trailers as possible, but there was not enough room for all. The men had found a shot-up German command car. With true Nebraska farm ability, they got the car, a Mercedes convertible, to work. They got some G.I. paint to convert it, painting a U.S. white star on the hood. We were ready to go in style, with the new car, the coffee I made on the road, and my chocolate.

We were moving along, getting more ovations, flowers, and various kinds of alcohol from the French who lined the road. My jeep's windshield was down so as not to reflect light and attract fire. It was covered by a heavy canvas which closed with a zipper. In this space, I kept a row of bottles—Calvados (our staple), wine, and anything else we were able to capture or receive.

Along the road for the breakout was the city of Mortain. Rommel had sent some of his best troops to cut off Patton's Third Army, to which we were now attached. By the time we arrived in the area, Panzer troops of "der Fuhrer" and "Deutschland" Regiments of the SS das Reich Division and taken Mortain from the 30th Division's 120th Infantry, which had been placed to protect the opening through which the Third Army was to pass into the heart of France. The remains of the 120th were surrounded. The chaplain and most of the medics had been captured. Planes had dropped medical and other supplies, but most of these had been collected by the Germans. Artillery tried to send in supplies in metal containers, but when they landed, they usually were smashed and their contents unusable. We knew that there were many wounded who needed help. Our job was to dislodge the Germans, keep the road open, and rescue the surrounded men of the 120th.

Our regiment attacked with tanks and infantry. We lost thirty-one of our fifty-five tanks. The German tanks had superior firepower, and they knew how to use it. These were elite troops we faced. The struggle was bloody and confused. For the first time, our red crosses meant nothing. Many of my aid men were wounded, though miraculously, no one was killed. My jeep acquired a couple of bullet holes, as did the red cross flag, but the jeep still ran. We had never been up against such ruthless adversaries. We were overwhelmed with severely wounded, though I believe that the tankers fared even worse than did our infantry. Surprisingly, we began to open a way for the Third Army to break through. The following day, my driver, "Gangster," and I decided that it was time for us to try to get to the wounded of 120th. We loaded our jeep and trailer with all kinds of supplies. While the battle was going on we had found a road that went toward the surrounded regiment. Steinbriner got the jeep going at full speed, broke into the open, and headed for the hill with the surrounded men. We drove right through the German lines! The Germans themselves were confused, since in this sector they were facing the surrounded

120th, and they did not expect action from their rear. When they realized that we were going through, they began to shoot at us, even though I had Red Cross flags flying, but we got through. As we were racing down the road I saw a number of our soldiers dead in the field in front of the hill that was our goal.

There were cheers from the men of the 120th when we arrived in their lines. In a quarry that had been converted to a vast aid area were men in need of plasma and other forms of medical help. Some had gangrenous lesions. Many of the wounds were horrible. The 120th's aid personnel and we rapidly put our supplies to work. My Calvados was most welcome, as were my cigarettes and chocolate. These men had had little to eat. It was not long before we had used up most of the supplies we had brought in. Wounded continued to arrive.

That night, under the flares of the Luftwaffe, the remaining men of our regiment reorganized and combined. At dawn, the infantry stormed Mortain and the ridge on which the 120th had been surrounded. The lost battalion was saved. I was so happy to see our men. By then, I had used up all my supplies, and I had been uncertain whether our regiment could prevail against the SS. I was exhausted and, in spite of having taken benzedrine, passed out. As our unit reformed, my men carefully put me on a litter and then loaded it onto our jeep. I awakened on the road.

That night we made camp and thought back on the previous couple of days. What did I remember most? On the race through the German lines, we passed an American soldier, dead in his foxhole, leaning over its forward edge. His helmet had fallen off to reveal brilliant red hair glowing in the sun. When we arrived at the area where the wounded had been collected, it looked like one of the worst scenes from the Civil War. The grateful reception we got from the wounded made the whole somewhat rash trip worthwhile. That day was one reason for which, much later, I got my first Bronze Star medal, as did my driver.

As we progressed along the road, we were met by wilder and wilder ovations. Often people were greeting us while there was fighting going on. For the first time, we began to run into the Free French who helped us by hitting the German rear guard from behind.

On our first night out of Mortain, I set up our station near a large and prosperous farm. For breakfast the next day, with our canned bacon, we had fresh eggs, still warm from the hens. This was our first fresh food in a long time. While at breakfast, we were able to see the owner's well-trained dogs herding sheep. This previously had been a stud farm and was kept up in a fashion reminiscent of the fine farms of a similar nature in the United States. There were acres of beautiful lawn spotted with bright flower beds, many of which formed designs. There were exercising rings, spotless stables, huge clean barns, beautiful carriages of all descriptions. The Germans had taken all the riding horses, but there were still a significant number of good looking work horses. There were two homes on the grounds, one owned by the caretaker and one by the administrator, who had been taken prisoner.

That night, I was quartered in the administrator's home. It had high ceilings, tall windows, and some lovely French provincial furniture. The wallpaper was bright and summery and went with the place. There were about fourteen rooms, and a room had been fixed up for me. The bed was comfortable with fresh linen and even a bright spread. There were clean towels, pitchers of water, and a wash basin, all of which had been set out by a housekeeper. The view from the window was lovely and framed by tall, lacy trees. Through them, I could see a smooth bright stream curving through brightly flowering bushes and shrubs.

At dinner, in a dining room, I opened my last bottle of wine, which was Champagne marked "nur fur der Wehrmacht." I was exhausted and slept, disturbed only occasionally by the firing of guns. This whole experience was so unbelievable. I had been sleeping on a litter or on the ground for weeks. Most of my food had been rations. This interlude from combat was like a dream, and I was determined to make the most of it. I remained in bed late and savored every minute. I was awakened by Clark, who said we were to move out in an hour. He was a tall quiet man from south Omaha who always seemed to have cigarette in his mouth. He did a good job of looking after me, along with Sergeant Banks.

What an incongruous night! It seemed strange to return to my jeep and my group, who also had found wonders in this farm, most certainly including some friendly women. The contrast between the small sea of wounded in the quarry where I had been only a day before and "the Horse Farm," as we called it, was unbelievable. One result of the crazy effort my driver and I made was that our men treated us with profound respect from then on.

PRESIDENTIAL CITATION:

The First Battalion, 320th Infantry, and the 737th Tank Battalion have been cited by President Truman for the rescue of the Lost Battalion, of the 30th Div., at Mortain.

Chapter 12

Letter to Dorothy

July 22, 1944
St. Lo

Dear Dotty,

You mentioned that people at home do not seem to know that there is a war going on.

Each citizen ought to spend a few minutes on a battlefield. The boys who are fighting the American people's war are under a constant threat of death, a death which in itself has little glory. This threat is a source of great nervous strain. At best, they fight for days with a couple of hours rest, eating when they can—often while walking. The food is usually cold. The great fatigue is something no civilian—not even an intern—can comprehend. Yet they go on, and when there is a halt in the fighting, there is a ready joke, and the strong try to bolster the weak.

The men here now realize that at least the French love them and would suffer privation for them. They have seen the Germans. They have discovered that the French will cheer them as they stand in the ruins of their own homes and of their total fortunes. The sincere gratitude of these people has done much to bolster the morale of our troops who often say "What the hell are we fighting for?" when they hear of strikes back home, or receive letters like the last you sent describing the home front, or hear of the social exploits of scions of New York society.

Love, John

Chapter 13

Le Mans

August 15, 1944

Leaving the Horse Farm we moved rapidly and without resistance of any significance to our first large city, Le Mans. All cities and towns had been declared "out of bounds" for troops in an effort to keep money, prostitution, drinking, and consumption of local food supplies under control. However, being a medic and having a vehicle, I was able to drive into Le Mans.

Despite the war, the French had made a definite effort to keep things up, perhaps to show the Germans that they could not be intimidated. The stores had bright fronts and were painted a variety of colors. The public buildings—including the Palais de Justice, fronted by its small, colorful garden—were elegant and graced by beautiful ironwork. My first view of the city was from the town square, which, interestingly, had a gravel center. One of the large buildings had been taken over by the Civil Affairs Department, and various civilians were being brought in for having collaborated with the Germans. Along the square were many cafes, most of which had neat tables on the broad sidewalk where wine and other drinks were being served to civilians and to the few fortunate soldiers, like myself, who managed to get into town at the risk of a fifty dollar fine.

The civilians were jovial and friendly. Though their city had not suffered much, their friends and relations had. I talked with a couple of escaped prisoners who had been working in coal mines in Germany. Their daily ration of food was 300 grams of bread, and a bowl of soup.

I had one of the Army French books to help us with the language. It was sadly inadequate. A very nice French girl helped me a bit with vocabulary. Speaking of French girls, they had some more "stuff" to me than the English women ever thought of having. They dressed, despite material shortages, in a style reminiscent of Southern California wearing bright colors and loose comfortable garments. They had ready smiles and in general, were much more friendly than the British. Of course, these were initial impressions, but time and experience sustained them.

The first evening of our stay I visited one of the great cathedrals of France, founded by and dedicated to St. Julian, who Christianized Le Mans in the Third Century. This Gothic structure dwarfed the largest I had ever seen. I entered through a high old wooden Twelfth Century door into a vast area where the ceiling soared overhead in Gothic arches. The place was breathtakingly beautiful. Certainly, I felt that I was in a house of God (whom I felt to be the same for all men), and to whom I offered a prayer of thanks for my safe keeping so far and of hope for a speedy victory.

It began to look like I might have a chance. I wrote to Ann to tell her I had made it through what I thought would be the worst. I was not permitted to mention where we were. I hoped that she had good news from her husband. However, I very much missed seeing her. I sent my love. Coincidentally, that very day, I received a charming and very concerned letter from her. She seemed to know just how to deal with our brief relationship with good sense, and I think with love. I wish I still had her letter.

The next morning, I returned for the high mass celebrating liberation. I arrived at the end of the service and saw the procession, detailed as only a Roman Catholic one can be, with beautifully colored vestments decorated with lovely French braid.

The choir boys came first, singing. They wore bright red gowns with white lace jackets. Then came the archbishop and the associate archbishop, followed by a large staff of elders, brothers, and others, each in his own elaborate dress denoting his rank.

The cathedral's beautifully stained windows, the oldest in France, had not been damaged by the war. The walls and ceiling were pure white. The oldest chapel was formed of varicolored stone from the countryside. Each doorway had a beautiful hand-carved wooden door. Over the main entrance was the main organ, and it was larger than many a small church and its woodwork was equally fine. One of the priests explained in English that the church had been added to and taken apart and rebuilt since the Twelfth Century. He also said that the first German speaking people here were Austrians, and that they attended mass occasionally, and the Germans, who came later, seldom came. He was surprised that we kept our troops out of the city, but I explained that we did not want to use their scarce stocks of merchandise. (I did not express our fears of drunkenness and venereal disease slowing up our troops in the speedy victory that we were seeking.)

Near this lovely city were the remains of a concentration camp once used for French civilians and soldiers and later, for French colonials. The Germans had a great distaste for the black French colonials, and German prisoners often asked us how we could have blacks in our army. I was surprised to see that the French people treated the black soldiers as equals, and that French women had no reluctance in associating with them. That was a source of great pleasure for our black troops who, for the most part, were not treated as equals in our own Army.

This city had only about a hundred thousand inhabitants, and it was just awakening from a long silence. Shutters were coming down. Shops were opening. This was a new world. The roads were lined by tall trees, and there were lovely residential districts with homes that had tall, sloping roofs. I liked the people and was sorry that I knew so little French. These people were impressed by our equipment and our efficiency. Of course, they were not aware of our fumbling start.

We had the impression that because we had broken out of Normandy, nothing could stop us. But there were some blips along the way and then our second major struggle.

Chapter 14

Chateaudun

August 19, 1944

When we left Le Mans, we drove along the road without encountering opposition. We approached the small city of Chateaudun in battle formation with two battalions abreast and one in reserve. As we neared the city, we were suddenly met with a hail of machine gun fire. There was a German airport in Chateaudun, and the troops protecting it were well-trained. They had directed their antiaircraft machine guns down the road on which we were approaching. We could also hear the rumble of Tiger tanks. We had not expected this. Soldiers broke for cover into the fruit trees that grew on either side of the road, but it was difficult to move vehicles out of the line of fire because the road was elevated, and there was a drop into the trees on either side of it. This change in our situation occurred in a matter of seconds.

Out in the open and near the road, I saw a G.I. fall, obviously hit in the chest. I grabbed an aid sack from my jeep and ran toward this wounded man. He was alive, but there was a gaping hole in his chest on the right side. His jacket had been torn and was stained with blood. I could hear air being sucked into the wound. That was the major problem with chest wounds: if air got into the chest cavity, it would cause the lung to collapse and make it difficult for the opposite lung to expand.

I cut off his outer clothes—a field jacket and a heavy woolen shirt—with the pair of heavy bandage scissors that I always carried. The wound had obviously been made by a fairly large bullet, probably from an antiaircraft gun. The gap was larger than my fist. There were bits of bone around it, but surprisingly, there was not a lot of bleeding. I covered the wound with a large G.I. dressing and sealed the edges with wide tape, hoping to keep more air from entering the chest cavity. All the while, I stayed as close to the ground as possible as machine gun bullets snapped over us. I dragged the wounded man to safety behind some trees and gave him a shot of morphine. I crawled to the jeep, got a bottle of plasma, and started it. All this did not take long, but was done under continuous fire from the German machine guns ahead.

As I have said, one of our most valuable tools in caring for wounded was blood plasma. Plasma is human blood from which red cells have been removed. Without blood cells the whole blood substitute would last much longer. Also, with plasma, there was a decreased risk of reaction to incompatible blood types. Of course, cross-matched whole blood would have been better, but that sort of therapy was found only in the field hospitals. The plasma helped to combat shock caused by blood loss, intense pain, or a combination of those. We tried to keep the soldiers out of shock, which was a life-endangering condition. Men in shock are classically pale, cold, and wet. They have a rapid, thready pulse and low blood pressure. When men reached my station in shock, I often pumped plasma into them with a blood pressure bulb. Plasma came in a corked glass bottle packed in a cardboard box. To set up the intravenous kit, two tubes were attached to the cork. One tube had a needle at one end to be injected into the patient; the other, with an air filter on its end, was for air intake. At times, I would attach the bulb to this air intake tube to increase pressure by pumping to make the plasma flow more rapidly. I do not know if others were doing that at that time, but certainly the hospitals were rapidly adopting this practice. Of course, in hospitals, the plasma or blood could be suspended at a height sufficient to speed up flow. Plasma was a life saver.

Then, I watched the man, who was having some trouble breathing. To my amazement, he asked for a cigarette. I had to tell him it would not be wise. He was quite young and was an infantry scout sent out routinely to secure our flanks as we progressed. Obviously, he had lost a good deal of breathing capacity, probably from the collapse of the right lung and pressure on the left. When I got a chance, I wrote a note to go with the wounded man, suggesting that a chest tube be placed with the exposed end under water. This would make possible the inflation of the lung until definitive surgery could be performed. As the man took breaths, air around the lungs would be forced out, creating a negative pressure that would expand the undamaged lung.

By this time, our battalion, now an experienced unit, had knocked out the German machine guns. The rumbling of the Tiger tanks had stopped, and there was heavy fire from our light artillery and bazookas. My men rushed to put my wounded patient on a litter, which they then placed on one of our jeeps. We sent him back to an ambulance that was not far away, and I directed it to take him directly to our clearing company. He was in fairly good shape, in spite of his shortness of breath and the significant hole in his chest. My heart was racing. I could feel it thumping away. When the shooting stopped, not more than a half hour later, I could not believe what I had done. My aid men congratulated me. At last, I was one of them, and I felt that, in a way, I had made up for my first time under fire when I had ducked for cover while my aid man remained standing by his patient and holding up that life-saving bottle of plasma. Delivering the baby showed professional skill, but this was being an Army medic.

The Free French helped us considerably by attacking the Germans' rear while we engaged them outside Chateaudun. My aid group was one of the first units into the city. With some fellow officers in our vehicles, we drove through mobs of cheering townspeople. They clapped, cheered, and kissed us and each other.

We set up our temporary aid station in the middle of the town square, ironically, near a rather artistic monument to the men of the Great War. I was then dragged off to the best cafe in town where wine (Musse, since the Germans had taken all the champagne) was on the house. All was excitement. It was a great day.

Well, we finally pulled ourselves away long enough to get our men established in a school, formerly a German barracks. Word had spread about my action under fire, and I was given a room in the best hotel in town. It had been the German Staff headquarters and was much nicer accommodation than what I had seen in England.

My room had apparently been occupied by one of the officers' ladies. It had a large comfortable double bed, modern chairs, tall French windows, a full carpet, a large mirror over the fireplace, which contained a porcelain stove, a wash basin with a large mirror, and a douche bowl, with which most of the rooms were equipped and which were standard in most hotels, I was told. I did not recall seeing one before. There was an adjoining bath (rarely to be found in English hotels). Outside was a balcony from which I could look out on the crowded, excited square.

I took a much needed bath in the huge tub. It was wonderful, even though the water was cold. After a cup of coffee and some stew that someone had fixed, I set out to look around. The hotel, though small, obviously was once luxurious. The lobby was of tile with a glass roof. In the large mirrored dining room, everything was in confusion, for the Germans had left in a hurry. Part of their last meal still was on plates, and the evening dishes had not been washed.

On entering the square, I could see that the town had suffered. Most of the shops and homes were closed. However, most of the cafes were open. I wandered through the mob that was cheering the vehicles of my battalion as they moved through town. There was a major furor when the girls who had slept with German officers were paraded through town with their hair shaved off. They were called collaboratrices.

I came upon a civilian aid station just off the square. The fact that I was a doctor was immediately recognized, since I had a red cross on my helmet and on my arm, and of course, I had a medical insignia on my shirt collar. The entire staff, led by a pleasant, plump, middle-aged woman came to greet me. They insisted that I come in and partake of some wine. The leader came from the cellar with two bottles of old champagne covered with cobwebs and dust. We drank many toasts, and my knowledge of French steadily grew, while my inhibitions melted away. The young nurses helped in all of this. I gave them cigarettes and gave their children a ration of chocolate. They were thrilled. Finally I left them, though the younger members escorted me through the square to see the excitement. I drew cheers from my men when I appeared with this group of young women.

I stopped in the square to talk with people, using my new French vocabulary, supplemented by all the English words I knew which ended in "tion." In the meantime, my men had found women and wine, and song was soon forthcoming. It was amazing that all of the men and I remained gentlemen in spite of everything we had been through, including the deprivation of the company of women. Some, of course, got mixed up with professionals, and I could not blame them. But everyone was having a wonderful time.

All of a sudden, higher rank made its appearance. Of course, we had been told that towns were out of bounds. I knew that trouble was at hand and that we would soon be ordered out of town. I returned to our hotel, which my men had begun to clean up. There was little to eat. Our rations were slow to come up. I had some German bread and coffee and cleaned up again. Then I headed back out into the town square.

I wandered into one of the principal cafes, where I noticed a very neat, well-behaved, and well-dressed little girl. She was about six, and she possessed a ready French smile. I said, "Bonsoir," and she was pleased. Some Hershey chocolate from my belt sealed our friendship. Her mother and father sat across from her. They, too, were well-dressed and seemed very nice. They insisted that I have some wine with them. The next thing I knew, they had me on the way to their home.

I soon learned that the little girl's father was a mechanical engineer of no mean repute. He seemed surprisingly young and before the war had been director of transportation in Paris. He had been imprisoned in Paris, but had escaped. I wasn't able to learn how this was accomplished, as my French was quite inadequate. I rather think that friends in high places were of great value to him at that time. The Germans had confiscated his Paris bank account, his three cars, and most of his belongings. He probably was Jewish, though that was never mentioned. Certainly, that is a subject that any Jew would be unlikely to discuss until the war was over.

The family's home consisted of about nine rooms and was well furnished in a modern manner. It was clean, neat, and comfortable. There was a joyous baby of about thirteen months. They showed me two bullet holes right over the baby's bassinet that had been made in our recent brief battle. The baby was thrilled with a piece of cellophane I gave him. All of this, of course, made my home seem closer. While the mother was fixing dinner aided by a maid, the father and I, with the aid of a French-English dictionary, soon learned a good deal about each other.

Then came dinner. Silverware glistened on a crisp linen tablecloth with a simple neat brown design. There were napkins to match. Small oil lamps supplemented the light that came through the tall French windows in the dusk. The father brought out his last two bottles of wine: one red and one white. They had vintage labels, but I did not recognize them. I tried to persuade him to save the wine, but he felt that the occasion deserved this nectar. The meal started with a meat pate served with cucumbers, slightly pickled and sprinkled with parsley, along with sliced tomatoes, also with chopped parsley. There was plenty of dark, wholesome bread, for which my host and hostess apologized. I guess they thought that an American doctor would have preferred something more elegant. I assured them that dark bread was a special treat for me. Next came a huge, fluffy omelet. I did not know what was in it, but it was delicious as it literally melted in my mouth. Unbelievably, next, came sirloin steaks, then noodles and cheese. For dessert came a fluffy, soft pastry with a brown, crisp crust sprinkled with coarse sugar. It was delicious, but I did not know what was in it. This was like a dream for one who had been living outdoors on Army rations for so long.

I did not smoke, but I always carried cigarettes, mostly for the wounded, but occasionally for barter. I certainly was glad that I had three packs with me. My host and hostess were thrilled to receive them. I also had a small can of Nescafe in my pocket. They wished to serve this after dinner, but since they were so overjoyed, I insisted that they save it for themselves. Though these people obviously lived fairly well, they had not tasted coffee for years. During and after the meal, we carried on a reasonably flowing conversation. I was able to use the little French I had learned, their dictionary, my Army phrase book (that was really quite poor), and my personal list of words that end in "tion."

After expressing great thanks, I left promising to return for lunch on the morrow. My plan was to bring with me things that were difficult, if not impossible, to get. I thought particularly of coffee and of small cans of food that came from home. The mail was one of our most remarkable support systems. When I returned to our hotel, I found that my men had somehow acquired a significant supply of wine. I drank some with them, then retired to my room. There was my luxurious bed with clean sheets on it (would wonders never cease?) probably in anticipation of occupancy by some German general. Between the wine and the luxurious comfort of the bed, I could hardly fall asleep. I had time to enjoy the sheets—unbelievable!

The contrast between this experience and living on the ground and eating G.I. rations with an occasional shot of Calvados was mind boggling. The night before, I had slept in a field behind a huge haystack with thick barricades about me. Though there seemed to be little need of such precaution, we who had survived to that point had learned that you must never let your guard down, even when everything seemed secure and safe.

One of the sights of the day was seeing the Free French "Patriots" march. They undoubtedly helped us to get into this city with minimum casualties. Certainly they helped the morale of the French people, who felt that the activities of the Free French made them part of the liberation. These parades were invariably led by groups of happy young women who marched in some sort of formation. These were the women who had nothing to do with the Germans.

The morning dawned with sad news: the city had been declared out of bounds. We had to leave. We were devastated. We had gotten ourselves organized. We had everything in the way of supplies, and we all had ideas of finding some female companionship. We felt that our fighting men were being asked to relinquish what they had won at some sacrifice. But Discipline had to be preserved, so farewell, Chateaudun!

I took my last remaining time in the city to visit the family that had been so kind to me. I brought them all I had: a can of chopped olives, some coffee (which was not easy to come by, even for us), and more cigarettes. They—even the children—seemed sad to see me go. They made me promise to return if possible. I told them that we were leaving town to preserve their supplies, which probably was partially true. But I felt the men deserved more than this one day of heaven.

My great regret in all of this was that I did not record the names and address of these wonderful people. Somehow or other, because of what we had been through, I felt that there was a good chance that I would not survive. Also, at that time, it was impossible, despite our recent successes, to predict an end to the war. We knew that the Germans were fighting a holding action so that they could reorganize and try to stop us. We respected their ability to do just that. They were to do more than we expected.

Chapter 15

Travel Across France

August, 1944

All of a sudden, the entire character of our war changed. Patton stressed mobility, and we moved. We moved so quickly that often we bypassed large numbers of German soldiers who had been taken prisoner. They represented a mixture of nationalities from countries overcome by the Germans, and most who we captured were a scruffy group, often malnourished. Occasionally, however, we got a classic German soldier. Those were well nourished and usually blond, or at least fair. These German soldiers wore decorations, unlike American combat soldiers, who rarely wore decorations, except combat infantry or combat medic's badges. Their uniforms were in good repair, and they usually had some food and other equipment with them. They carried themselves in a haughty way.

It was unusual to see one of these men as a walking prisoner. They either escaped or fought to the end. So, those we saw were usually wounded. The others were falling back with their equipment whenever possible. In contrast were troops that had been recruited from captive countries, like Poland, Hungary, and Czechoslovakia. Those soldiers were happy to be captured and to be out of the war. Of course, when supervised by experienced officers, they did fight, but they seemed ready to surrender if given a chance.

By now, the weather was fine. The canvas cover of my windshield was always stuffed with bottles of wine. We were able to get some real food, which we sponged off of major units nearby. As we grew more relaxed, we began to crave female companionship, but our leaders made every effort to keep us away from the civilians. We rarely camped near a major city, and we moved almost daily. With all that, to my surprise, I continually had to treat GIs with gonorrhea. The first case I saw was before we got to St. Lo. I could not imagine how the man could find sex while all that combat was going on.

We raced across France. It almost seemed like a tourist trip. On occasion, I had a chance to visit other units, and I even had a pleasant though brief visit at a field hospital where I knew some of their personnel. We had some drinks. I was jealous, especially because there were nurses on the staff, one of whom I knew. We passed south of Paris through Orleans, Trois, Joinville, and Nancy, where our division stopped to regroup and prepare to end the war.

Nancy is a lovely city, and its town center is quite wonderful, surrounded by elegant iron fencing with gold decoration, triumphal arch, and palatial buildings. We drove through this magnificent site and through old city's gate fixed between two round towers with small windows, presumably for archers, and bearing the Cross of Lorraine, for Nancy was the capitol of that province.

We were assigned a small home for our group. It was a simple home, but comfortable. It had four windows across the second floor. The lower floor with its windows was obscured by bushes and trees. The entrance to the street was marked by two concrete pillars, and lateral to them was a substantial iron fence. I was assigned to a small but bright room just above the front entrance. There was no furniture in the room. Someone had found me an army cot and a simple wooden chair. The room looked out on the small front garden between the street fence and its shrubs and the house. I had a small bathroom with a rather crude metal-lined shower. I was late getting settled, so I ate and went to bed.

That night, I was suddenly hit with intense nausea. I vomited repeatedly. Then I was struck with a tremendous fever. I thought that I had some sort of food poisoning and should try to wait things out. The next day, the whites of my eyes were yellow, my urine was brown, and my temperature was 104 degrees. I could barely move.

I rather lost contact with reality, but I did manage to call Peacock, a fellow officer from the collecting company and a man for whom I had respect as a physician. He was tall, dour, and did not flap. He thought, as I did, that I had acute hepatitis. I was so weak that I could not walk. My men put me on a litter so that I could be taken to a field hospital in one of our ambulances.

The diagnosis there was hepatitis, about which no one knew very much. In any event, they put me to bed. I do not remember the next few days. I do believe they gave me some I.V. fluid. I seemed to recover a bit and to note my surroundings. After a few days, I was able to take fluid by mouth. Around me were men who were seriously wounded. I did not receive much attention: the nurses and corpsmen had more important things to do. My major food was canned grapefruit juice, which I seemed to tolerate, and I lost a great deal of weight. After six days, I was able to eat other simple food.

The doctor who cared for me was not much older than I was. He thought that I might have been infected with hepatitis virus in some farm house. I had been in the habit, particularly in Normandy, of taking my rations to any inhabited farm house, where the farm wife might add some eggs and some garden vegetables to make what to me was a delicious meal. In return, I would give the farm family coffee and cigarettes and, occasionally, some chocolate.

There was also the possibility that I had gotten the virus from one of the many immunizations I had received. Before every battle, we all got tetanus shots in addition to all the other immunizations, and our technique for sterilizing needles was not effective at that time. Needles were boiled and occasionally soaked in antiseptic solutions. Viruses are tough and if caught in an air pocket in the needle they could survive. In fact, there had been a large number of hepatitis cases in the service. In any event, the doctor said that I was about to be discharged, and that I would be sent to a reassignment pool within the next few days. Interestingly ,my urine was still brown and it continued to be for the rest of the year. No one seemed to know much about hepatitis back then.

Then, I made one of the important decisions of my life. I decided to leave the hospital A. W. O. L. to return to my unit. I felt that at least I would know what to expect there. I had been through a great deal with that team, and it seemed reasonable to try to finish the war with those who knew me. I knew that I might regret this decision and that I might be missing a great opportunity to get a better assignment. I got together my few belongings and just walked away from the hospital tent as if I were on some mission in the area. A passing jeep picked me up and was happy to deliver me "home" without question.

I reported to my commanding officer and had a magnificent homecoming. There were nineteen letters, a *Time* magazine, a copy of the *San Francisco Chronicle*, and a bottle of White Horse Scotch. In those days, people did not feel that alcohol was so terrible for hepatitis patients, though, I of course was a bit cautious about it. My commander said he had a special surprise for me.

Later that day, our commanding general came to present me with a medal for my efforts in Normandy. It was a Bronze Star, awarded for valor and hard work in the face of the enemy. Apparently my actions at Mortain, when my jeep driver and I crossed through enemy lines to bring medical supplies to the surrounded 30th division, had been cited. There were some other actions also mentioned, particularly the long hard hours I had put in during the battle for Normandy. It was a much bigger honor than I had expected. There was a second honor: I received the Combat Medical Badge for my work as a battalion surgeon. I also was notified that I had been promoted to captain. Finally, I was returned to my old outfit, the collecting company.

Although I was not happy leaving the men whose lives I had shared so intimately, the collecting company had real food, more space, and less risk. The battalion aid station was usually close to the front lines, and the living conditions were those of the forward infantry. The collecting company was usually at least a thousand yards farther to the rear, where there was less chance of being hit by small arms and even by mortars. In addition, because the collecting company was a larger unit, there was a kitchen truck that had more varied food and more ways to prepare it. The better food was important in my recovery from the hepatitis as was the more sheltered living. I began, for the first time, to believe that I could survive this war. I was naive; we had to face some very bad times.

We had a celebration. Two of my fellow officers also had been promoted. One was in charge of the administration of the company. I was to be in charge of medical matters. There also was a new addition to our command group. Members of my aid station came to join the celebration. I broke out a bottle of Old Crow that I had brought all the way from England. Of course we had acquired all kinds of wine, most of which had been captured from the Germans and marked "nur fur der Wehrmacht." It was a happy, wild evening with much singing and reminiscing and with many a toast to missing friends. The recent days had been so quiet and we had made such progress across France that we thought that the worst was over and that some of us would head home by Christmas. We were all so wrong.

The next day was Yom Kippur, the most holy day in the Jewish calendar. I thought it would be good to go to services and to thank God for my good fortune to date. I really had not been into Nancy before. I was one of two Jews in our entire unit. The other was my good friend David Roth. Dave had no interest in religion. He had never been a battalion surgeon. I had been in a much worse spot than he. His experience in Normandy had made him feel, as many soldiers did, that there could be no God, given the horrors we had seen.

This was an Orthodox service. I had grown up in a Reform congregation in San Francisco, but this was my first chance to be at a Jewish service of any kind since leaving home. The temple was located near the edge of the city on a broad boulevard and had once been a lovely building. It was shaped like a long hall with an arched roof, and there were traditional balconies for women all around the interior walls, except over the bima. The huge organ located on the balcony had been maliciously and completely destroyed. The altar and all its associated decorations were completely ruined. All religious symbols had been removed. There was no arc to hold the Torah scrolls. A large table had been placed on the bima, which filled most of the end of the room. The Germans had used the temple as a medical supply depot, and they had gutted it.

There was no rabbi. A cantor performed the service. At first, we gathered in a small adjacent chapel, but soon had to move to the main temple house, because the congregation was so large. It was impressive to be witness to the first service in that temple in four years and to see the number and variety of Jewish soldiers, men from all branches and all ranks, privates to generals. Most of them understood the Hebrew service and were able to partake with greater ease than I could. My knowledge of Hebrew was minimal, even though in my youth I had attended Hebrew school in Boston for a short time. Nevertheless, I felt good being at the service.

There were also a few civilians in the congregation. Jews had either been sent to concentration camps or to work camps, so I do not know how these had survived. They were enthusiastic in taking part in the ritual and occasionally smiled at us, though they made no special overtures of friendship.

After services, I took my first tour of the Nancy since the day we arrived, stopping first at a place near the railroad station. There were trees and grass in the middle of the square, and about it were hotels and nice cafes. I stopped at one of the cafes. It was modern, clean, and neat. The people were in general in a gay mood.

For them, the war was over. Although they were faced with major problems in recovery, their city had not suffered the bombing and destruction that we had seen elsewhere, particularly in Normandy. As had happened so often before, I was asked to join a group. Of course, there was little to eat. All I could contribute was some chocolate that I, as always, had in my pocket and which they carefully divided. It was a source of great pleasure. Such chocolate had not been seen here in years.

After lunch, I continued my tour of the city, which was quite beautiful. What hurt was to see how it had been allowed to deteriorate over the four years of war. The beautiful buildings showed complete lack of care. Many shops were boarded up. Probably they had belonged to Jews. In spite of all of this, it was the most lovely city I had yet seen in France.

I wandered into a department store. It was built like other stores of its kind at the time, each floor with and open area in the middle from which you looked down to the main floor. The stores generally had little merchandise, and the prices were high. Interestingly though, the clothes for women and children were quite stylish. I had pictures taken in one of those machines (six pictures for twelve francs) and noted in my letter home that I could be recognized by my thinning hair, prominent nose, and silly grin.

We were issued Army paper francs that were honored by the French. The problem was that, except for the money we sent home, we were paid in francs worth just about half of the value of the francs in circulation. So it was foolish for us to buy anything that was not necessary. (Much later the French authorities recognized this problem and supplemented our incomes.) Like a good soldier, I resorted to barter. I always had cigarettes. As an officer, I got a carton of cigarettes every week, even in combat. A pack of cigarettes was a valuable commodity. I did not smoke and could easily trade a pack of cigarettes for a meal with wine. It was also a pleasure to give a cigarette to anyone who was friendly.

Outside the shopping district, I found the university, one of the largest in France. It had five major faculties and a beautiful library built just before the war. One of the professors showed me around. He spoke good English. The university had suffered, like the rest of France, which had gone to seed for four years. The medical school was in another part of the city, and I planned to see it; for it was the home of a great obstetrician, Tarnier. Because there was little fighting at this point, and because there were very few casualties, I resolved to see as much of Nancy as possible before we moved to our next offensive.

Chapter 16

Nancy

September–October, 1944

    We were in a holding pattern. Our scouts had occasional contact with the Germans, but there were few casualties, and consequently, we had little work to do. That being so, I decided to see as much of Nancy as possible before we moved out. We had no clue as to when we would move or for what reason we had stopped. However, here we were in the largest city I had been in since leaving home.

    I had only a brief view of the town center on the way into the city before I was hospitalized. I now wanted to see more while things were quiet. There was the Place Stanislas, with its lovely bronze statue groups in each corner of the square and at the center, the grand statue of Stanislas, last Duke of Lorraine. The government buildings had a palatial elegance that we Americans tried to emulate, but just missed, and the triumphal arch just outside the square extended a parkway with beautiful neoclassical government buildings along the way and at the end, the superb government palace and Pepiniere. I visited the magnificent cathedral, and thanked God for protecting me to this point. The stained glass windows were undisturbed by the war and the most beautiful I had seen in France.

    On the way back, I stopped at a real barber's and had the works. Until this time, my haircuts had been done by one of my aid

Classification cancelled 8 Feb 45 by authority of VOCG, 35th Infantry Division, by

RICHARD A. BURKE
MOJ) USA

C O N F I D E N T I A L

CITATION FOR THE BRONZE STAR MEDAL

To CAPTAIN JOHN A KAPSTEIN, 0511180, Company "D", 110th Medical Battalion, on detached service with the Medical Detachment, 320th Infantry, for meritorious service in connection with military operations against an enemy of the United States in France during the period 31 July to 3 September 1944. Throughout the period mentioned, Captain Kapstein, as Battalion Surgeon, has performed his duties in an outstandingly meritorious manner in every operation in which the 320th Combat Team has been engaged. His technical and professional skill, rendered with devotion to duty and tireless energy through long hours under the most trying combat conditions, have not only been a material contribution to the prompt treatment and evacuation of the wounded, but reflect credit upon his character as an officer and upon the Medical Corps of the Army. Entered military service from California.

GO No 40
Hq 35th Inf Div
5 Oct 44

Note: Obviously, Captain John A. Kapstein and John Kerner, M.D., are one and the same.

men who had had some experience as a barber. He was a fairly heavy man of Italian descent and was obviously not prepared emotionally for what we had been through. He was called Tony, and in England was all smiles and tolerated all jokes about him. However, as the fighting progressed, convinced he would not make it back home, he became more withdrawn. In any event, there I was with haircut, shampoo, shave, massage, and smelling like a perfume department of a five and ten cent store. I felt cleaner than I had felt in a very long time.

Even though I had a new assignment, I continued to be quartered in the same small house where I had become ill and which I had barely seen before my illness. There was the same Army cot and plain wooden chair in my room looking out on the small garden, the same small bathroom and rather crude metal-lined shower. This house held no evidence of the people who had lived there. All the contents had been removed, even pictures and clothing.

The next day, after a peaceful night in my own bed, I went to one of the hospitals in Nancy and had a wonderful, non-rushed, hot shower, and I got some clean clothes. I was then ready to do a bit more touring in the city. It was Sunday, and everyone looked his and her best. The well-dressed women mostly wore hats reminiscent of the Lilly Dache type, large with sloping brims. Their clothes were smart and to me seemed provocative in contrast to the clothing we saw in England. Though cloth was very expensive and scarce, the women seemed to get what they needed.

The men's clothing was tremendously varied, from gaudy to proper and a bit stiff. The younger men—I cannot explain how they avoided military duty—liked dark, solid- colored shirts and knickers fastened at the ankle. They wore white socks. Their hair was greasy. They had drab ties. Their jackets were worn over their shoulders. Arms were never seen in coat sleeves. I had thought of these guys as a bit "sissy," but, of course, I had little knowledge of the local culture. More and more French were appearing in uniforms of which there was a huge variety, and it was difficult to know who was really serving and who was trying to make himself

```
                                  From
No.____        To                      Capt. John A. Kapstein 0-51118(
                                         (Sender's name)
               Mrs. S. Kapstein        Co. C, 110 Med Bn
                                         (Sender's address)
               1963 Clay Street        APO 35, c/o Postmaster
               San Francisco, 9        New York, N.Y.
               California              24 Sept 44
                                             (Date)
(CENSOR'S STAMP)
```

DEAR MOM,
   WE ARE NOW PERMITTED TO MENTION ANY TOWN WE HAVE VISITED. HOWEVER, WE CANNOT MENTION ANY TOWN WITHIN TWENTY-FIVE MILES. SO, GET OUT YOUR MAP, AND TAKE A LOOK SEE.
   THE FIRST CITY I VISITED WAS ST. LO, THERE WASN'T MUCH TO SEE. YOU'VE PROBABLY SEEN PICTURES OF WHAT HAPPENED TO THAT CITY. I SPENT A VERY LITTLE TIME IN TORIGNI, IT HAD MANY OF THE CHARACTERS OF ST. LO, BUT IT WAS MUCH SMALLER. I SPENT A LITTLE TIME IN VILLEDIEU, BUT IT WAS NIGHT, AND THE FRENCH TOWNS LOOK UP TIGHT IN THE DARK. A BRIEF VISIT TO ST. HILAIRE DU HARCOUET REVEALED SOMETHING OF OUR POWER. MORTAIN WAS A LOVELY CITY, BUT ONE WHICH MOST OF US WOULD JUST HAVE SOON NEVER HAVE VISITED. LE MANS WAS THE PLACE WHERE I VISITED THAT CATHEDRAL OF WHICH I TOLD YOU. IT CERTAINLY WAS A LOVELY CHURCH. CHATEAUDUN WAS THE PLACE WHERE I MET THE NICE PEOPLE WHO THREW THAT LOVELY DINNER FOR ME AND WHERE I SLEPT IN THAT HOTEL BED BETWEEN SHEETS. THAT WAS THE HIGH POINT OF MY VISIT TO FRANCE, TO DATE. I HAD A BIT OF TIME IN THE TOWN OF PITHIVIERS, BUT IT WAS SMALL AND UNINTERESTING. IT WAS THERE THAT WE STAYED ON XXX THE FARM OF A COLLABORATOR. (I JOINED THE BATTALION AS A BATTALION SURGEON SHORTLY BEFORE WE GOT TO TORIGNI) MONTARGIS WAS A CITY WHERE I SPENT A LITTLE MORE TIME THAN IN MOST. IT WAS THE CITY WITH THE BEAUTIFUL GOVERNMENT BUILDINGS. TROYES WAS SIMILAR, BUT I HAD LITTLE MORE TIME THAN TO BUY A DRINK AND LOOK AROUND. AT BRIENNE LE CHATEAU I HAD A CHANCE TO VISIT THAT LARGE CHATEAU OF NAPOLEON. AT JOINVILLE, I LEFT THE AID STATION AD RETURNED TO THE COLLECTING COMPANY. IT WAS IN THAT CITY, THAT I GOT THE CHANCE TO SEE AND ENJOY A GOOD OLD AMERICAN MOVIE, ALSO AT THAT CITY I HAD THAT LOVELY LUNCH WITH THE RESTAURANT PROPRIETORS I HAVE A COAT OF ARMS OF JOINVILLE AND I WILL SEND IT ALONG. I'LL ALSO SND ONE FROM STRASSBOURG, THOUGH I HAVEN'T BEEN THERE. ROSIER WAS THE TOWN WHERE I HAD THAT SUPPER BEDROOM ON THE STUD HORSE FARM.
   IN THE NEXT ISSUE, I HOPE TO BE ABLE TO GIVE MORE TOWNS. AS YOU CAN SEE, I'VE MANAGED TO MISS SOME OF THE GREATEST CITIES OF FRANCE FOR WHICH I'M VERY SORRY. HOWEVER I GUESS WE CAME OVER HERE TO FIGHT THE WAR. HOWEVER, IT ALWAYS DIGUSTS US THAT THE HIGHER ECHELONS GET TO SPEND TIME IN THE CITIES WHILE WE SET UP OUT IN A FIELD OR SOMETHING SIMILAR. THERE IS ONE ADVANTAGE TO BEING A GENERAL.
   I HOPE THAT THIS LETTER WILL SATISFY SOME OF YOUR CURIOSITY.
                                    ALL MY LOVE,
                                          Johnny

look like a hero. Interestingly, there were Frenchmen in U.S. uniforms and some in English uniforms. Whatever the type of uniform, I felt the more the better. As far as the people of Nancy were concerned, the war was over, except for the missing men. I for one, had a strong feeling that the war was not over, though I must say, I did not have an inkling of how bad it would be.

Sunday in Nancy was like Saturday night at home. There was still blackout at night, and it got dark at about 7:00 PM. It was now mid-October. There was a strict curfew for soldiers at night. So, social activities had to end by 7:00 or, at the latest, at 8:00. The cafes were jammed. There were more and more orchestras in the cafes. The most popular music was American, mostly swing, but there were often old favorites of a slower nature. The only European music played was popular international waltzes.

The most elegant cafe was in the Grand Hotel. It was an L-shaped room with a ten-piece orchestra raised in the corner and backed by a large window facing the street. The musicians wore white fluffy shirts of the Cuban rumba type. Black trousers, patent leather shoes, and very slick, shiny hair completed their costume. The place was jammed, and though it seemed to be able to seat about four hundred, people were constantly going up and down between the tables hunting for seats.

To my surprise, the people of this area drank mostly beer. Their beer tasted much like American and it was served cold, unlike the British, which tasted flat, and was always warm. Those who did not drink beer, drank mostly vin rouge; since it was the cheapest wine, and wine was expensive in this area.

But these people really were not out to drink: they just wanted to be with a large group. I rather think they were celebrating their liberation and their survival. Until their liberation, the people of Nancy had not been permitted to assemble in groups, as, I think, was German policy throughout France. Certainly, this city seemed to have sustained less damage than many, perhaps because of its proximity to Germany, where there had been no major battles, where there were no major factories or military bases.

APO 35, c/o Postmaster
New York, N.Y.
22 Oct. 44

(CENSOR'S STAMP)

DEAR DOROTHY,
   IT BEGINS TO LOOK LIKE THE NEWSCASTERS AND THE "WISE MONEY" AT HOME WERE WRONG AS USUAL. I HOPE THAT THEY ARE JUST AS WRONG ON THE PRESIDENTIAL RACE, AND THAT DEWEY WINS. ALL THIS IS MESSEY. I OPENED REFERRING TO PROGNOSIS FOR THE TERMINATION OF THE WAR.
   THIS LETTER IS IN REPLY TO YOUR LETTER OF SEPT. FOURTEENTH WHICH JUST CAME YESTERDAY; THOUGH I HAVE RECEIVED MORE RECENT MAIL FROM YOU. YOUR LETTER SPENDS A GOOD DEAL OF SPACE ON COUSIN SHERWIN WHO IS APPARENTLY GETTING EXCEEDINGLY GOOD TREATMENT FROM THE FAMILY. I AGREE THAT OUR RELATIONS STILL HAVEN'T LEARNED HOW TO ENJOY LIFE. I THINK THAT THE YOUNGER GENERATION HAS BEEN TOO BUSY IN TRYING TO EITHER MAKE MONEY OR TO GET AN EDUCATION. IN EITHER CASE, THEY HAVE FORGOTTEN WHAT THE MONEY AND THE EDUCATION ARE FOR. AS FAR AS I'M CONCERNED, AT LEAST, THE REASON FOR EVERYTHING WE ACHIEVE IS TO ENJOY LIFE MORE. THAT IS PROBABLY POOR ENGLISH, BUT YOU MUST GET MY IDEA. IF YOU MAKE MONEY, AND DON'T ENJOY LIFE MORE FOR IT YOU MIGHT JUST AS WELL NOT HAVE IT. AND, SIMILARLY IF YOU HAVE EDUCATION AND IT DOESN'T MAKE YOUR LIFE MORE ENJOYABLE WHAT THE HELL GOOD IS IT. WHATEVER THE FAULTS OF THIS LITTLE JAUNT OF MINE, CERTAINLY IT HAS CONTRIBUTED TO MY KNOWLEDGE. I MAY NOT HAVE LEARNED MORE MEDICINE, BUT I'VE LEARNED A BIT ABOUT HOW THE REST OF THE WORLD LIVES. I'VE LEARNED TO APPRECIATE MANY THINGS I TOOK FOR GRANTED. BUT MOST OF ALL I'VE LEARNED TO APPRECIATE PEOPLE. I THINK THAT I'LL ENJOY LIFE A LOT MORE FOR THIS EXPERIENCE.
   AS I TELL MOM, I REALLY HAVE BEEN ABLE TO KEEP BUSY. THERE HAS BEEN NO TIME LATELY WHEN I WONDER WHAT TO DO. ALL THAT THOUGH WE HAVE HAD PRACTICALLY NO PROFESSIONAL WORK TO DO. THERE HAS BEEN LETTER WRITING, READING (MAGAZINES, BOOKS, JOURNALS), TRIPS TO TOWN, OUR NEW RADIO (THE NEWEST AND BEST ACQUISITION THOUGH IT DOESN'T WORK DURING THE DAY, AND THE GERMANS OFTEN MESS IT UP DURING THE NIGHT), AND VISITING.
   I NEVER READ SO MUCH, YET I ALWAYS SEEM BEHIND. I READ THE NEW YORKER FROM COVER TO COVER INCLUDING THE ADS. TIME IS MY FAVORITE, AND IT TOO (IN THE PONY EXPRESS FORM) IS READ FROM COVER TO COVER. I CAN HARDLY KEEP UP WITH THE JOURNALS. I'VE READ SEVERAL BOOKS: THE BEST, "GOOD NIGHT, SWEET PRINCE", THE OLDEST "VANITY FAIR" (WHICH SOMEHOW I MISSED), SHORT STORIES, ETC.
   I ALSO RECEIVE THE DAILY NEWSPAPER FROM SAN FRANCISCO. I'M SURE THAT I KNOW MUCH MORE ABOUT WHAT IS GOING ON IN THE CITY THAN I EVER KNEW WHEN I LIVED THERE. SURPRISINGLY ENOUGH, I FEEL THAT I KNOW THE UNITED STATES MUCH BETTER SINCE I'VE COME TO FRANCE.
   IN SPITE OF OUR RELATIVE LUXURY IN OUR PRESENT POSITION, AND THOUGH I HAVE PLENTY TO KEEP ME BUSY, I STILL GET UNHAPPY AT TIMES. PERHAPS IT IS THE RAIN AND MUD, OR MORE LIKELY IT IS THE FEELING OF GETTING OLDER WITH SO MUCH TO DO YET AND HERE GO THE BEST MONTHS AND YEARS. YOU SEE THE CONTRAST IS GREAT. UNTIL MY ENTRY INTO THE ARMY, MY LIFE WAS PLANNED. EACH YEAR WAS PLANNED IN DETAIL AHEAD AND THE LOGICAL ALWAYS HAPPENED. EVERYTHING WENT SMOOTHLY. NOW, THE FUTURE IS SO INDEFINITE.
   OF COURSE, THERE ARE SOME REALLY FINE THINGS LIKE THE VISITS TO TOWN, THE MONTHLY RATION OF A QUART OF WHITE HORSE SCOTCH AND A HALF OR MORE OF A BOTTLE OF GORDON'S GIN, PUTTERING AROUND IN THE LITTLE SHOPS AND GETTING A DOLLAR A PACKAGE FOR CIGARETTES IN EXCHANGE.   ENOUGH TALK, LOADS OF LOVE TO YOU ALL,

V-MAIL

Interestingly, this cafe provided music and drink, but not meals. Food was difficult to obtain, and probably the management had decided not to bother much with it since they did so well selling drink. The cafe was really like a huge bar. There were other large restaurants where the scene was quite similar and which also were jammed, this being Sunday. Of course, I had not had an opportunity to see the scene on weekdays, but I heard that the mood of celebration was present even then.

Some of the restaurants did serve food, but in small quantities and at considerable cost. They too, were jammed. As I wandered about with my friend, Goodson, a tall young doctor from Portland, we got more and more hungry. We stumbled on a restaurant which did not seem to be playing to the mobs. It appeared to be nice, and we decided to give it a try. Booths separated by carved wooden partitions lined the walls. Along one side and at one end of the room were windows. The far end of the room was filled with lovely wooden cabinets with rows of bright colored plates standing on edge. The walls were decorated with famous French sayings in bright red: like "Liberte, Egalite, Fraternite" and "C'est la Guerre!" Between those were glistening copper containers of various sorts. The tables were covered with bright colored table cloths, though the effect was compromised by squares of white paper in the center of each table. Of course, that was necessary, as laundry was difficult, and soap was in very short supply.

The meal: sauerkraut with some tasty sausage, a very good veal steak, browned potatoes, fresh carrots, mirabelles (cherry plums, yellow and characteristic of this region) served stewed. There was a bottle of red wine that was not bad at all. The price was high—165 francs, or about $33—which, for us, was a good amount. The quality of the meal suggested better times in the past and, I hoped, in those to come. It became obvious that it was best to go to places where the well-dressed French went, rather than where the soldiers went, which were those with the most noise and the greatest likelihood of finding single women. I was interested in single women, but I hoped to find nonprofessionals.

The city had rows and rows of shops—seemingly more than one would expect in a city of this size, but I rather thought that Nancy was a district center with customers from the surrounding countryside. That government buildings were a major source of pride, evident from the care they received. The local color was more present here than at any place we had seen in Europe. I looked forward to visiting the medical school and the university which were famous. I would have loved to return here in better times.

A source of wealth for me were the free rations that we received every week. These included four to ten packs of cigarettes, one to four bars of tropical chocolate, one to five packages of gum. The most valuable for me were the cigarettes that I could trade for anything.

Civilian movies had just reopened, and there were long lines of people anxious to see anything. The Army, of course, had free movies for soldiers, and many were quite good. It is difficult to remember what movies were being shown, but I did get the impression that though there was a war going on, some French movies were being made. The soldiers were often given the newest possible movies, and often some fairly recently made ones. All of them made us think of home. We went whenever we had a chance.

This was a strange time. There was no professional work to do. I had more time to read than ever. I enjoyed visiting the city. But there was so much that was difficult. Until my entry into the Army, my life had been planned. Each year had its goal, and the future seemed clearly defined. Now, all was uncertainty. We knew there was fighting going on just beyond the city, but the fact that we were stuck in Nancy was unexplained.

There was another disturbing feeling. I longed for female companionship, though I do not think that sex was what I was looking for. That was available for a price and for me had no appeal. In France, young women—except for the professionals—were carefully protected by their strict families. Of course there were occasional female entertainers. Usually, the major shows did not come as close as we were to the front lines.

Marlene Dietrich and her troop were the exception. They put on a show near our company in a large barn. The troupe had Joe Fay, a tenor, a good accordionist, a girl who did novelty numbers, a comedian, and Marlene. There was also a good orchestra from our division. The humor was good, and it was good to hear the boys laugh and to laugh myself. The music was always good to hear. Marlene may have been getting older, but she still looked good to us. She wore a full length tight fitting white dress with long sleeves, high neck, and a sort of jacket. It had sequins of silver and gold. It was quite elegant—especially here within range of German guns. She sang. Her voice was not too good, but it was fine to listen to "See What the Boys In the Back Room Will Have" (from *Destry Rides Again*), and "Lily Marlene," which had been a particular success with the troops in Italy and Africa. Interestingly, the German troops loved it, too, even though Marlene did not sing it for them. Fascinatingly, she also played a musical saw. Those two hours took us away for a wonderful break.

This break from combat was also a time to find old friends. My closest friend, Dave Roth, had a job similar to mine, but he did not have front line experience. He reported to me that a friend of ours from medical school, Helmut, had had a good job in a field hospital, but like me, he was sent to fill a position in a battalion aid station. He was captured by the Germans, and while being taken to the rear in a German train, he was killed by our bombers. Helmut was probably the best prospect for being a great surgeon in our class. I think Dave and I drank a bit too much in toasting Helmut and others we knew who had been killed.

It finally happened. I met a girl.

Dave and I had gone to a movie, *Janie*, which was quite nostalgic for most of the audience. Then, we went to an excellent stage show by one of the divisions—dirty, but good. Then we went to the Red Cross Canteen for doughnuts and coffee. There I met this lovely French girl.

Colette was a Red Cross nurse and worked as a volunteer in the canteen. She invited me home to meet her family. They lived in a beautiful building that had once been an abbey. The windows and stairways were splendid with carved stone decorations depicting various religious motifs and ornate ironwork. (Apparently, this region was particularly skilled in that art.) It turned out that her father was a professor of medicine in the medical school, which was a position of importance. All of her family spoke some English, but they encouraged me to speak in French. It was surprising how well I could get along. I enjoyed meeting the family, although, unfortunately, visits were not long because the 6:00 P.M. curfew was still in effect. But a new dimension had been added to my life.

At the end of each work day, I would walk Colette home. She and I often would play bridge with her younger sister and her mother until it was time for me to leave. They usually served cake and Cointreau. The only time we were alone together was on the walk home.

Colette was attractive. Her hair was auburn, and she wore it in a stylish, short bob. Even in her Red Cross uniform, which fit well, she looked more fashionable than the women I had met in England. She wore her hat in a perky fashion. Perhaps this attraction was enhanced by my long lack of female companionship.

Her father invited me to the first banquet to be held in this city since the beginning of the war. All of the city's dignitaries were to be there. It was planned, because of curfew, at midday on the anniversary of the Armistice of World War I. The host would be the chief of surgery of the medical school.

One evening, soon after I met Colette, a great addition was made to the Red Cross Canteen: an orchestra. Colette was permitted some time away from her duties dispensing doughnuts, and she danced surprisingly well, since there had been little opportunity to dance during the war. For me, it was wonderful. I had not danced since England, and they were playing mostly American prewar music.

It was getting late; so I again walked Colette home; only this time at the door we kissed, first just gently but then, more passionately. It was the first time I had ever had a woman insert her tongue into my mouth. It was a wonderful sensation, and I, of course, became tremendously aroused. It was dark. I began to unbutton her blouse and shirt and just began to fondle her splendid breasts, when she pushed me away gently. We both knew it was late. After another wonderful kiss, she said, "Demain," and left.

Me in Nancy, France
after my release from the hospital

I rushed away. There was just enough time to catch transportation back to my quarters. I jumped onto a four by four (a two and a half ton truck) just as it was about to leave and spent the time riding back trying to figure a way to be alone with Colette before curfew.

When I arrived in my quarters, there was an envelope on my bed marked Top Secret. Inside was an order for the 110th Medical Battalion to move out at 700 hours on the following day. We were to support the 320th Infantry Regiment in action. We were not to communicate with anyone, not even in our own unit, in any way. Of course, I expected that we would move out as soon as we had reorganized, and as always facing battle, I had some anxiety, though much less than when I was in a battalion aid station. But what drove me frantic was the terrible timing. Just when my relationship with Colette was maturing to something wonderful. It seemed to me that the gods were conspiring against me, and I neglected to remind myself that I had the good fortune to survive to this point and to meet this lovely woman. Fortunately I had her address. When I did not show at the canteen on the next day, Colette would know why, because by that time, troop movements would be in evidence.

Chapter 17

Lorraine

November–December, 1944

We left the lovely city of Nancy not really knowing what to expect. Heavy rain had begun. Though I had been living in relative luxury, combat had continued around the city. Our infantry supported by tanks and artillery continued to capture high ground and river crossings around Nancy.

The Germans, intent on slowing our progress, tried a stratagem. They permitted my old battalion to cross the Meur River nearby, and then hid twenty tanks with support infantry in some woods. Their intention was to cut off the battalion, which would have been a disaster. Fortunately, an artillery spotter in a small plane saw the Germans and called for artillery. All the artillery in the division focused on that area, and the Germans were decimated. There were no casualties among our troops. After that, our troops captured increasing numbers of prisoners, and we had few casualties.

My unit for a time was relatively superfluous; since the combat was so close to Nancy that wounded could be brought from the field to a hospital in the city where many of our division doctors were stationed for the time being. But all of that changed as we left town to advance. Our regiment was to lead an attack on the Saar.

Our first order was to take the town of Fresnes. We became involved in a terrible battle. The Germans had had time to prepare their positions thoroughly. Their holding actions had succeeded. All of the roads and open spaces had been strewn with mines. There were barbed wire entanglements and planned lines of fire for the German automatic weapons. They had in typical fashion set up good positions for their effective mortars and frightful 88s. They had support of their excellent tanks, which also had had time to regroup.

The majority of their tanks were superior to our best. Their more powerful guns could engage our tanks from a safe distance. The Germans' armor was stronger and more impenetrable than ours. On the other hand, we had greater numbers of tanks and artillery. This situation demanded great skill in maneuvering, and our tankers had learned a great deal since Normandy; so that they could at least keep the Germans in check and could often advance against them. Fortunately, not all their tanks were Tigers, and our newer tanks had more powerful guns, though they were not the equal of the Tigers'. Our tankers and their commanders learned to exploit the German weaknesses whenever possible, hitting the tanks' sides and tracks.

The fight to gain Fresnes was bitter. This was a profound shock to all of us. The wounded poured in. These were the worst casualties since Normandy. The men were often covered with mud, and it was difficult to clean wounds adequately. Using heavy bandage scissors, we cut the men's clothes away from wounds, cleaned the wounds with large amounts of water and soap, then put on dressings. We were afraid of tetanus spores in the mud as well as other agents that would interfere with wound healing. We evacuated now to the division clearing station which was back in action; since Nancy was too far away.

We had set up our station in a badly damaged but sturdy farmhouse. There was a deep cellar with strong walls and a huge supply of potatoes. It was bitter cold. We found stoves and assembled them in one of the rooms of the farmhouse. The pipes from these stoves were run across the ceiling and provided heat, which helped to keep the wounded comfortable. From then on, we always carried stoves and pipe with us. These were tied onto our front fenders, so that we looked more like gypsies than soldiers.

Because of the incoming shells fired from a nearby forest, we slept in the basement where we were accompanied by huge rats that often jumped on our sleeping bags and made rather loud squeaking noises. Fortunately, they seemed more interested in the potatoes and other food than in us, but this was still most unpleasant. I had never had such an experience. Rats are abhorrent to most of us, and we knew that they carried all sorts of disease. But we traded unpleasantness for the knowledge that we were unlikely to be wounded in the cellar while sleeping.

Food was sent to us from the rear. Most of it was cold. We kept coffee on the stove, but it was difficult to keep enough. We had no real containers and mostly used canteen cups in which our canteens were carried on our belts. It was so depressing. We had sailed across France after Mortain, and we had thought the back of the German army had been broken. Now, I was no longer the naive young lieutenant who landed with a footlocker of booze. Our worst fears were being realized. We were facing a miserable winter.

Whatever else I had learned, I knew that to survive mentally, I had to have some sense that I was providing some sort of comfort for myself. You just could not give in to the horror and discomfort of the cold, the mud, the enemy fire, and despair. My personal belongings were scattered over my three quarter-ton truck. In the trailer attached to it was a duffel bag containing extra clothes, but mostly the sort that I would not be needing. I had a valpak with my dress clothes in it, but was sorry that I had brought it along. Although the need for such stuff was remote, my conservative nature kept me from just throwing away those expensive things. In the front of the truck, I had hung an assortment of bags. My friends teased me about them, but to me they were important. They contained extra underwear, extra socks, an extra field uniform, soap, tools, and food. In a built in box near the front seat, I kept my mess kit, a C ration, a couple of D rations (true field rations, which were dense chocolate bars), my last bottle of Haig and Haig (reserved for victory), toilet articles, and a German fur hat which I wore under my G.I. helmet. There was also a small pick, a map case, a Blum's candy tin containing my camera and some film that I had acquired in Nancy, a first-aid kit, field glasses, a cup, and a canteen. Under my seat I kept a military web belt with compass, a first-aid kit, and a canteen with a field cup in a case. Periodically it was necessary to check this stuff to know what was where in case of an emergency. Our situation was unpredictable. A stray shell could hit us or near us at any time, particularly now when we were trying to advance through the Saar into Germany. Now the Germans were protecting their homeland.

Prior to leaving Nancy, I had everything washable laundered. I had a large supply of clean clothes, probably enough to last me through the winter, as long as my truck was not hit by a shell. Because of my supplies, the enlisted men recognized me as sort of a Montgomery Ward. They often came and got socks or a shirt or some other piece of equipment. They did not have the storage areas that I had, and they also were not as provident. Typical situation: my chief technician asked if there was any coffee around, with a significant look at me. I said, "You'll find a tin and a jar of coffee in the upper inside bag in front of the truck." Many just gave up and slogged along in a depressed sort of way, including my fellow officers who obsessed about people at home, who, under no threat, were practicing medicine, making money, and generally living it up. It was especially difficult to accept this lot of seeing fine young men wounded and covered with mud and of trying to make progress through mud in vehicles which were not designed for this sort of weather.

Gradually we began to use chains on our wheels so that we could make progress through the mud. We learned to get together decent meals whenever possible. We would set up some sort of a kitchen and send men to the rear to search for fresh food. We tried to feed our men and anyone in the vicinity with at least one hot meal a day.

Our regiment drove forward against stiff resistance and against well trained troops. We continued to suffer casualties, and they seemed to us, worse than Normandy, perhaps because of the wet and mud, and because we were emotionally exhausted. We were also confronted with many cases of trench foot, which is closely related to frostbite. Essentially when shoes and socks get wet, the skin begins to break down, and there is considerable discomfort and swelling. If there is cold, blood vessels tend to close off, which may lead to gangrene. This serious problem could have been prevented by waterproof boots, but such footwear did not reach us until weeks later. Also, changing socks often would help, but few men thought to carry a lot of extra socks, as I did.

Our army was not prepared for a winter war. The men in combat just would not take enough gear to protect themselves from the wet and cold. If they could not move quickly, they might not live. They were thoroughly miserable; wet, cold, tired, ill fed, and unprepared for these conditions. Nevertheless, we moved ahead capturing town after town, moving steadily, but slowly, toward Germany.

We finally got over the line barely into Germany to the city of Sarrgemunes. We found a mostly intact building that had been officers' quarters for the Germans. It was dry. There was running water and even a working fireplace. We set up a first rate station. I was glad that I was here and not with the infantry battalion. We were able to clean up, dry out, and take decent care of the wounded. I found my friend Dave Roth, who was with a neighboring unit, and invited him for a real meal. I broke out some good French Champagne that I had cooled in the snow. We found some glasses that had been made in this area. We drank to the defeat of the Germans and threw the glasses into the fireplace.

In the midst of this revelry, there was a sudden influx of wounded. As I was surveying the men when they came in, I noted that a number were from a neighboring division. I was cleaning up one of them, a man with a bad scalp wound where a bullet had penetrated his helmet, and he had shattered his left wrist. It dawned on me that he was an old friend from San Francisco, Bill.

We had grown up together, played poker together, gone to parties, and done all the things that young friends do. He was in mild shock. We started some plasma. Though his scalp wound was deep and bleeding profusely, his skull was intact. I was able to control bleeding in that area with a pressure dressing using an ace bandage. With the wrist shattered, I was unsure whether his hand could be saved. We cleaned that area, carefully dressed it, and splinted the area with a wire splint. I hoped the hand could be saved. At least one major artery was intact.

Bill gradually came around. He was incredulous to see me and thought he was fantasizing. However, he soon realized that all of this was for real. He had yet to realize that his war was over. He got a tetanus booster, morphine, and a cigarette, followed by some hot coffee. There was little time to find out what had happened. He was an infantry officer, and apparently a sniper wounded him in the head, and a second shot hit his wrist.

I rushed him to the next ambulance, hoping that the division hospital could do something more to save his hand. I did not know if there was a field hospital close by. Fortunately, there was was one, and he did well. His hand was saved, but it was almost useless. Certainly he would not be able to work in his profession, ophthalmology. On the other hand, he was alive. I was able to get word to his parents before the Army did.

The roads were muddy, and the fields quagmires. But, we had been successful in capturing a large number of Germans along with equipment. Our commanding general of the Third Army, George Patton, now with four stars, saw a chance to finish the Germans off. He ordered an advance. We came to a major intersection where there was a traffic pile-up. There was General Patton standing up in his jeep which bore a sign indicating his four stars. His helmet was shining. He had pistols on his hips. He was directing traffic!

Our troops strove to move forward, but we began running out of gas. We did not know that most supplies to the Third Army, were being sent to Montgomery for his failed attack on Arnheim. Finally, General Patton ordered men out of their vehicles to walk forward. But on foot, we were just not able to make significant progress.

Quite unexpectedly, we were informed that our division was to be relieved. We had had serious losses against increasing resistance as we approached Germany. We were to go to Metz over Christmas, get some rest, take on reinforcements, and be reequipped. My unit was put in a school building in Metz. The city had taken a beating in various battles and bombings, but this school building was intact.

It was Christmas Eve. We put up a Christmas tree and decorated it with all kinds of stuff, including cotton. Until then, since leaving Nancy, we had lived mostly on rations that came in cans or boxes and were essentially the same day after day: beans, concentrated eggs, chopped corned beef, cookies, hard candy, and coffee. We had no fresh vegetables or fresh fruit, and still none of us had the good sense to drink the powdered fruit juice fortified with vitamin C that was provided with some rations to prevent scurvy. In Normandy and crossing France, we often had apples, which helped our vitamin supply.

This Christmas Eve meal included turkey, cranberry sauce, sweet potatoes, etc. I still do not know how they got it to us. During that wonderful dinner, we received word that all plans were changed. The Germans had broken through our lines, had surrounded Bastogne, and were headed for the sea. As part of Patton's Third Army, we were to stop them and relieve Bastogne. There were to be no reinforcements, no rest, and no refitting. It had been snowing for some time and it was bitter cold.

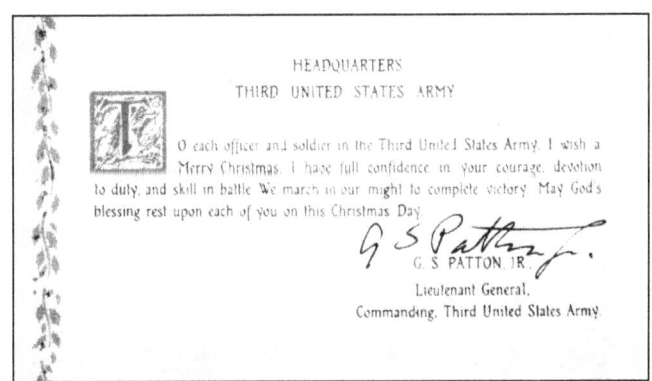

Christmas greetings from Patton

KAPPY'S NEWS
(Take it or leave it)

AMERICAN FIRST ARMY TROOPS HAVE CAPTURED WEISWEILER AND WERE LAST NIGHT ABOUT A MILE BEYOND IT ON THE GREAT MOTOR ROAD TO COLOGNE. AMERICAN THIRD ARMY TROOPS SUPPORTED BY TWO THOUSAND FIGHTER BOMBERS MADE SUBSTANTIAL ADVANCES YESTERDAY. FURTHER SOUTH, THE ENEMY WERE IN FULL RETREAT TOWARDS THE RHINE. ALLIED PLANES HAD A BIG DAY SHOOTING UP TRAFFIC BEHIND THE GERMAN LINES AND BOMBING PONTOON BRIDGES ACROSS THE RIVER.

R.A.F. LANCASTERS ATTACTED TARGETS IN WESTERN GERMANY YESTERDAY AND ALL RETURNED. OVER ELEVEN HUNDRED AMERICAN HEAVIES FROM BRITAIN ESCORTED BY SEVEN HUNDRED FIGHTERS ATTACKED TARGETS IN NORTHWESTERN GERMANY INTRUDIN INCLUDING GERMANY'S LARGEST REMAINING OIL PLANT AT HANOVER AND THE RAIL YARDS AT HAMM. THE RAIDERS KNOCKOUT A TOTAL 129 FIGHTERS OF THE ENEMY. AMERICAN LOSSES WERE 37 BOMBERS AND 13 FIGHTERS.

THE VICTORIA CROSS HAS BEEN AWARDED TO MAJOR DAVID V. CURRY OF THE 29th CANADIAN ARMOURED RECON. REGT. FOR HIS LEADERSHIP IN CUTTING ONE OF THE MAIN GERMAN ESCAPE ROUTES FROM CALAIS POCKET. IN NORMANDY LAST AUGUST.

GENERAL SIR HENRY MAITLAND WILSON IS GOING TO WASHINGTON TO TAKE A PLACE OF THE LATE FIELD MARSHAL SIR JOHN DILL AS HEAD OF THE BRITISH JOINT STAFF MISSION. HE WILL ACT ALSO AS MR. CHURCHILL'S PERSONAL MILITARY REPRESENTATIVE TO MR. ROOSEVELT. GENERAL ALEXANDER IS PROMOTED TO THE RANK OF FIELD MARSHAL FROM JUNE FOURTH THE DAY HIS ARMY CAPTURED ROME. XXX IS NOW SUPREME IN THE MEDITERRANEAN. GENERAL MARK CLARK TAKES THE NEW FIELD MARSHAL'S PLACE.
THE RUSSIANS HAVE TAKEN A RAIL JUNCTION LESS THAN 30 MILES FROMX NORTHEAST OF BUDAPEST.

YESTERDAY, SUPER FORTERSSES FROM SAIPAN ATTACKED TOKYO THAT WAS THE XXXXXX SECOND RAID IN FOUR DAYS. SUPER FORTRESSES FROM INDIA BOMBED BANKOCK IN INDO CHINA.

BRITISH FOURTEENTH ARMY TROOPS IN A NEW DRIVE INTO NORTHWESTERN BURMA HAVE PUSHED TWELVE MILES BEYOND THE UPPER CHIN WIN.

ANNOUNCEMENTS
THERE WILL BE CHURCH SERVICES AT 1230 today. SERVICES WILL BE IN THE LARGE ROOM.

EDITORIAL
MAY WE TAKE THIS OCCASION TO QUOTE A MEMORANDUM RECEIVED LAST EVENING BY SPECIAL MESSENGER FROM OUR HEADQUARTERS: "....... THE SUPREME COMMANDER WISHES TO EMPHASIZE THE IMPORTANCE OF THE CONDUCT OF TROOPS IN THEIR RELATIONSHIPS WITH THE CITIZENS OF LIBERATED COUNTRIES WHICH MUST BE SUCH AS TO INSURE THE GOOD NAME OF THE AMERICAN ARMY BEING HELD IN HIGH REGARD."
27 November 44

-30-

Chapter 18

Bastogne

December 25, 1944

    The whole situation was terrifying. The Army always is full of rumors. We heard that the Germans had broken through our lines with a major force, and that our line across the Ardennes had collapsed. We had no air cover because of the weather. The 101st Airborne Division was surrounded in Bastogne. The American Army had tremendous casualties, and we did not know how many had been captured. We had moved across France so rapidly that we thought the war was all but over. We began to think otherwise in the Saar. None of us expected anything like this.

    We were upset at having to leave Metz and our plans for a pleasant Christmas. We hurriedly repacked our vehicles. Fortunately, I had accumulated a good supply of warm clothes, and I needed them all. My truck had no doors, so that we were exposed to the air. I put on two suits of long underwear, two pairs of socks, wool pants and shirt, a field jacket, an overcoat, two pairs of gloves, and a fur hat covered by my helmet. Still, I was none too warm.

    We took off in the dark, driving north into Luxembourg amid sounds of small arms and artillery fire. Around midnight, we got to a small, seemingly deserted town, Boulaide. I spotted one faint light and led my unit toward it. As we drove through the

Pass for Germans to surrender

town, we saw a number of German flags. Apparently, the Germans had taken this town during their offensive, but our division had driven them out just before we got there. I heard that some of our men waded through a freezing cold river to get at the Germans.

The small light I had seen was in the home of a farmer who was there waiting for us. He had hidden out in his cellar. He had a roaring fire going and had slaughtered a pig. He had brought out a huge sausage. He had large loaves of fresh-baked bread. We did not know how he had been able to provide all of this, but we were grateful, to say the least. We hastened to set up a station, sampling the delicious food as we worked.

We hardly had set up when combat soldiers began coming in. A few were wounded, and all had various degrees of frostbite. Having been in the Ski Troops, I knew how serious frostbite is. The severe cases I put in a warm room, wearing the most dry clothes available and leaving their frostbitten parts exposed, while I kept their bodies warm. I planned to evacuate them. The more mild cases I warmed up and fed. Those, I expected could go back to duty with proper clothing, if I could get it. Finally, after three hours or so, ready to collapse, I arranged shifts to care for whoever came in and found a place to drop my bedroll. Some Christmas Day!

At dawn, I was up. The farmer had been up most of the night. He had cut the coat-of-arms from the center of a Luxembourg coin which he presented to me. He knew we were going to move out; so he gave me this huge sausage which had a very strong odor of garlic. Obviously, I was grateful to this man, and I regretted not getting his name and address. I still have the cutout coin.

Just before we pulled out, a full colonel came by to check on wounded. He went around to encourage them. However, when he saw the men that I had planned to evacuate, he asked, "What's wrong with these men?"

I answered, "They have severe frostbite, sir."

"Warm them up and send them back to duty. I need every man I can get."

"I'm sorry, sir. If these men go back to duty, there is a good chance they will lose a hand or a foot."

"I'm ordering you to send these men back to duty."

"I'm sorry, sir, I can't do that."

"I'll recommend that you face court-martial."

"Very well, sir."

He left. Later on, these men received Purple Hearts, when at higher echelons it was realized how dangerous severe frostbite was.

We pulled out early the next morning, having arranged for the evacuation of the wounded by leaving one of our ambulances to shuttle and later to catch up. There were sounds of fire fighting all around us. We weren't sure where the front was, but obviously our division had somehow made progress that morning, and we got word to set up a station in Nagen, a town in Belgium. On the way there, we drove through the beautiful city of Luxembourg with its deep valley going through the middle of the town. The bridges over it were intact.

By late morning we were in Nagen, which had been badly battered. There was the rattle of small arms fire and the horrible sound of German burp guns, their rapid-fire submachine guns. We also heard the crunch of landing shells and the clatter of tank treads. We were never sure whether they were the Germans' or ours. On Christmas morning, the sky suddenly cleared. We began to see our planes with long trails behind them. There were bombers going for the rear and fighter bombers diving. It was a wonderful sight, and we all cheered. This was the first good news in days.

We set up an aid station. Incongruously, superimposed on this clean, peaceful, friendly country was a dirty unpleasant war. The smooth valleys were marred by stacks of ammunition boxes, gun emplacements, shot-up trucks, tanks, and everywhere, miles of communication wire. The wire was strung from trees, from poles, and on the ground. The roads had been torn up by the heavy vehicles of both armies. Here and there, a tree had been violently knocked down. There was a never ending roar of guns polluting the otherwise pristine air. We noticed that the people of this town had taken in citizens of nearby towns that had been devastated in the furious battle as the Germans drove ahead toward Bastogne and, they hoped, to the sea to cut the Allied Armies in half.

We had chosen this town because it had sustained relatively little damage and consequently could provide a good site for care of the wounded. Unfortunately ,while scouting for a site, one of my fellow medical officers was wounded and evacuated. That left me to deal with the wounded of a regiment of over five thousand. I never worked so hard, even in Normandy.

My main job was to get the seriously wounded in good enough shape to be transported to the rear in ambulances, which meant stopping hemorrhage and often giving plasma. They were brought to my station, a restaurant, by jeeps fitted with litter racks and by ambulances coming from the smaller units. The wounded were all cold, and their wounds were horrible. We saw many of the worst wounded, for many with minor wounds had returned to duty. We were short of men, and the need to break the circle around Bastogne was urgent.

The people of the town were friendly. They had disliked the Germans in the past and hated them even more now. They brought us food and firewood and helped to get us water, so urgently needed in cleaning the wounded. The stove I had brought with me was very useful when added to the one in the restaurant. I had learned always to take a fairly large wood stove tied to the fender of my truck, along with pipe which we ran from the stove around the room and then outside. This provided warmth, which was so needed.

We had to remove most of the clothing from the wounded in order to care for their wounds. A pile of torn clothes, bandages, sponges, and other debris was a constant problem. But we managed. We soon had a large rubbish heap outside. We hated to open the door; because we would lose heat. We put on adequate bandages. We started plasma often. Many of the wounded were in shock, and frequently I found it necessary to start I.V.s in the femoral vein. I still seemed to be the only one in our unit who could manage that. For this reason, I had the aid men do a lot of the other chores.

When wounded were brought in, it was important to evaluate each man and assess the urgency of his condition. Fortunately, I had been able to load up on supplies in Metz on Christmas Eve. My favorite bit of equipment was the elastic bandage, which in Normandy I had found to be so versatile. We used untold numbers of syrettes of morphine. Fortunately, I had saved a large supply of cigarettes, which were gratefully received by the wounded. We made gallons of hot coffee using the stoves in the restaurant. We were able to get some reasonably decent food, but for us, there was little time to eat. In many ways, it was worse than Normandy. Although we had a better setup for our station, winter made the field conditions worse. It was extremely difficult to evacuate wounded men through the snow even with chains on jeeps and ambulances. There also was the problem of men literally freezing before the aid men could get to them with first aid and evacuation. I taught the aid men to make sleds which had a low profile and moved through the snow easily.

The worst thing about our situation was that we did not understand exactly what was going on. We were frightened and disheartened. We had thought the war was about over, and now we seemed to be fighting for survival. Morale was low. On our first evening, I broke out one of the bottles of Scotch that I had brought from England. I divided this among my exhausted aid men. I think it helped.

Beginning in Normandy, to keep my sanity, I made a big effort to act as much as possible as though I were in a much better environment. I continued to shave daily. The standard issue Army helmet had a liner that was easily removed, leaving the helmet like a big basin. I warmed water over my little German stove, and with that was able to shave. I also was in the habit of setting up some sort of table on which to eat, even when I was in a foxhole. When possible, I supplemented our simple G.I. fare with some wine or Calvados. I tried to wear clean, dry clothes. I brushed my teeth. Whenever possible, I had water heated to a boiling point in a large can and had the men dip their mess equipment into it to avoid gastrointestinal problems by killing viruses and bacteria. In these ways, I tried to set an example for my men, who were often discouraged and inclined to neglect themselves.

One of the most amazing facts of this terrible battle was that our troops could keep fighting on. I don't know how they were able to dig foxholes in this cold ground or how they were able to use their firearms in the miserable weather. They often used abandoned German foxholes, and they sometimes broke the frozen ground with hand grenades. Most of the men were inadequately clothed. They had been issued a type of rubber boot with leather tops. These were good for mud and wet, but not good for real cold. Feet sweated in them, and then when the soldiers stopped to fight, their feet tended to freeze. Our quartermasters had a lot to learn. They had not anticipated the needs of a winter war.

We leapfrogged toward Bastogne. As we got closer, the fighting grew more bitter. The German Tiger tanks were tough to stop. We now faced elite German troops. We even picked up some of their wounded, who actually were better dressed against the cold than our men. They wore helmets lined with fur. Their clothing was of heavier wool than that of our men. They often wore a sort of white jump-suit over their clothes for camouflage. That extra layer added warmth. They often had wool sweaters under their field jackets. They all carried extra heavy wool socks, and many had gloves with provision for freeing the trigger finger. Many of these men had been on the eastern front in Russia.

When we got close to Bastogne, an infantry major came by and said that the troops surrounded in Bastogne were low in medical supplies and in medical officers. Did I think I could help? He said that they planned to force their way into the city, putting some infantry on the outside of tanks, and perhaps we could load a tank or two with medical supplies, a couple of aid men, and an officer, if available. Well, I figured, what the hell—I'll try it.

They brought a tank to our station, and we loaded supplies onto it. I took two volunteers with me: Volkman, who was a tech sergeant and quite gentle, and Bradford who was a tough veteran and a leader. I put on my full winter gear: two pairs of long underwear, a wool uniform, two pairs of wool socks with leather boots, a field jacket, my overcoat, and my fur hat with ear flaps, covered by my helmet. We moved out.

It was obvious that the tankers were trying to protect me and my men. They put their other tanks in a position to protect us, one on either side of the supply tank onto which we climbed and got as low as possible, using the gear fastened to it as cover. The tankers carried their bedrolls, extra treads, and extra clothing on the outside of their vehicles, while extra ammunition and fuel were protected by armor whenever possible. Much to our surprise, the commander had found a route to Bastogne that was concealed, and we encountered little fire. What there was had a tremendous response from our group which consisted of four tanks, a tank destroyer, and, of all things, a command jeep containing the scouts who had found the route.

I heard a story when we made a brief stop near an infantry company. In this "white jungle" close-quarter fighting in the winter-bound fir forests, soldiers on both sides sometimes had sluggish reactions. T/Sergeant McLaughlin of Black Rock, Arkansas, an E Company platoon sergeant, set off at dark to contact G company. He encountered some soldiers digging into the frozen ground. "G Company?" he asked. Just as he spoke he realized these were Germans. "Nix" one of the German soldiers replied as he continued chipping at the ground. McLaughlin pivoted slowly, and trudged off through the snow. He was well back to his company before the Nazis opened up in his direction.

Within a few hours, we were in Bastogne passing cheering troops of the 101st Airborne. We had travelled eighty-five miles in a bit less than two days against stiff opposition. Though we had some wounded, we did not have a man killed from Metz to Bastogne. That was remarkable considering the conditions, and it was noted in the news. It was the kind of mobility that our division was known for. During that time, we went through parts of three countries: France, Belgium, and Luxembourg. We had crossed rivers where the bridges had been destroyed, and we dealt with the horrible conditions. We had reason to be proud of the 35th, but we were too busy doing our jobs and staying alive to reflect on our accomplishments.

We set up in the main railroad station. We took over the command jeep to transport wounded and to bring supplies to the various aid stations. Almost immediately wounded poured in. These were the less badly hurt who had been willing to defer care to the more seriously wounded. The wounded had first been attended in battalion aid stations, from which they were transported to our station, which was enclosed, warm, and better equipped. Because of the difficult transport through snow, evacuation of the more severely wounded to our station had priority. There was real danger of those men freezing to death. The less seriously wounded were helped back to the station afterward, unless they were able to get there on their own. The jeep driver worked overtime bringing supplies, transferring wounded, and being a messenger.

By nightfall we were exhausted, but we knew Bastogne had held. The Germans had been stopped. We didn't know how soon our troops could recover enough to begin to move toward Germany again, and I think we would just as soon have stopped to wait for spring.

The next morning, it was obvious that other troops were getting into Bastogne. Their shoulder patches were different from our Wagon Wheels. But fighting was far from over. A medical officer came in. He was fresh, had a clean uniform, and told me he had been bored in a field hospital and he would like to see some action. He had had a good medical education at Cornell, and we had a lot to talk about since I had spent some time at Cornell not much more than a year before. He had been assigned to a battalion aid station of an infantry battalion just outside of town. I thought he was out of his mind to leave that safe place for this. He was brought into the station that evening with the top of his skull blown away. We treated him with care, and he was the first person I evacuated immediately to the rear along a newly opened route. I never knew if he lived. The poor guy did not know how to survive in a combat area. The situation with this man was not unusual for replacements. All of them were inadequately trained. They were assigned to various duties, but there was not enough time to teach them how to stay alive. Few replacements lasted more than a few days.

Our lines having held, our generals, particularly Patton, thought this was an ideal time to destroy the German Army. So, instead of resting and reorganizing, he decided that we would attack. All of us in Bastogne were terribly angry. We and the troops around us were exhausted. The cold and deep snow were terrible. The soldiers we faced were elite Germans who, though defeated in their attempt to cut our armies in half, still knew how to fight and to take advantage of the terrain. They were defending Germany now, and their supply lines were shorter and better than ours. It was difficult to believe that we were entering a battle that for us was worse than Normandy or Bastogne. General Patton wanted to surround the Germans, cutting off their supplies, but Eisenhower the supreme commander, wanted to advance on a broad front. At least that was my understanding. Each had his reasons, but I had learned to respect Patton, even though he was highly demanding of his troops. In retrospect, I think Patton was right.

My truck. Note the "Bags Miscellaneous."

My truck outside of Bastogne

Woodcome, me and Cook dressed for the bitter cold near Bastogne

Metz to the Ardennez

Chapter 19

Roer

January 14, 1945

Around January 14, everything seemed to change. The casualties had dropped to a few and they were mostly victims of frostbite. I made a twenty-eight mile trip for a hot shower, taking with me as many of our aid men as could be spared. The showers were our first since Christmas.

When we took a shower, we first stored our valuables and turned in all our clothes. After a long and luxurious shower, we were issued all new clothes from the skin out, and they did not do a bad job in fitting you. My clothes were the same as the enlisted men's, though, of course, I later put my insignia on the collar and my combat medic badge over my left shirt pocket.

Around that time, I heard that I had been put in for another decoration, in part for getting supplies into Bastogne on that tank ride. I was pleased, of course, but I decided never to wear the ribbons in a combat area. There were thousands who deserved medals more than I did. I truly believed this. Just surviving during the last couple of weeks in the bitter cold was terrible for the enlisted men, while in addition, they had to contend with fear of the Germans and to fight desperately for their own lives. They did that and did it very well.

Bastogne had been badly damaged in the battle. It was full of debris that had not been cleaned up, and almost every building had been damaged by incoming shells. Bastogne was not especially beautiful. There were no notably attractive buildings, no impressive parks. The stores were uninteresting and had practically nothing in them. There were few civilians around.

I found my good friend Dave not far away. His collecting company had been less involved in the battle because his regiment had been held in reserve in case the Germans broke through. He had made camp in a bar, not surprisingly, and in the bar was a piano. Some source sent us supplies of paperback books quite regularly (as if we had had a lot of time to read). There were often included books of music of popular songs. I stored most of this stuff for better times, if they ever came. I broke out the music and some captured cognac marked "nur fur der Wehrmacht" and began to play. I had played the piano for years, and had a pile of lessons, but I was never very good. To the GIs in Bastogne, I was Liberace. I played on and on. More and more men came in and sang the songs, and polished off my cognac. The contrast with what we had been through was unbelievable.

It had been an eventful day but an important one for me. I had heard of my second decoration from a tech sergeant who worked at regimental headquarters. The shower and new clothes made me feel good. I returned to my quarters in the railroad station, which was warm from the stove in the corner, and replaced the blanket that lined my sleeping bag with a clean one that I got at the shower. I had even washed the pillow cover that I had brought from home with a "baby pillow" which I had taken everywhere. I don't remember how I got it khaki-colored. I had made a cot out of a litter on which I spread my sleeping bag.

As I lay there comfortably, I assessed my situation. Because we had driven the Germans back from this major drive, no matter the terrible losses, I was sure the war was over. It would just be a matter of time. For once, I felt that I could survive. Early on, I had the feeling that I probably wouldn't make it through, that I would be killed or wounded, so why not take some chances? Now I felt differently, and my conscious decision was "just do my job. Be careful. Don't do anything stupid, like trying to go through enemy lines or riding on the outside of a tank. Don't volunteer. I've done that." A number of my enlisted men had adopted the same attitude long before. Privates would refuse promotion, wanting only to do their jobs and look after themselves. They did not want responsibility for others, along with the increased risks that came with leading a squad, platoon, or any unit. Though there was talk about rotation, the only sign of that seemed to be with higher ranking officers. It became clear to me that there was no way to get out of the infantry, except by being wounded.

Despite the bitter cold and inadequate equipment (particularly clothing), the men who had relieved Bastogne were ordered to pursue the Germans. The forests in that area gave great advantage to the defenders. The Germans in the area included some of their best soldiers. The toll on our men proved to be worse than in Normandy.

My unit was just getting used to Bastogne when we got orders to move in a hurry to back up troops who were being pushed about in northeastern France. We were assigned to join a combat command that included my medical platoon, two regiments, and supporting artillery. The rest of the division remained with the task of pursuing the Germans.

Our division had developed a reputation for being able to move fast and to adjust speedily to situations. We had to travel two hundred fifty miles quickly. My driver, a portly Italian-American nicknamed Tony, had built plywood sides and doors on our three-quarter ton truck. I did not know where he got the materials, but they protected us from the bitter cold. Always on one fender was lashed the wood-burning stove and on the other fender some lengths of stove pipe. All of those things helped to save us and the wounded for whom we cared.

I found myself in command of a platoon of the collecting company. There were about a hundred men, ten ambulances, four three-quarter ton trucks, two jeeps, various and sundry trailers, and a two and a half ton kitchen truck. We had all become quite experienced and could set up without any orders being given.

By the time we had moved to our new position, the Germans had already withdrawn. It was obvious that they were moving back to establish a defense line to protect "the Fatherland." So, we were on the move again, this time to Holland. The British had been trying to move the Germans out of eastern Holland, particularly Maastricht, but they were not having much success. Our division moved in with remarkable spirit and we drove the Germans out in a couple of days. There were casualties, but the number was remarkably low, for which we were all grateful. That is not to say that the fighting was easy. These Germans were some of the best we had faced, and they knew how to use the terrain to their advantage. Their main purpose was to hold us up so that they could set up a major defensive position.

The weather conditions were terrible. It was cold, and there was snow. The men still did not have as good equipment as they needed, though at least we had fresh uniforms. They had begun to get boots with the lower portion of rubber. I wore leather paratroopers boots with two pairs of woolen socks, and I tried to get my men to do something similar.

I set up a station in a rather large restaurant-bar in Maastrict. Within a few hours of our arrival, the citizens were busy scrubbing out all evidence of the Germans. The women were washing their windows, and so help me, they were even washing the streets with soap and water. God only knows where they got the soap and why they were willing to use some of their very precious commodity in this fashion. They wanted to erase any sign of the hated Germans.

We saw women and old men, but no young men. There were very few children. The reasons were two-fold. First, most of the young men had been taken to labor camps in Germany. Second, the population had been terribly malnourished, with the result that, the young women did not ovulate and could not often conceive.

Further, if they did conceive, neonatal mortality was high because of the malnutrition of the mothers and inadequate feeding of their infants. The Germans had been ruthless in taking almost all of the food produced, and if any person tried to hide part of his produce, he could be shot on the spot. The people greeted us with unbelievable joy. They had little to offer but gratitude, and we gave away all the food we could spare. We gave special attention to women with small children, all of whom looked emaciated.

We were hardly settled, when we were ordered to move again. This was another long trip. We were to relieve some British troops who had been having a terrible time in a battle for the Roer River. This river was a sort of defense line in western Germany. Part of the Siegfried Line, the Germans were determined to hold it. We arrived and took over the British positions in one sector, and the British used those troops to reinforce those to the north.

I set up our station in a rather nice home. It was modern and sturdily built with a deep, dry cellar. Word was out that we would be there for awhile. It became clear that we would build up in preparation for the invasion of Germany. Whereas, in the previous fall, we felt we could sail in, we now realized that the Germans had had time to build defenses on the Roer and the Rhine. We all knew that the allies had wasted time, energy, and initiative in the failed British drive to the north.

We had time at last to lick our wounds. We restocked. I took groups of men to showers and for new clean clothes. I was able to get some real food, when we set up a good field kitchen. I even began to think of going to Brussels, which was about a hundred and fifty miles to the west.

One day, I loaded an ambulance with men who had been in most danger and headed for Brussels. With a population of over a million, it was the largest city I had been in. Brussels seemed to be laid out roughly in circles and was surrounded by many parks. Of course, in winter the trees were bare. We left our vehicle in a garage and walked to what seemed the main street. it reminded me of Market Street in San Francisco.

There were shops, a few cafes, and some government buildings. It was Sunday and restaurants were closed but cafes were open. It seemed that everyone was out in his Sunday best. Sunday afternoon there seemed to be like Saturday night at home. I wandered around and finally found an officers' club. I could not believe the elegance, and there I was in my combat clothes. The main room had a towering ceiling with crystal chandeliers. There was a lovely bar and tea dancing to a good orchestra. It was almost unbearable. The tables had spotless linen, and there were waiters dressed in tails. The whole thing reminded me of the Palace Court. I had picked up Goodson. He had been through most of the war to date with me, but in a different platoon. He was tall, dour, often depressed, and I think he drank too much. He had a young wife and child, and his principle goal was just to get back home. He was very intelligent and could be good company. The food was remarkably good, and that was especially so when compared with that available to most of the population, and to us on the line. It was served with wine, which gave it a proper touch.

Somehow Dave Roth found us, and he and his commanding officer joined us at a rather festive table. All of us could hardly believe that this had been going on while we were freezing in the mud and snow. Then a British Colonel joined us. He called us PBIs, poor bloody infantry. After lunch, he showed Dave and me around a bit and even introduced us to a couple of charming young women. Somehow, we broke up, and one of the women took me on a tour, including the Golden Square, with its ornate and gilded medieval buildings with their multiple steeples, towers, and domes. These buildings, their entrances guarded by lions, were built around a large cobblestone square and housed government or guild headquarters. From here, we went to see "the Piss Boy," the famous fountain, at a street corner featuring a statue of a small boy urinating under an elaborately carved stone alcove. Then we did a brief tour of the shopping district, where, at least from the outside, the stores and their windows were the equal of the best of New York.

It being Sunday, the better cafes began to open at 3:30. First, we took in the more fashionable afternoon spots where city residents went on Sunday afternoon. There they are entertained by good music and fairly good entertainers. At 5:30, the night clubs opened. To conserve electricity, curfew was at 10:00. There was dancing to good orchestras and entertainment. The best clubs reminded me of the Copacabana in New York, being two floors with a cafe upstairs entertainment by an orchestra, singers, story tellers, and other kinds of performers. Downstairs, as in a typical night-club were a small dance floor, a bar, many tables, a good orchestra. These night-clubs were expensive whereas the best meal in the officers' club cost about $.50.

There was an acute male shortage; so I was welcome, even in my combat clothes. Young girls of well-to-do families were in groups at the better clubs, chaperoned by either a mother or some other older woman. There were also unescorted women, more than any of us had seen in over a year. But passes were up, and I had to leave at 7:00 in the evening, just when it was getting good. The young woman who had taken me around was pleasant enough and attractive, though not fashionable. She worked in a minor government job and apparently had not been able to buy much in the way of clothes. I said that I would try to call her if I were able to get back to Brussels, but who knew when that might be.

Now we had to drive back. It was winter and already dark. To my surprise, all the men returned as they had been told. The penalties were harsh for anyone who did not return to duty. On the other hand, my men were all in various stages of drunkenness. Though it was against military law for an officer to drive a vehicle, it was obvious that I would have to drive. I took off my bars and got into the driver's seat. An Army ambulance was heavy and not the easiest vehicle to drive. As soon as we got out of Brussels the roads became progressively bad. We were not permitted to use headlights, only blackout lights, small, blue lights which did not light the road but could not be seen from the air. A vehicle approaching could see the blackout lights and avoid collision. Road signs were few; because most had been removed to impede the Germans at the time of the breakthrough. From time to time, I got lost, but fortunately I found help from small G.I. groups and even occasionally from locals. Somehow, I got us back.

It was disturbing, after the luxury of Brussels, to return to battlefront conditions. Overhead, we heard again and again the burping noise of V-1 rockets, which we called "buzz-bombs." It was frightening when their motors stopped, because at that point, they started their descent—who knew where. We had seen these rockets increasingly in the daytime. They moved a bit faster than a plane, and were about the size of a small plane. There was a flame from their tails. Fighters tried to shoot them down, and occasionally, they succeeded. The antiaircraft gunners also took shots at them and were sometimes successful. They worried us, and we had begun to hear about the V-2s hitting England. Those could not be seen until they hit. We wondered if these rockets might change the war and we hoped to get to their source before they destroyed us.

In Belgium and occasionally in northern France, German jet planes flew very low over us. We had never heard of this kind of aircraft. They made a frightening noise and although they sprayed us with machine gun fire, they did surprisingly little damage. We also worried that, should those planes be produced in large numbers, our forces would be in real trouble. German propaganda broadcast the threats to us of the V-1 buzz bombs, the V-2 rockets, and these new jet planes. We had nothing like them. A few days later, we were permitted to return to Brussels. On our first trip, we had parked near a movie theater, and I had asked directions from a pleasant young woman who was the cashier. This time, there she was again. She remembered me. I asked her what time she got off work. In mid-afternoon, she told me with a pleasing smile. She was well nourished, but not heavy. I remember mostly her striking blue eyes. Seeing that she got off at a relatively early time, I asked if she would join me. She was pleased at the suggestion, so I returned shortly to pick her up and invited her to dinner. I spoke a little French, and she spoke a little English, probably having learned it in the movies. We managed communication.

We went to a small restaurant in the neighborhood. Everything was expensive, since our dollar was undervalued in Belgium. We essentially got about half of what it was worth, so I bartered. I always had cigarettes. We ordered a simple dinner that was a huge success with the young woman; perhaps it was more elegant than she was used to. My tip for the waiter was some cigarettes, with which he was ecstatic. After dinner we wandered around, talking a bit. Finally, she stopped us at a small but attractive hotel and surprised me by asking for a room. The man at the desk was courteous, and, to my surprise, did not charge us.

The room was pleasant. After a brief embrace, she began to take off her clothes; and so did I. I had not been with a woman for months. She was charming and kind, and though our lovemaking was not passionate, it was enthusiastic, and we both seemed to have a good time in the process. We left in just enough time to get me back to where we had parked the ambulance. I got all kinds of whistles and wolf calls from the men as they saw me approaching with this attractive young woman on my arm. Her name was Jenine. The memory of that evening sustained me for longer than I expected.

It often seemed strange to me that I did not keep a record of the many kind and friendly people I met. But, I thought the chances of my surviving the war were only fair. It was also impossible for me to see myself in a civilian situation. We suspected that if we had the good fortune to survive the war in Europe, the invasion of Japan loomed. That was a horrendous prospect. Oh, how I regretted not being more careful to keep names and addresses!

Again, I drove back from Brussels, because no enlisted man was fit to do so. This time I did not get lost. On returning, I found that we were to move out in about forty-eight hours. So, after a brief rest and some packing, I decided to make a last run to Brussels. I got a jeep and driver from the motor pool, probably illegally. The driver was happy to get a chance to go to Brussels. I went to the theater where Jenine worked to find that she was not there. Her replacement could not tell me where she lived. I walked the streets in despair. We returned earlier than usual to be sure all was ready for our next troop move.

We had just become comfortable in our location. We had set up a kitchen. We had established good relations with our British Army neighbors. I was invited to tea one day. Their officers lived in relative luxury. Tea was served in a large cellar with table cloths, china, and crystal glassware. Even though I had heard that the English did this sort of thing, I still found it hard to believe. While we were there, we also had a visit from one of the officers who had supervised our training at Carlisle so long before. He had become a sort of medical inspector general. We had rarely seen any high ranking medical officers in our areas. He was impressed with how we set up and with our knowledge of our function. I pointed out the many ways in which we had modified what we had been taught. This was not the war that he and his fellow officers had planned for.

It was time to move on. We had to cross the Roer River. We had built up a significant force, and though the Germans had set up defensive positions, it was obvious that they wished to delay us so that they could set up major positions on the Rhine. There were casualties. But we had the best support we had had so far with field hospitals not too far back.

Men were killed and badly wounded, particularly the engineers who had to bridge the river. Their bravery was remarkable. They could not fight back when shot at, since their job was to build a bridge and adequate approaches. Our infantry men were supposed to cover them with support from our artillery. But those engineers had no real cover, and the Germans knew that. The Germans also knew that it was important for us to bridge the Roer. It was a bitter fight.

A task force consisting of our regiment, some field artillery, a tank destroyer battalion, some engineers, and a Negro tank battalion was formed with our division commander in command.

This was an unusual situation. The only black soldiers we had seen were drivers for "the Red Ball Express." That unit was a series of trucks that brought supplies to us as we advanced across France. The drivers would come to our units and unload as quickly as they could; then hightail it back to the rear to get away from the shooting.

This Negro tank battalion was an entirely different sort of group. Black troops were segregated, and although their commanding officer was white, all of their noncommissioned officers were black. These men were proud of their unit and anxious to show their worth. Interestingly, their tanks were Shermans, which were the best we had, even though they were out gunned by German Tiger Tanks. This task force was mobile and experienced. We moved fast, and got behind the Siegfried Line. We took over from the British who had unsuccessfully tried to liberate the eastern Dutch city of Venlo. We did it rather quickly, but at considerable cost.

The townspeople were ecstatic to see us. We were there no more than a few hours, when the women began washing the streets and their windows, just as they had done in Maastrict. These people were even more enthusiastic at seeing us than the French had been. They obviously were intrigued by the Negro troops. Most of them had never seen a black man. These soldiers loved all of this, for they were being treated at least as equals.

I began to hear of some of the heroics that got us there. The most heroic story was of a tank platoon leader in a lead tank. He had a bullet hole in his left leg and his right leg was almost blown off by an antitank gun shell. He kept on shooting, killing the antitank gunners and capturing their officer, before he was evacuated to us for care. Another man, a staff sergeant, though he had four bullets in him, three in his chest, and one in his abdomen, kept his squad together, two of whom were also hit. They were on the outside of a tank and kept on firing until our aid men could get to them. We cared for these heroes as best we could, waiting for the chance to evacuate them to a field hospital.

We also saw a number of German casualties. There were all sorts. Some were rather pleasant conscripts from conquered countries. Germans were more arrogant. For the first time, we saw wounded SS. To our surprise, they seemed to be frightened. I felt it was because they were famous for all sorts of terrible things, like machine gunning civilians and, certainly, for firing on my aid men near Mortain. I think they thought that we would execute them on the spot.

At one time, I had compassion for "the heinies," but by now I had lost it. They had violated all the Geneva Convention rules, particularly when they had fired upon my aid men doing their jobs. However, we continued to treat wounded Germans and to risk the lives of our aid men when they went to the aid of German wounded. We could not remove the feeling of fair play from Americans, which was something to be proud of. I suspected that the Germans probably called us soft because of our compassion.

The liberation of Venlo, was a minor triumph. Some scouts had found a bridge over the Roer to which explosives had been attached. They disconnected the explosives and dumped them into the river below, knowing that at any time the explosives could go off, killing them and demolishing the bridge. Such were the men of our infantry. I could never get over their bravery in action and when they were wounded.

The drive to liberate Venlo was no picnic. Though we thought the Germans were running out of manpower, that was not the case, and the fighting was fierce in terrible conditions of cold and mud. Finally, though, we began to get proper winter clothes, including long underwear and waterproof boots. This sort of equipment would have been of huge value when we were near Bastogne, but I suspect that the planners thought the war would have been over before winter. What a laugh! We were seeing more casualties than ever. We were approaching and trying to get behind the Siegfried Line. The Germans knew this area and their 88s were devastating to personnel, tanks, and vehicles. They fired those high-powered guns with the accuracy of rifles. Venlo was an attractive city, and we hoped to get some rest there and a chance to regroup, but we were told to head for the Rhine.

We were now in Germany. Some of the people were actually friendly. Knowing the function of my unit, they sometimes helped in setting up the aid station and in getting us connections to water and, electric power. Our usual source of light had been the Coleman lantern. Fuel was put into its base and pumped to put it under pressure. The lantern contained an element of hard clay which, when lit, produced a good light. The problems were that these elements were fragile and that they were surrounded by glass.

There were great contrasts. One town would seem pleasant with minimal damage, while the next we came to would be ruined. There often were faces in windows watching us. Over the doors of most of the homes in this area were bold black-and-white signs "German Family." The countryside from then on was torn up violently. It was very muddy. There were dead cattle scattered about. There were old gun emplacements, scattered shell cases, barbed wire entanglements, old defensive lines.

Chapter 20

Paris

March 20, 1945

Somewhere after Bastogne, I threw my name into a hat with a group who had survived that battle. Our reward, if our names were drawn, was to be a trip to Paris. As we were preparing for the assault on the Rhine, I received notice that my name was one of those drawn. Like the other major changes in my life over the last year or so, this one was sudden. I had about four hours to prepare to leave for Paris.

I had no dress clothes. So, I prepared with clean G.I. clothes and took with me a musette bag with some clean underwear, socks, a clean shirt, and toilet articles. I wasn't permitted much more. I also took all the money I had and all that I could borrow, which was not much, as we sent most of our money home. I also took a carton of cigarettes.

I arrived in Paris after a long, fatiguing trip, first on a train with hard wooden seats then by a two-by-four truck from Rheims. Being the senior officer in this group, I was in the front seat of the truck. We drove along the right bank of the Seine into Paris. We could see the towers of Notre Dame in the late afternoon sunlight with the Eiffel Tower in the background. It was unbelievable. We had been in other cities, but none were like Paris, and none had such glamour.

RESTRICTED

110th Medical Battalion APO 35
(Unit)

JOHN   A.   KAPSTEIN   0511180   Capt. MC
(First)   (Middle)   (Name)   (ASN)   (Rank/Grade)*

a member of   Co., C., 110th Med. Bn.   , is authorized a 72 hour**Leave/
                    (Unit)

Pass* effective 1600 hours, 15 March 1945.   in Paris, France,
                                   (Date)

He will report to the American Red Cross (Central Booking Office), American Express
Building, corner Rue Auber and Rue Scribe, Paris, on or before the date noted above.

*** 1700 hours   And 1900   hours   date
     (Arrived ARC Club)   (Departed ARC Club)

        (Commanding Unit)   (Army Group Liaison Officer)
     MILLARD W. HALL
NOTE: Lt. Col., MC, Commanding.

Permission pass to buy in PX in Paris

The old Montmartre

With some other officers, I was quartered in the Lafayette Club, which was a couple of blocks from the opera and seemed to have been a small hotel prior to the war. We registered at about 6:30 in the evening, went to our rooms, cleaned up, and went to dinner in the club dining room. By this time, we felt much better. The dinner, although G.I. food, was surprisingly well prepared and with French accenting, better than any we had had since leaving home.

None of us had been to Paris before, and certainly we were naive. So, we headed for the best night club, which had just reopened a couple of days before, the Bal Tabarin in Pigalle, an area just below Montmartre and popular with soldiers. The club was much like our larger night clubs, shaped like a horseshoe with a bar slung along one side, tables around the dance floor, and a stage at one end. The orchestra was in a corner near the stage.

The show was mind boggling for us on our first night's leave from a combat zone. It was the most elaborate show I had ever seen, even at the Copacabana in New York. Of course, there were girls in beautiful, lavish costumes and no conservation of materials. There were elaborate head dresses, often with plumes, and dresses with long trains which came off for dancing. Most of the women were bare breasted. The sets were quite wonderful, intriguing lit fabrications suggesting the facades of beautiful Parisian buildings. I had never seen so much done on such a small stage.

The show ran from 10:00 to 1:00 with breaks for dancing. There were plenty of women about. They were all dressed extremely well, in spite of the outrageous prices there. We could not help comparing them with the women in England, who never seemed to be stylish, except perhaps in their Waves or Wrens uniforms. We liked the Bal Tabarin so much that we stayed until 2:00.

It was a pleasant spring night, and when we split up, I hired an open carriage and rode around for a long time trying to get the feel of the city. I was exhausted, and even though I would have loved the company of a woman, I decided at last to return to the Lafayette Club and I collapsed into bed.

At 9:15 the following morning, I took a bus tour of the city, provided by the Red Cross. I had the company of a pleasant nurse, which was all right with me, since it was the first time for each of us in Paris, and we felt at ease with each other. Also, struggling with my inadequate French was not necessary.

The tour, about two hours long, included the Opera, the Madeline, Place de la Concorde, Place Vendome, Champs Élysées, Arc de Triumph, Tuilleries, and Eiffel Tower. When we got out at the Arc, its massive and triumphant sculpture recalled to mind two intense images: first, the picture I had seen of the German Army marching up to the Arc with French people watching and crying; second, the American Army marching, much more recently, up the same route. Napoleon's tomb at Les Invalides was another reminder of France's past glory, which, after two cataclysmic wars this century, seemed unlikely to be revived.

We also got out at Notre Dame, and though I had seen pictures of it, this monumental structure was almost overwhelming. The rose window over the entrance was especially beautiful, lit from behind by sunlight. We also got out at the Trocadero, with its famous vista of the Eiffel Tower before returning to the club for lunch.

That afternoon, I went to the PX to see the gift department and the values there and compare these with what I saw in the Paris stores. The PX allowed each soldier on pass to buy one gift, one bottle of perfume, and one scarf. The gifts were very good, and they were at cost (without the usual retail mark-up plus black market kickback). I picked out a bag that I had seen in a store for forty-eight hundred Francs ($98) for very much less and a bottle of Houbigant, which I remembered to be a favorite of my mother. I sent her these, trying to make her feel that I was on a modified tour of Europe. The scarf, I sent to Ann. Actually, in the back of my mind was always the knowledge that I had to return to face the crossing of the Rhine, and God only knew what weapons the

Germans would use to keep us from entering their heartland. The whole exciting scene in Paris seemed unreal.

From the PX, I went to the Champs Élysées to look at some of the shops. Much more beautiful than those in Brussels, they were furnished in light-colored wood and many mirrors, often with interesting designs that I saw only in France.

I stopped at an officer's clothing store, where I picked up some ribbons to which I was entitled, and I got a cloth overseas cap and a tie. M.P.s had stopped me to say that I was out of uniform, as I had no hat, and ties were required in this area. When I arrived in Paris, the only hat I had was a helmet, and of course I did not have a tie. It would have been absurd to buy anything more knowing my visit would be short.

I also picked out a book for my sister, On Ne Badine Pas Avec L'Amour by De R. Peynet. It cost a considerable number of francs, so I bargained for it. Because a cigarette was the first request of a wounded man—pain came later—I always carried cigarettes in one of my pockets—I always carried morphine, too, even in Paris—and so, invariably had the means to barter.

The city had been planned for beauty and charm. Even in this short time, I knew that Paris was far and away the most beautiful city I had ever seen, and even with the austerity of the war, the shops were at least as good as and perhaps better than those in New York. There was no vista that was not pleasing. Continually recalling the devastation I had seen, I just could not get over all of this.

Toward the afternoon of that first day, on my way back to the Lafayette Club, I got a little lost on the Metro. A well-dressed man stopped to help me and offered to take me to my destination. As it turned out, he was going in my direction, toward the neighborhood of the opera.

There were some unusual things about this man. He spoke English with only a faint accent. He was well dressed. He was relatively young. How had he avoided military service or labor camps? He was most pleasant and suggested that on the following morning he would show me a bit of Paris which I might not otherwise see. He worked at the Louvre, and much later I learned that he was one of that small group who had hidden major works of the Louvre from the Nazis. I looked forward to the next morning.

After dinner, I picked up the nurse whom I had met in the morning, and we went to the Follies Bergere. All of the seats had been sold well in advance. However for a couple of packs of cigarettes, I soon found us in comfortable leather seats in the first row.

The show was much better than I had expected. The costumes and sets were magnificent, and the girls were beautiful. This was a much more elegant show than I had seen on our first night. The chorus was larger, and the costumes were even more elaborate than at the Bal Tabarin, with bright materials, lots of feathers, and, in most instances, bare breasts. The comedy was superior, with a minimum of spoken French because of a preponderance of American soldiers in the audience.

After the show, we found ourselves making the rounds of the night clubs: the Lido, Chantilly, Paradise, Moulin Rouge, and others. Some were open until 6:00 A.M. My companion, who was from a field hospital in Eastern Belgium, was pleasant, reasonably attractive, and about my height. She had short blond hair, a well proportioned figure, and a good sense of humor. Though we had no immediate sexual attraction, we did enjoy ourselves.

On the following morning, my new French friend picked me up, and we went to Montmartre. Few soldiers went there. It was a bit out of the way. Montmartre is at the highest point in the city, and the views from there are splendid. First we visited the church, Sacre Coeur. We climbed its highest tower to get an even more beautiful view of the city on that clear winter day. From there we walked to the oldest part of Montmartre, where the cafes had not changed much in hundreds of years. The small square in the center section, even with war going on, had its own government: the Independent Republic of the Montmartre. In the center of this area was La Place Tertre, a small square with many trees. Here artists at work set their easels, and the great of the city came to observe and to buy. I gathered that there were many fewer artists at this time than when France was at peace. We saw mostly old men and an occasional woman. There were few soldiers. Around the square were the Mairie and cafes, including the Cafe des Poulbots, which, once a week, served free meals to the little poulbots, the children of the area. The area was charming, and took my mind off of the war. I guess that was why I had been sent to Paris.

Early in the afternoon, I wandered through the shops for awhile before returning to the Lafayette Club to clean up before going to my new friend's for tea. I went there in a carriage, making excellent use of the barter system, for it was a long ride. There were no cabs, and the vehicles that were not military were mostly small cars with trailers. Certainly, they did not use petrol, which could only be obtained on the black market. The petrol in civilian use at that time was usually stolen from the American Army, either by cutting holes in the fuel lines or by stealing the fuel cans, "Jerry cans," they were called.

My host lived in an elegant apartment overlooking the Seine near the Isle St. Louis. It was the home of one of the great sculptors of France. He had made all of the door knobs and hinges. The walls of the study were of beautiful tooled leather and wood— also the work of this sculptor. Each piece of furniture or decoration was of museum quality. The other guests were especially interesting to me, for I had met few upper class French people. Most of them spoke some English. I brought a bottle of Champagne for the hostess.

Tea was enjoyable, with toasted French rolls, jam, and butter. Later we had the champagne I had brought. The hostess was most pleasant and was surprisingly shy, as were the other women. It was surprising because most women we met in Paris were anything but shy. Their home contained some lovely silver and a collection of magnificent fans of which the hostess was particularly fond. I was impressed with the elegance and style of the women's clothes, despite the high prices of goods. These women seemed to know what to buy. Shoes were all of the wedgy type which often were covered with the same material as the women's coats. The French were much more lavish with clothes than Americans were, particularly during the war. The women seemed to be built to look good in most anything. Of course, they had walked much and eaten less during the war.

I was surprised and upset to hear that many of these people and their friends were unhappy with the current situation in Paris. Apparently, they expected everything to be perfect when the Americans arrived, and they expected us to do everything for their comfort. They complained that conditions for them were worse at this time than when the Germans were there, which is probably true, for the Germans catered to the upper class Parisians. These people lamented the physical conditions.

Hearing them complain when they were doing so little to help themselves was unendurable. There I was in combat clothes, fresh from the front being told that "Things were better when the Germans were here." I could not believe that they placed so little value on their freedom and on what we soldiers had done to provide them with it. These could not be the same French who were willing to lay down their lives to stop the Germans. I took polite leave of the hostess and my friend, not being able to stand any more of this conversation.

That evening, I returned to Montmartre. None of my friends—who were more interested in the nightclubs—wanted to go along. So, I went alone. I walked into a little bar in the Place Tertre. There I was greeted in a cheery and friendly way by everyone present. There was a private who could play the piano beautifully. He and I played songs that the people there liked. We sang and they often joined in. He and I were the only Americans there, though another, hearing our music, wandered in. Drinks were less than a quarter of what they were in places soldiers usually frequented—particularly in Pigalle—and they were much better. After a while most of the drinks were on the house.

On the walls of this little cafe were murals painted by famous artists in the area, probably in exchange for drinks and food. Standing about and hanging on the walls were pictures also done by artists in the colony and put up for the opinions of their fellows. The bartender looked like Paul Lucas. It was a colorful group with whom I felt so much more at ease than I had earlier in the day with those elegant Parisians. It was early morning when I found my way back to the Lafayette Club.

The next morning my friend the art expert, looking quite dapper in a well made suit, brought along a pleasant and surprisingly shy young woman to join us on the day's tour. His wife joined us later. We visited the Cemetiere du Pere Lechaise, where many of France's great are buried. There were the tombs of Sara Bernhardt, de Musset, Chopin, and all of the great French artists I had ever heard of and many more. It was a beautiful, sunny day, and the trees were beginning to show little green leaves.

That afternoon, I returned again to Montmartre. I was beginning to feel at home there. It was a lovely sunny day. On the way, I stopped at the Lapin Agile, a cafe that I had heard about. It was on a sloping street and was fronted by a fence of trimmed branches. The cafe was a simple wooden structure with plain wooden tables and chairs. There were checked tablecloths, some red and some blue. Inside were only a couple of older Frenchmen sipping some sort of aperitif. I had a cool drink and soaked up the charm.

Though we were not supposed to take pictures in combat areas, I had kept my small vest pocket Kodak, and whenever I could find film, I bought it, even if, as often was the case, it was long out of date. Here and elsewhere I took pictures which I still treasure. I sat at a little table in the Place Tertre and watched people walk by, hoping that some day I could return here.

I stopped by the little bar where I had played the piano and again thanked the owner. He knew I would be returning to the combat zone and kissed me on both cheeks. On the way back to my hotel, I stopped at the opera and caught the last act of Romeo and

Juliet. The place was splendid. Even with the war going on, the grand staircase was lined on both sides with soldiers in plumed helmets and bright silver chest plates. Inside were layered boxes in gold and the beautiful domed ceiling.

Afterward, I met some friends at the Cafe de la Paix just adjacent to the opera. They mostly talked of their sexual experiences, and here I had just been soaking up Paris. At another table alone having an aperitif was the nurse with whom I had toured on my first day. I left my group to sit with her. We began comparing notes, and somehow we felt like old friends.

Her name was Joan. She was a surgical nurse, and she had seen the horrible effects of combat. She had been overseas longer than I had and was returning to duty in the evacuation hospital. Somehow, she looked better to me that day. We agreed to have our final dinner in Paris together.

We got as dressed up as was possible and headed for a pleasant restaurant we had seen in the area. It was expensive, but the host seemed to recognize that we were not the sort of soldiers who were stationed in Paris. So, in a very un-French way, he presented us with a bottle of wine as a gift. The menu was limited, but the food was the best that either of us had tasted since leaving home. The host suggested sweetbreads en croute. I had never eaten sweetbreads, and they were wonderful. The dessert, a Tarte Tatin, was another excellent experience. On the way out I gave the host a package of Camels, instead of money. He seemed pleased.

Feeling good from the wine and the food, we headed toward our quarters. Joan's hotel was not far from mine. In a matter-of-fact way, she asked if I would like to see her room. Of course, I accepted the offer. The room was spartan, with a washbasin and a bidet behind a screen. It did not take long before we were in her single bed together. We knew it was unlikely that we ever would see each other again, and our lovemaking was enthusiastic, if it was also a bit desperate. I was grateful and remember her fondly. I wish, as I so often did during the war, that I'd had the good judgment to record her name and address.

The group I arrived with was picked up early the following morning by an Army two and a half. I sat next to the driver and slept sitting up until we reached the railhead north of Paris. We rode back to Germany in the same type of railway car, with seats of hard wood slats, that we had come in. I slept most of the way.

When I arrived back at the same station I had left just days before, the war was still on, and the trip to Paris had seemed like a dream.

Chapter 21

Rhine

April, 1945

We now confronted the Siegfried Line. With enough veterans to maintain organization, our division had become a mature fighting force. We developed a reputation for being able to move quickly and efficiently. My unit had become so knowledgeable that once I had selected a site for a station, no further orders were needed. We set up a warm area for the wounded, using our ever-present wood burning stove. A kitchen area was organized, which certainly was much more luxurious than the rations I lived on for so long. It was easier to have such a set-up now, because there was almost always a relatively sound building for us to use, as opposed to the situation in Normandy, where we usually had to be out in the fields or, at best, to use ruined structures.

We moved.

After Venlo, in one German town, we found a pile of newly printed German brochures with our division insignia on them telling us that the Siegfried Line we were about to approach was impregnable. Our general set up a task force that went around the line. We were met with bitter resistance, but with cool efficiency we fought our way through.

This progress was costly, and we had many casualties. In the vicinity of Geilenkirchen, we went through some of the bloodiest battlefields of the war. Most of the towns were leveled or almost so. There were no civilians in these towns. The fields were torn up with craters, foxholes, gun emplacements, and barriers.

Once we had passed the Siegfried Line, our progress was much different from what we expected. It was more like the sweep across France—faster and with little resistance. I noted that most of the wounded were replacements. Many had only joined us after Bastogne. That was not surprising, but it was sad and wasteful. Instead of taking us off of the line to rest and refit as had been considered in Metz, we were kept in combat positions, even when we had sustained terrible casualties. This practice demanded that we accept replacements for the killed and wounded who were poorly trained and did not know how to survive in the field, so they became casualties shortly after joining us. There just was not enough time to train them. It was like putting a high school football player in the line in a pro football game—but here life and limb were at stake. We had a similar situation in Bastogne, but it was probably more urgent then to put replacements on the line.

Once again, my life had changed. Returning to my collecting company from the battalion aid station represented a tremendous improvement in my life and in my chances of surviving. At the same time, it made clear to me that I was never going to be assigned to a hospital. I had become too good at what I was doing, and the United States Army rewarded its fighting men by giving them more chances to fight.

In Normandy, we were continually under fire. Here, in a collecting company, we were only subjected to occasional artillery. On the other hand, when we were on the move, or when I was scouting for a new location, which was often, we were in as much danger as the infantry, but with no means of firing back.

We progressed rather rapidly into Germany, and it was not hard to tell what had happened to most of the good things in Europe. They were there in Germany. The homes were equipped in a modern manner, and the moderately well-to-do had luxuries which we did not find in Belgium or France, even in the most wealthy homes. Such things as bathroom fixtures, clothing, and food were all of surprisingly high quality. These things had not been looted, of course. Despite the war, German production of consumer goods had obviously continued.

We were in smaller cities, rather than towns, with many civilians. Our feelings toward them were slow to crystallize. Certainly they did not harm any of us, and most made attempts to be helpful. Civilians were treated sternly, but not brutally, and we were forbidden by military law to be friendly with any of them. We spent a night in the home of an arch Nazi. The place was well-furnished in a modern style. His bookcase held all the Nazi literature ever written, and his closets contained the uniforms and paraphernalia of a SS troop officer and of an army infantry officer. We used his living room and dining room for our station, and there was now good American blood spattered around the place. We showed his home little mercy; the bronze bust of Hitler did not survive long.

The GIs, who had seen so much destruction in Allied countries, at first were inclined to pilfer and destroy, even works of art. Many thought that was as it should be, that "the bastards deserve no better." I wondered, "Sure, whip their army, show no mercy to the party machine, but what of the rest? Treat them firmly, but let us not be like them," and that is what I told my men. Gradually, this idea prevailed.

We now approached larger towns as well as small cities. The approaches were marked by numerous white flags. There were droves of prisoners who were led by all sorts of soldiers, even medics. We next set up in Rhineberg in a large cafe that was also in the home of the owner and his family. I told the father of the house which rooms he could have and which we would take. I was sure that he expected much worse. He and his family were soon helping to prepare our station, building a fire in the furnace for heat for our patients and being as helpful as possible. They remained out of the way.

Before long, we moved to a hospital. The Catholic sisters were most obliging, and rapidly cleared a large section for us. For the officers, they provided clean sheets, room service, and fresh eggs. For our chaplain, nothing was too good, especially after he said mass for them. We moved on to another cafe in a small town near the Rhine. Here again, we had similar experiences, and we prepared for many more casualties, for we were about to try to cross the Rhine.

This was a time for considering the future. Although I knew the war was virtually won, the steady stream of casualties was a continuous reminder that it was still dangerous out there. Early on, I really did not believe I could survive. There was so much killing. Normandy was horrendous, but there was some romance in being part of history. All romance left in the Ardennes. A combination of fear, exhaustion, and bitter cold seemed to enfeeble even the will to survive.

Now, on top of all of this and knowing that I would never be in a hospital—at least as a doctor—I missed feminine companionship. It was not only that there was no sex, but I also longed for female conversations and company. The brief visit to Brussels probably made this longing more intense. Even the trip to Paris lasted only for three days, and there was so much to see, that I felt I just scratched the surface. Female companionship had been an afterthought on that trip.

The next job was to cross the Rhine. There were two bridges in our sector, and the fighting to protect them was fierce. But by now, we were more hardened.

I changed the way my unit worked. If there was a hospital at all nearby, I would bypass my station and even the division clearing station and take the wounded directly to the hospital. This was not according to the Army plan, but with the good roads we found in Germany, it seemed foolish to unload, check dressing, give more plasma, send the wounded to the division clearing station, then on to a hospital. So the seriously wounded were taken directly to field hospitals. If we got a man alive to a hospital, with our first aid and the proximity of hospitals, his chance of surviving was above ninety percent. At first, my commanding officer was unhappy with me, but he soon saw the appropriateness of this decision.

In Germany, our living conditions improved. We found a coal mine that had wonderful bathing facilities. The area was spotless. There were excellent showers and even tubs for officers. It was the first time in Europe that I had been in a bathtub with hot water, and that was pure luxury, for it was still cold and muddy off the roads. I found much more favorable facilities for my aid station. Restaurants with living quarters were perfect when they were available. The dining area was perfect for treating wounded who were not immediately sent to hospitals, and the living areas were much better than any we had seen.

We could see the Rhine. The Germans were being pounded. In the evening, we could see the bombing going on, on the other side of the river. The sky was overcast with low clouds and lit huge numbers of searchlights spreading out in enormous fan shapes like the ones at home on festive occasions. There was a steady drone of planes overhead. Every now and then, there was a huge flash over the target area; seconds later, we could hear the huge "crumpf" of the exploding bombs. The sky was frequently lit with the flash from our artillery, followed shortly by the explosion of our guns going off. After a while we could hear the crashing of the shells on targets. At one point there were a series of explosions, almost like a string of huge firecrackers. This, we learned later, was the Germans blowing up the magnificent bridges we had seen.

Though I knew the war was almost won, I remained pessimistic. Churchill was talking victory, but I knew the men of my division still had a lot to face. We had expected that the Germans would give up. But now we were in their homeland, and they were still fighting on.

Many of the civilians complained bitterly about minor inconveniences; others were very helpful; others were sullen. None troubled us. It was the first time we had close contact with civilians, except for the nuns in the hospital. All of us remained guarded, although it seemed to me that it would be increasingly difficult to stay aloof, regardless of Army law. What can you do when you see that some of the patients in the hospital are children who have been burned—forbid them dressings and medicines?

It was all very confusing. I knew the Germans were catching hell. I hoped desperately that they could see the end and stop this horror.

After a tremendous barrage, our engineers were able to construct a pontoon bridge over the Rhine. When our 320th infantry, crossed in the dark and set up a beachhead, they found that others from our 134th Infantry had done the same. My unit followed close behind. We were particularly proud of our engineers, who built that bridge under fire.

Though the enemy fired upon us, we had few casualties. I began to get the feeling that we were home free. We, with other troops from the south, rapidly formed a ring around the Rhur, which was the heart of German industry. The cities like Munster and Essen had taken terrible beatings from bombing, but we saw factories outside the cities in relatively good condition.

Amazingly to us, the Germans around us acted as if the war was over. The officials cooperated with our staff. They were already cleaning up and organizing their cities. In the countryside, we saw farmers filling foxholes and trenches so that they could do their spring planting. Yet with all of that, the German Army had not given up.

Shortly after crossing, while setting up a station in a restaurant, my men found a huge wine cellar with fine German and French wine and cognac. Everyone in my company got a share, but we packed a major portion into our trailers which were carefully guarded from then on. This supply of alcoholic drinks was extremely valuable as trading material in the Army and of course, for drinking. Our cook, traded two bottles of cognac for a side of beef from somewhere. On top of the good news about this valuable find, I received a welcome letter from Doctor Traut, stating that I would have a job in his department when I returned. Obviously, I hoped to be able to accept his offer—some day.

As we began to push further into the Ruhr, there was surprisingly heavy resistance. The Germans began firing on us with antiaircraft guns, which had been used to protect this industrial area. However, our division was now experienced in combat and knew how to use our artillery and tanks much more effectively than in France. Unfortunately, their skill could not prevent loss of life and severe wounds.

The fighting now began to take place in cities, and that was an entirely new experience which forced troops to learn new techniques and strategies. An example of our new technique: with roadblocks of heavy concrete, the Germans had surrounded Bottrop, a city with a prewar population of 87,000. They laid down fire from substantial buildings and thus made the city a fortress. Our regimental commander called for smoke to be laid down over the area. He then sent bulldozers to break up the roadblocks, covering them with heavy fire from one of our companies. When the roadblocks were broken, he sent in tanks. Behind the tanks came our infantry. This strategy worked and soon, with relatively few casualties, we had the city.

I took over the headquarters building of the huge Rhinebaden factory for use as a clearing station. Surprisingly, it had flowing water and even some coal-powered central heating. It was quite luxurious.

Our general, in cooperation with others, decided that it would be better to surround the entire Ruhr area than to take each city, one at a time. They surrounded twenty-one enemy divisions with 10,000 to 14,000 men in each division. There were three Panzers (tanks), one Panzer Grenadiers (elite soldiers in mobile units), and three parachute divisions, who were among Germany's best. Since they were cut off from supplies, they surrendered. Over 317,000 prisoners of war were captured, including twenty-four generals and one admiral. Many tanks and more than seven hundred fifty guns were destroyed or taken. We were so grateful for this splendid maneuver. If we had to take one town or city at a time, those forces would have exacted a tremendous toll.

I felt that now for sure, the war would end. I could not believe that, having had this horrific loss, the Germans would continue to fight.

Military Government Germany.

Supreme Commander's Area of Control

NOTICE

I. Military Government has been established. You will obey immediately and without question all of its enactments and orders.

II. All civilians will remain in their homes, bomb shelters, or places of employment at all times until further notified and thereafter except:

    1. From 0900 hours to 1200 hours one person per household may leave his home to procure food or water.

    2. Or by written permit signed by a Military Government Officer.

III. Complete blackout will be observed from sunset until sunrise.

IV. Use of cameras or binoculars is prohibited.

V. Apparatus or other means of transmitting messages, firearms, ammunition, explosives or other war materia' will be delivered to the military authorities, and it is unlawful to possess or control any thereof except that police so authorized by a permit signed by a Military Government Officer may possess and carry small arms and ammunition in order to enforce law and order.

VI. Persons convicted of the following offenses are liable to any lawful punishment including death:

1. Communication with German forces.
2. Armed attack on, or armed resistance to, the Allied Forces.
3. Killing or assaulting any member of the Allied Forces.
4. Unlawful possession or control of any property described in paragraph V above.
5. Assisting any member of the German forces to avoid capture.
6. Interference with transportation or communication.
7. Sabotage of any war material of the Allied Forces.
8. Wilful destruction, removal, interference with, or concealment of, records or archives of any nature.
9. Plunder, pillage or looting.
10. Wilfully interfering with or misleading any member of the Allied Forces.
11. Any other act in aid of the enemy or endangering the security of the Allied Forces.

VII. Violators of any of the foregoing provisions will be punished by a Military Court.

VIII. The complete enactments of Military Government will be posted in the near future.

By Order of the Military Commander.

Chapter 22

To Meet The Russians

April 19, 1945

Now came a most dramatic change. My medical company was made part of a combat team. Our usual assignments were within our own infantry division. This new team consisted of the 320th infantry regiment from our Division, a combat unit of tanks from an armored division, some support artillery, and our medical company. The assignment was simple: go as quickly as possible and meet the Russians.

The unit of almost 5,000 organized quickly. As we took off, I understood how the Germans must have felt during their blitzkrieg. The top canvas of the front of my truck was down, and I often stood up in the front seat to watch our dramatic progress. In one day, we traveled 220 miles. We passed thousands of German soldiers who were so surprised to see us that they did not fire a shot. We passed cities and towns that were all but leveled by our bombing. We felt that they had it coming.

It was obvious that there was much hunger. Approaching one town, we met some slight resistance which our lead tank eliminated. In the process a horse was shot. In the short time, it took for my group to reach town, the horse had been cleaned of skin, meat, even internal organs.

The most terrible experience occurred in the course of this blitz. As we were progressing along the autobahn, our scouts noted some smoke off the road to the north. Our commanding officer sent scouts to learn the source of the smoke. When he got the report, he stopped the column and diverted it to the area from which the smoke was rising. This surprised us; since we knew his orders were to go as far as possible as fast as possible.

The reason for the stop was Gardelegen. This was a camp for slave laborers. It had held about a thousand Jews, Gypsies, and other "undesirables." When the SS saw us coming, they put the entire thousand in a large barn, poured oil on them and on the barn. They then set the entire area afire with incendiary bullets. Those who tried to escape were shot. Others around the area were beaten to death.

I photographed the scene and eventually got the pictures home so that people could see the kind of people we had been facing. The pictures are still in my possession. It is my tendency to bring them out whenever people argue that the terrible things done by the Germans were exaggerations.

Our commanding officer went to the mayor of the neighboring town who denied knowing of the conditions in Gardelegen. The general then had all able bodied persons in the town—old men, women, and older children—come to the camp with clean sheets. He had them bury each body separately in a sheet. He wanted the townspeople to be sure to know what had happened there. He was able to accomplish this objective in a relatively short time, so that we could move on. It was difficult for me and, I guess, most others to realize that humans could be so terrible to humans.

We stopped in a small town. It was a warm, sunny late afternoon. I took my shirt and undershirt off. I balanced my typewriter on a gas can to write about the horrors of the day while they were still fresh in my mind.

The men, took advantage of the break. They washed clothes and aired them. Everyone was busy. Some were working on a generator that they had rigged up on one of our trailers that was made from the engine of a ruined German car. Others repaired a

German ambulance and painted it with G.I. paint, so that it could be added to our evacuation potential. Cooks were preparing dinner. Our men were farm boys, and as I said before, they knew about machinery and worked with amazing speed. We felt safe, for as medics, we were put in the center of a protected area. We heard distant fire of guns, but we were not sure who was firing. We knew they were howitzers; since they had a sound like a deep cough followed by a big explosion.

Children wandered into our area. They did not seem to fear us, and they were the best mannered we had seen. This town had sustained little damage. There was a small hospital with many patients most of whom had been brought here from some distance.

The next day, we traveled another seventy-five miles to the Elbe. We passed through rural areas where people were working hard in the fields. Women, old men, and children worked side by side. Spring planting was urgent, and they knew it. Our general sent scouts across the river, and we made camp again. We had passed from Waltrop through Hamlin, Hanover, and Peine. We were now in Zerbst and were now the closest American unit to Berlin.

The cities had taken a terrible beating, and most bridges had been put out of action. Our engineers did a remarkable job of constructing functional temporary bridges for our advance. To our surprise, the people seemed glad to see us and, for the most part, were not hostile, perhaps because we treated them so much better than did the freed prisoners and forced laborers who wandered the countryside by the hundreds. The Germans were now paying the price of having used forced labor.

The whole situation with the Polish laborers was quite interesting. Many of them helped us, and in return, we fed them and helped them in any way we could. They tore down the roadblocks that the Germans had put up. They helped our engineers build their bridges. I am sure that they worked with more vigor at these tasks than they had putting up the roadblocks under the supervision of the SS.

These people faced a dilemma. Many of them had worked on the farms where they were fed. Now liberated, most did not want to work for the Germans. At the same time, who was going to feed them? Our unit had brought little surplus provisions. So some of the former forced laborers decided that for now, at least, it was better to keep working on the farms. They knew that if crops were not planted, it would hurt not only the Germans, but also the Poles. Interestingly, some of these workers were treated better in Germany than they had been in parts of Poland, and the more poorly educated Poles often did not realize that they might be better off working on German farms until after the war.

Spring was in the air. The weather was beautiful and, certainly, it had been wonderful for our progress. Flowers were in bloom. Fields were green. The trees were in blossom. The plowing and planting accentuated this atmosphere of renewal, and we felt wonderful.

I had a friend in our company who had joined us as a replacement. He was a wonderful pianist, and, whereas in the evening I often played popular music for the men if there was a piano around, he played first rate classical music. I used sheet music which the Army distributed. He carried his music in his head.

My friend thought he would like to explore the town. He had not had a chance to do much touring. Those of us who were more experienced, felt we had survived to this point, and we did not want to take any chances. Well, someone took a shot at my friend and shattered his right hand. Our aid men brought him in, and I did my best to dress this horrendous wound. Bone was shattered, and some blood vessels were damaged, though, fortunately, no major vessel had been torn. Still, I was sure that he would never have much use of that hand for playing the piano.

It would be difficult to evacuate him. We were three hundred miles from a field hospital. Finally, two of our aid men volunteered to take him back, for we now had an extra ambulance. They knew there was risk involved, but that was the kind of men who made up our unit. After they left, I turned on my radio to hear the very sad news that President Roosevelt had died. I didn't feel that his death would change the war in Europe, but I worried about Truman's ability to deal with Churchill and Stalin. All of us only wanted peace.

Of course, I continued to write my daily "Kappy's News" with the the material I got from the daily BBC. It was broadcast all over Europe. Now, more than ever, people came to read the information I was able to provide.

Gradually, we moved our entire unit across the Elbe. We took many prisoners (1,759 in one day). But our patrols still ran into German patrols, and there were casualties. The artillery continued to be active, as were the tanks. One day, we captured SS Major General Heinz Jost and the Clauswitz Task Force commander, Lt. General Unrein. Jost was listed in SHAEF's Who's Who In Nazi Germany. We also captured the head of the Gestapo in foreign countries. He was in civilian clothes and was riding a bicycle. We captured huge stores of enemy supplies. We freed a large group of American prisoners of war with much celebration. Some of my men saw some smoke that led them to a huge store of captured French cognac, cordials, and wine. This more than replenished our stocks. They found a German two-and-a-half ton truck, got it going, loaded it, and repainted it. Guards were placed on the truck. I wanted to maintain control of this alcohol to avoid problems, and it was kept as secret as possible.

Because my German was reasonably good, I occasionally talked with the captured officers. One said to me, "If you do not want any of our land, why do you fight us?" Such a question after I had seen Gardelegen!

One night, just as we were settling in, a large patrol of Russian troops appeared. They too were veterans. Interesting to us was the presence of a significant number of women in their ranks. These women were quite unlike any I had known. They were very sturdy, and they had obviously been part of this combat unit. Their uniforms were similar to the men's. The losses in the Russian army had been great, and it was reasonable to put women in the ranks, though that was not the practice in any other Allied army.

The mere presence of women seemed to make our celebration more fun. Well, we were in a celebrating mood. We brought out a good supply of our fine liquor, and they brought out their home-brewed vodka. Our cooks got some food together, and we had one wild celebration with singing, dancing, and of course, eating and drinking. None of them spoke English, and none of us spoke Russian, but we understood enough to be thrilled that we had met. We exchanged insignia and bits of uniforms. It was a grand night.

Early the next day, in full uniform and carrying a large white flag, a German delegation approached. They asked for our commander, who appeared in his combat clothes. In good English, they said that they would like to arrange for the surrender of Berlin to the American troops. Our commander radioed headquarters. He was told that Berlin was to be taken by the Russians. We were to go back across the Elbe. We obeyed, but without having a chance to say good-bye to our Russian friends. It turned out that the Russians destroyed a major part of Berlin in the process of taking it.

Continuing west, we did not stop at the Elbe. Though our division was mostly from Kansas and Nebraska, it was called the Santa Fe Division. The road to our next stop was marked by our scouts with signs which said Santa Fe Trail. This time, we did not see many German soldiers, but the civilian population was much more active than before. They were busy repairing their cities, working in the fields, and repairing railroads and bridges. The work was, of course, still being done by women, older men, and young boys, and all were working with enthusiasm. There was little obvious hostility to us, but neither did we receive enthusiastic greetings.

We set up in Hanover where my unit took over a beautiful large home outside the city. We had just set up when we heard the war was over. It was hard to believe that after all we had been through, this was the end.

We were ready to celebrate, and we did. We distributed to our company of about a hundred men a bottle of some kind of liquor to each. This hardly put a dent in our supply. It was a wild celebration. There was an air raid siren on the roof of the house. Someone turned on the "all clear" signal and it reverberated over the countryside. A general came from headquarters to demand an explanation for our outlandish behavior and threatened some sort of reprimand. I apologized and explained that we had survived 264 days of combat and had traveled more than any other division. I gave him a few bottles of champagne and cognac and more for the men who were traveling with him. He left us a happy man with no more threats. However, we did turn off the siren.

In my multiple "bags miscellaneous," I had kept a bottle of Old Grandad bourbon whiskey. In the course of the morning, I drank the entire bottle. Soon, I could not stand; so I retired to my bed. For the first time in my life, I was really drunk. I held onto the bed fearing I would fall out. It was a terrible feeling. I also was sick to my stomach. I never drank bourbon again. I awakened in the afternoon with a great thirst. Otherwise, I did not feel as bad as I expected. The room was bright and airy and overlooked a lovely garden with large trees bearing bright new green leaves. There were even birds singing. I drank a lot of water, shaved, and faced a new life.

My good friend Dave came around with his commanding officer. They had become close friends. His commander was a tall handsome man tending to be bald. He was a bit older than we were. He was a physician who had been in general practice in rural Iowa prior to the war. We decided that my unit of the collecting company would host a party that evening for all the officers in our battalion. We had a beautiful location and a huge supply of liquor.

Before the group assembled, I went to Jewish religious services held nearby. It was strange, for this was the first time since leaving home that I had been at Army-sponsored Jewish services. The services in Nancy were performed by the local civilian Jewish survivors. The service was much more Orthodox than I was used to. However, there was a lot for which to thank God. I must confess that it often had crossed our minds to question if there was a God, and if so, how He could have allowed what we had just been through. On the other hand, there I was. I was grateful to be alive, and I felt that in living, I had an obligation to represent those who had not been so fortunate.

That evening we had our party for the officers of the battalion. There were three companies and headquarters. Each had its officers. So, there were about forty of us in the course of the evening, and most of these officers had survived from the landing. I was the only one who had put in time as a battalion surgeon. We set up a large table with a clean white tablecloth. We had hard boiled eggs cut in half and food I had received from home: olives, whole and chopped, anchovies, and cheese. Of course there was bread, and the usual G.I. food. At another table I set up my bar. There were at least thirty bottles of liquor: Cognac, Scotch, brandy, all kinds of liqueurs, such as creme de menthe, cognac, and Benedictine. It really was a sight in that lovely garden. The feature of the evening and the initiation drink was a "blood and guts." It had a good shot of cognac, tomato juice, and salt and pepper. That was sort of a misuse of good cognac, but it was what the men wanted. There was a good deal of singing and good fellowship.

We ended up playing poker. I had played little of that game since leaving home, but I had great experience. In spite of my somewhat debilitated state, I won a good deal. In any gambling game played by combat troops, all sorts of money was used: American dollars, occupation marks of Germany, occupation francs of France, Luxembourg, and Belgium, and even some pounds. Every soldier could easily figure the value of each quickly enough to bet accordingly.

We were now embarking on a different life. We felt great being alive and in this place. Fortunately, the possibility of going to the Pacific was way in the back of our minds. We wondered what was next.

Bodies at Gardelegen

V.E. Day

V.E. Day

Chapter 23

Occupation

May, 1945

The day after V.E. Day was wonderful for us. It was fittingly beautiful, clear, and bright—almost like summer. In the morning, I sat on the balcony outside my room soaking up the sun and glorying in the fact that there was no danger. It was 10:15, May 8, 1945. The radio was going steadily with the great news and with the reactions of the world. We, probably more than most, were aware that there was still a war in the Pacific.

In 264 days of combat, our division had suffered some 25,000 casualties including replacements, a huge number, since when we landed, the division consisted of about 14,000. We felt that we had a rest coming. Our hope was that we would return to the States. There we hoped to get leave or even to stay, although we knew that most available ships, supplies, and men would go to the Pacific. In the back of my mind was the fear that, as an experienced division, we would be rushed to the Pacific to help with the invasion of Japan. I tried not to let that thought take over. So, good soldier that I had become, I decided to make the most of what we had. In any case, we thought it unlikely that we would be rushed home, and as far as I was concerned that was fine. Our present location was magnificent. Further, it was a joy not to worry about casualties and combat risks.

In my mail on that day was a letter from Sam Ziegler who was serving in the Pacific under General Stilwell. It was he who helped me get my first uniforms so long before. His job was to train Chinese troops to work with the Americans constructing the Burma Road over which supplies could be brought to those Americans and Chinese who were forcing the Japanese from Southeast Asia. Sam said that before he could train the men assigned to him, he had to get them nourished and physically built up to face the challenges of building a road and fighting off the Japanese who were trying to impede their way. It sounded as though Sam's living conditions were worse than ours had been, certainly worse than ours were at that time. It was miraculous that a letter from Sam dated April 27 got to me on May 10.

I purchased a new uniform at a temporary PX that had been set up, and I got a local tailor to fit it. He put on the various insignia—a big improvement on my sewing. This uniform had standard type Army pants and shirt, but included a new item, the Eisenhower Jacket, which went to the waist with a wool strap there. It was fitted so the lapels spread to show shirt and, of all things, a tie. The tie was beige rather than the black like we had had in the past. All of this was in preparation for a parade which we were to hold in honor of our Colonel, but there was also to be a parade to celebrate the victory in Europe.

I just could not get enough of the leisure. I lay in the sun. I read a book. But, I also was put in charge of arrangements for a special evening for the colonel. He had been in the Army for five years, and had served in World War I. He had not been too well, and he wished to return to practice as an obstetrician-gynecologist. He was a nice old man. He had seen to it that I returned to the collecting company when a replacement was found for me in the battalion. It may well have saved my life. Certainly it meant that in the Ardennes and the Hurtgen Forest, I was with the collecting company rather than the battalion—a thousand or more yards back of the battalion aid station and with living conditions better by far.

The plan for the day was to have a parade of our battalion in honor of the colonel and to have a dinner in his honor that evening.

Medics are never too good at marching, and our men were no exception, especially after having done no marching in over a year. Someone got a band together from regiment, and that gave our parade a little more class. We had the parade in a beautiful soccer field nearby.

I arranged the dinner. I had more experience at that sort of thing than anyone else. My mother was superb at entertaining, and even at an early age, I helped do things like set the table. We ate in the garden which was necessary because of the number of men. The table was set with silverware I had found in the house. There was a clean white table-cloth and napkins and lovely white Bavarian china. The table was decorated with containers of lilies of the valley. I am not sure many of the men had seen such a fancy table ever. Before dinner there were drinks from our relatively bottomless store.

We served a fine Liebfraumilch 1920 with it, and in addition to the usual G.I. food, we had venison steaks from deer shot in the neighboring wood, which had been a private preserve of Herman Goering. We also had a wonderful mushroom omelet, for there were plenty of eggs, and the cook had found some mushrooms.

After dinner there were speeches, and we gave the colonel a plaque with the antlers from one of the deer shot that day. The inscription on the plaque read: "E. T. 1944-1945 to Colonel Willard W. Hall, Leader, Physician, and Friend, from the Officers of the 110th Medical Battalion." In the course of conversation, the Colonel asked for my home address, since he thought he might get to San Francisco. He did see me later. It was a pleasant dinner, and I am sure that we all began to realize that war in Europe was really over. The convincing change was the fact that blackout was no longer required. Vehicles being driven at night with lights on was something we had not seen in well over a year.

The evening ended up with another poker game. This was a little more serious than the last one; we were all more sober. The game reinforced my sense that the war in Europe was over, and I continued to force thoughts of the war in the Pacific to the back of my mind.

I had now been overseas for a year and wore two gold bars on the sleeve of my Eisenhower Jacket. I now also had a European Theater ribbon with five battle stars, my first Bronze Star, and my particular pride, a Combat Medic Badge, which none of the others had. Our unit had also been awarded a presidential citation that was indicated by a gold wreath over the right pocket whereas other decorations were over the left pocket.

We had a chance to look around and were somewhat surprised at the attitude of the local population. They had had many sleepless nights because of bombing. So they celebrated with us the end of the war. They were cooperative. They also appreciated our presence, since the country-side was overrun with liberated prisoners of all sorts, and the Germans feared retaliation. There were thousands of displaced persons, most of whom were trying to find their way home: Russians, Poles, Belgians, French, Hollanders, and many others. Many had set up small tents or made shelters out of any materials they could find, including old boxes. They were not being spoiled. People everywhere were trying to construct at least one room from their ruined homes. There were still miles of prison camps enclosing German soldiers by the thousands. The absence of men to form a police force created a serious problem. American troops provided military police until some local government could be restored.

The area around Hanover was quite beautiful, and I wondered how the Germans, having such lovely areas, would want more. In spite of this beauty and in spite of our luxury in having real beds, linen, bath tubs, and reasonably good food, we all ached for some sort of social life. There were no Red Cross canteens. We saw many lovely young women, most of whom reminded us of Americans more than did the French or Belgians, probably because the Germans were better nourished. But we were not permitted to fraternize with the German women. We could not even say "Good morning." The Germans accepted that. They were so happy that we were not the Russians.

We found out about the point system: there was one point for each month served, two for a month overseas, five for each decoration. A total of seventy or over made it likely that a soldier could be discharged. At this time I had only fifty. I had five battle stars, counted as decorations, and two other decorations. (I later got a second Bronze Star.) Besides, I had not been in the Army long. So, I knew that I had no hope of being discharged. We were shown a film about the war in the Pacific, and I began to think of how I could avoid going there.

After the film, we met our new commanding officer. He was strictly "G.I.," meaning "government issue." Loosely, that meant that he would operate only according to the rules. His regime promised to be strict with an accent on "spit and polish." All of that might be tolerable, but the men felt that they were entitled to a bit of relaxation after months of combat and the possibility of more. Our old colonel had been through it all with us. This man came from the rear echelon, really far back, and he had had no combat experience. He was a poor choice to command this group. We felt that one of our officers should have been promoted to C. O. One of his first orders was for us to get rid of the truck in which we had stored our captured cognac and wine. He also gave our wonderful Mercedes command car to our commanding general. We were furious and helpless. He did not know about our supply of liquor, which we proceeded to store in our trailers and any other available area. We got rid of a quantity of medical supplies that we were sure we would not need until the Pacific, and we were sure we could get more if such a move came to pass. At this point, we felt our liquor supply was our greatest asset.

In the early evening, we saw a Russian show put on by performers who, while entertaining Russian soldiers, were captured by the Germans. Our division freed them. The show had the usual singing, guitars, jugglers, dancers, acrobats, and skits, with an American commentator (a private from the infantry who spoke Russian). We thoroughly enjoyed the show, and felt that, for the most part, the Russians were better than the Americans who came to entertain us, though perhaps at this point, we were just more relaxed than we had been in many months.

After the show, we adjourned to my friend Dave Roth's company with a group of officers that we particularly liked. Another party ensued. When we had consumed all of their liquor, we adjourned to our company area, for we still had our unlimited supply, and continued partying until daylight. It is difficult to believe how much alcohol was consumed. We had developed such a tolerance.

It was interesting that after all this time together, a group of friends had emerged. Our group was a fine group of young doctors, all out of their usual environment, but all of whom had adjusted in one way or another. We had also added a medical administrative officer. Because so many doctors had been killed or wounded in forward areas, the Army added this new category. Medical administrative officers were trained in first aid and probably were better qualified than we doctors when we first started.

Now, however, we were experienced, and that counted for a lot, although, unfortunately, the Army liked to use experienced personnel. The old guard had taken all the good positions, and we, the last to join, had been given the least attractive duty. The old guard looked after its own, and the young men like me were the ones who did the real medical work, such as it was, at this level. We saw that the experienced were not promoted, but rather that new commanders came from above. At this point, we were all looking for a way to break out of this trap, knowing that it would not be easy. We knew what was our most likely fate. But, we had survived, and thank God, our sense of humor had survived with us.

To our dismay, the stay in Hanover was a short one. On the 17th of May, we were relieved of governing and policing duties by a British unit and by the American 94th Division. We moved south and west to Recklinghausen. There is not much to say about Recklinghausen. We adjusted to our changed circumstances. There really was nothing special to do. We were on the edge of a small city, and we were discouraged from going anywhere in the area unless it was on Army business. We went to movies, which provided some diversion. During the day, I read a great deal and wrote letters. Most evenings we played poker, at which I continued to do well. We all worried about more combat in the Pacific. There were always rumors, and it seemed that the most likely thing for us to do was to sail for the Pacific via Marseilles.

After a short time in Recklinghausen, again we gave up the area to the British. My unit did not look too impressive. I led with a three quarter ton truck. Tied on to the right front fender was a footlocker which the men called "the Captain's Box." It contained the most important things that I needed to set up quickly. There were various Army bags attached to the side of the front seat. The sides of the truck were open, the rear was covered with canvas. We pulled a trailer that contained the medical supplies and some of our huge store of alcoholic beverages. I sat between the driver and my first sergeant, Banks, who was squeezed on the outside. On top of the trailer was a "three seater" latrine which we had had made by a carpenter in Hanover and which we would place over a ditch when we stopped. There were toilet seats with covers and a back rest. The three seater was comfortable, but got too much attention, so, we covered it with a canvas tarp. On the side of my truck were still the names of my three nieces: Julie, Jeanne, and Renee. Most soldiers who saw these names assumed they were the names of girl friends. In the back of my truck rode some of the aid men. Behind my truck was a captured German truck painted OD, which our commanding officer had ordered us to discard. This truck had been loaded with Cognac, champagne, and other captured liquor. Now it was empty, and we were searching for a good place to leave it. Then came four ambulances followed by the captured command car, also painted OD, that contained the rest of my aid men and which we were bringing to our commanding general.

As we moved along toward our next destination, Koblenz, we passed through a number of German cities in the Ruhr manufacturing area, such as Munster, Essen, Rhineberg, Gelsenkirchen, and Dortmund. These cities had taken a terrible beating. Often when we stopped at the top of a hill, we could see nothing but ruined buildings. The devastation was much worse than we had expected. We saw horse-drawn wagons, but few vehicles that were not our Army's. There were masses of people moving. They pulled possessions on small carts. Some had bicycles, and a few lucky ones piled onto trucks.

The local people were already vigorously trying to clean up the mess caused by our heavy bombardment and to construct shelters for themselves. They had cleared the streets and stacked bricks. Yet, one thing that I noted in dismay was that though the cities had been devastated, huge factories outside them seemed to be intact and even functioning. The Krupp Works did not seem damaged in any way.

In thinking about our victory over Germany, we often ask ourselves whether it had been worth the cost in lives, suffering, and destruction. All around us we could see what happened to Germany. The great cities we passed through, many the size of San Francisco, lay in ruins. In Munster, a city of 200,000, there was hardly a wall standing. We thought about the people who had been killed in those cities. We thought of the dead of all the armies, particularly our own, and the horrible wounds which led to death or complicated survival. Those who talk about "the next war" should be forced to see what cities like Dortmund, Essen, and Munster looked like after this one. The San Francisco earthquake was a picnic compared with what we saw. One "gain" from this war will be to show future generations how terrible war can be. As we saw it, Germany had been converted from a country of city dwellers to a country of farmers, at least for the time being.

Of one thing we felt proud: we had destroyed a government that sponsored extermination camps much worse than imagined at the time in the United States. The Germans made racial prejudice a key part of their agenda. We had destroyed the government; but had we destroyed the ideas on which it had built its power?

Almost every German officer that I talked with felt that we would end up fighting the Russians and that the Germans would join us. We, on the other hand, felt that the Russians had saved us from a much more difficult campaign. We were outraged that we had been separated from the Russians, since we felt that camaraderie was in order between our two armies and even that fraternization among the lower ranks might work toward the top and prevent confrontation in the future. Obviously the generals and politicians thought differently. Our papers showed the meeting of "Joe and Ivan," but we had been separated from each other almost immediately.

Finally, near Dusseldorf, we crossed the Rhine. This was a different experience from our first crossing. The river did not seem as wide as it had when we first crossed it. There were no German planes attacking us. There were no antiaircraft guns firing. Certainly, there was no need for a mad dash. We used a very solid pontoon bridge that our engineers had constructed.

Cologne was the first city that we entered on the west bank of the Rhine. The parks, squares and buildings left standing suggested what a beautiful city it had been. It was larger than San Francisco and had been ruined. We passed the famous cathedral. It showed signs of damage, but its main structure—including the magnificent steeples—was intact, probably owing to sound construction. We hoped that our airmen had deliberately spared this church. We drove through Bonn, where there had been a famous university. This city had also suffered heavy damage, but probably less than what we saw in the Ruhr cities. We passed Remagen where stood the famous bridge that we captured.

Then, the land became more hilly. There were old castles on many of the hilltops and some relatively newer ones that probably were occupied. There were many excursion boats along the river. None moved, and many had obviously been damaged. We then drove south toward Koblenz, but turned away from that city and went west along the Mosel river. Located, at the juncture of the Rhine with the Mosel, Koblenz' site is beautiful. This city, too, had sustained damage, but not the devastation we saw in the Ruhr area.

We then turned west along the Mosel and passed through lovely little towns that had not been at all damaged. These towns were resorts and wine making centers with lovely small farms scattered about them. The hills rolled down to the river. We saw the terraced vineyards, with terraces of native stone, from which came the famous Mosel wines. The hills surrounding the valley rolled down to the river. Most of the quaint little towns were situated among the hills near the river.

There were Gothic churches, often placed just above the towns and pleasant guest houses everywhere. These had porches with tables and chairs, and evidently had been planned to provide food, drink, and magnificent views. The vines had been planted with military precision around the towns, and in spite of the war, appeared to have had tender loving care. The people of the area knew how valuable these vines were. Later on when I was permitted to talk to the Germans, I found that these vines had been started from slips from California. After a terrible blight following World War I, the Mosel growers learned that these California vines were resistant to that blight and used them to replant the entire valley.

Where there were no vines there were lush green fields and woods resembling parks. As we moved along we continually saw beautiful old castles against the sky, and where there were no castles, there were watch towers, some of which dated back to Roman times. In the larger towns, like Bad Ems, were luxury hotels, small inns, and guest houses. These were to be occupied by sections of our division, particularly our 320th Infantry Regiment. In this lovely area, we were to be occupation troops, for how long we did not know, though we felt the longer the better, since we wanted to postpone being reassigned to the Pacific.

I had studied German in high school for three and a half years. I had an excellent teacher who had stressed conversation. Because she was from Koblenz, I spoke with the local accent and could converse and even talk a bit of philosophy. So, I often became interpreter. We took over administration and medical supervision of the area. This was a new challenge.

The most beautiful area was Brodenbach, a small town which was to be the home of my company. When I got out of my truck, I could look up to a hill high above us, and on that hill was an old ruined castle with two crenelated towers set dramatically against the sky. Downhill from the castle and around the town were those well tended vineyards. I soon learned we grew the vines in the United States for world famous Mosel wine called Schwartze Katze. In the town square was a statue of a black cat, the image of which we soon recognized on labels of the wine from our area.

Looking down from the town one could get glimpses of the river. It was not wide, but it certainly was more than a stream. Our company was put up in what had been a youth hostel. It was in an ideal situation in the woods just outside of town. There were large washrooms with sinks, tiled showers, a large kitchen, a spacious mess hall, and a pleasant day room. Importantly, there was hot and cold running water and electricity.

I had a room to myself. It was a corner room with windows looking through the forest to bright green fields and another set of windows looking down over vineyards to the river. My room was about twelve by fifteen, with a sink, mirror, clothes closet, and simple commode for my stuff. Apparently I had lucked out, or perhaps one of my men gave a bottle of cognac to whoever was assigning rooms. Off the room was a fairly large sitting room that I was to share with other officers. Like the other buildings in town, the youth hostel had a split timber, brick, and plaster facade and a pitched slate roof.

After I got myself settled in, I took a brief walk around the town. It had a population of twelve hundred and had not been damaged in any way by the war. It was interesting to see such a place for it was an entirely new experience. The streets were winding, with no particular pattern. The church was the smallest I had seen. From a distance, it looked almost like a toy. It had a slate roof and a little steeple. Most of the homes appeared to be quite old and all had charm. Inside, their ceilings were low. These homes had been built centuries ago when people were shorter than in our generation. Even though I was only about five feet six, I had to watch out not to bump my head in doorways. The windows were always sparkling, and the brass polished. The sidewalks in front of the homes were clean. The curtains usually white, were fresh looking. Some of the homes had little shops in them. The largest building in town, in this predominantly Catholic area of the Rhine

Land, was the church. There was also a fairly large hospital for tubercular children. Surrounding the town beyond the vineyards were green fields, mostly pastures, divided by hedgerows similar to those in Normandy. The horizon was neatly bordered by trees. There was a small stream flowing slowly just beyond our garden, through the nearest field, and down toward the river. It was packed with frogs who kept up a steady croaking day and night. It was spring, therefore mating season.

As I wandered through the town my first evening, I noted that each home had at least one person at a window looking out. That person was usually a woman and usually a young one. There were slave laborers in the vicinity, but there were no young German men and even very few older ones. Everywhere there were droves of children, evidently conceived before the men had gone to war. We saw no babies. It was rare to see anyone who seemed to resent our presence. People often made friendly advances, but we were forced to ignore them, which was not easy for me. That was Germany for us, then. There were other small, lovely towns in the area. The cities had taken a terrible beating but here all had been peaceful. Certainly, this was not the area of industry, and so it was left alone. They had huge stores of food and clothing. This was in contrast to the small towns we had seen in France and Belgium where the people existed from day to day often short of food and adequate clothing. Germany at this point had to look to its farmers to help restore the country. I had felt that the cities might be the home of communists now, but these people were conservative Catholics.

It seemed that we would be here for awhile, in the vicinity of the Eck where the Rhine and Mosel meet. I placed a tourist map on the wall of my room and it said, "So schon ist die Mosel vor Koblenz," and it was right. On our first morning, we got some furniture from the Burgomeister. Here was the first time that I really used my German. Our sitting room had a carpet, a large couch, and some overstuffed chairs—not elegant, but comfortable. I added to my room a large plain cabinet that I placed along the wall away from the windows opposite my bed. I now also had three chairs and a desk. With all that, I still had plenty of room, and I found it hard to believe my good fortune. Certainly, I had had nothing so luxurious since leaving home.

The commanding officer of our company, Jackson, had a corner room like mine, but smaller. I had known him since summer camp in 1941. We were together in the medical school R. O. T. C. and at Fort Ord outside of Monterey. He had been with the company since we landed, but had not spent any time in a battalion aid station, as I had done. He was promoted when our previous commanding officer was sent home after V.E. Day. He was an all right man, but our friendship was superficial.

After getting settled, some of my old friends came around, and we had a somewhat hilarious poker game, funny probably because six of us downed fifteen bottles of Mosel wine, and we found that this wine had a tremendous kick. I did not feel that I was becoming a drunkard, but certainly a bit of alcohol helped relieve the continuing, if fading tension. We had grown taut with the fighting and then the consideration of more was constantly on our minds.

We were promised chances to go to rest centers in Luxembourg or Belgium. Of course, the men were pleased, to put it mildly. For the first time in over a year, they had beds with springs. The eight stall showers were a true luxury. Also, the row of sinks and toilets was a wonder that none of them had in years.

I was interested in seeing the countryside. My first trip was to Bad Ems. It was on the Lan river, which also runs into the Rhine below Koblenz. To get there I first traveled down the Mosel. Every time I looked at the valley, it seemed more beautiful. The little towns along the rivers were like Christmas cards. There were lovely little churches of assorted Gothic design. There were many very old buildings that had been lovingly maintained. The roads were bordered with cherry trees loaded with bright red fruit. Above the towns rose hills of the valley, each with an old castle or watch-tower. Everywhere were the beautifully cared-for vineyard terraces.

As we drove down the Rhine, we could see that the small towns had not fared as well as those in the Mosel Valley. Bombs directed at bridges and shipping on the Rhine often missed their targets and hit areas close by. When we turned up the Lan River, we found a different sort of valley. It was more narrow than the Mosel, but it too was quite beautiful, and its small towns were undamaged and surrounded by vineyards and guarded by castles.

Bad Ems had grown because of its famous baths. The many large and beautiful hotels, fallen into mild disrepair because of the war, were still lovely. There were also small hotels and pensions. The shops were open, and the town was the most normal I had seen in Germany, France, or Belgium. There were some troops stationed in this town, but not many, as our division was spread over the countryside without large concentrations.

We returned to Brodenbach for dinner. Afterward, three of us went for a walk along the banks of the river, eating cherries as we went. It was a splendid evening. We walked out onto a promontory and watched the Mosel course by. We could see small ferry boats taking people and vehicles across the river, using cables, and the force of the current, and proper angles to get the ferries across. When we returned, we gathered a couple of friends and talked into the night. We all found the area overwhelmingly beautiful, and the contrast with where we had been was acute. Of course, there was always talk about what might happen and always about home.

There seemed to be little purpose in our lives, but we had learned not to complain when things were so pleasant, I read a good deal. I gave lectures to the enlisted men about the area, about the Russians, with a bit of history thrown in. I crossed the river in one of the ferries with a fellow officer. There were cherry trees on the other side, too, and the cherries tasted sinfully good. We went through some of the little villages. The north side of the Mosel was not so prosperous as the south side, perhaps because the road was quite poor, while on the south side the highway, though not wide, was an excellent road. For some reason the north side of the river had changed less over the years. There were a good number of buildings with door stones bearing dates from the seventeenth century. Grottoes along the road had even earlier dates. They seemed to be almost made of lime; since they had been painted with so many layers of whitewash over the centuries and were elaborately decorated. The towns were decorated with garlands, paper bows, and paper rosettes. Apparently these decorations were dedicated to the patron saint who looked after the vineyards in the area. Walking along in the early evening occasionally one would see a fish flip out of the water after an insect. The local people, usually old men, fished along the shores and caught trout. Those of our men who tried fishing had little success. Obviously, local knowledge helped.

I had the opportunity to visit a winery just outside of town. It was operated by monks. The monk who took us in hand was interested in where I had come from, and when I said I was from California, he was surprised that I found his wine so good. He thought California wines much better than German or French; since his vines had come from California.

One afternoon, shortly after our arrival, I went down to the river with a box of water colors provided by one of my aid men who had been an art teacher before the war. He came along. Being an aid man was a typical job for such a man, who also was a bit older than the rest of us. It was only a short walk. We sat on a small pier with our feet in the water and painted. My first production was not bad, and one of our group liked it so much that he bought it from me. This was my first attempt. There were only seven colors; so I had to do a lot of mixing, but I enjoyed it. I had a desire to create something, although I was not sure what. After seeing so much destruction, to be creative was therapeutic. I also thought of trying to write, but my early success encouraged me to continue painting. Interestingly, the art teacher looked at what I had done and told me what he liked, but he did not direct me. His painting was more relaxed than mine and obviously much more professional.

One evening shortly after my first try at painting, I walked up a little valley cut by the stream that flows into the Mosel close to our quarters and from whose very banks rolling hills rose rather steeply. The hillsides were covered with trees except for areas cleared for vineyards. In the folds between the hills were cottages.

The road back

Essen

Near the end of the valley was a small village, and behind it, a mountain shaped like a sugar loaf. At its summit was the most beautiful castle I had seen in Germany. Walking late one afternoon, I rounded a bend in the road and saw it for the first time, beautifully lit by the setting sun and rising against pink clouds that shaded to violet against a soft blue sky.

Surrounded by trees, the castle rose above three tiers of ancient battlements. At one end was a huge circular tower topped with crenelations, at the other a rectangular tower rising above the massive structure, its shape suggesting the command tower of an aircraft carrier. Old slate-roofed houses with small vegetable gardens behind and between them clustered against the circular tower. I would liked to have known how such a massive structure was built so long ago and under what circumstances. From this vantage point one could look down and see the Mosel curving toward our village nestled into folds of the hills. I returned to our village crossing an ancient stone bridge. High above was the castle guarding the people of our town and those of a forgotten age.

I was given a new job: examining troops in the vicinity for further service in the Pacific. To reach the examination station, I traveled along the Rhine as far as St. Goar. It was a lovely trip. The road follows the winding banks of the river. On the higher hills in this area were old castles, but more modern than those near where we were billeted. The old towns along the Rhine, originally river stops, were more prosperous than those on the Mosel. Because of their relatively small size and because they were distant from industry and bridges, they had not been damaged.

One evening, I went to an outfit quartered in a hotel perched on top of a mountain looking toward Koblenz. From the terraces of this hotel, I could look up and down the Rhine for many miles. At dusk, the towns looked hardly damaged, and the only signs of war were the ruined Rhine bridges.

I examined men and officers, one of whom was familiar with San Francisco, even though he was a New Yorker. In examining any true veteran, I tried diligently to find something that would keep him from further combat. I just could not see sending anyone who had survived from Normandy or through the Ardennes on to more fighting. After examinations, the officers invited me to their rooms where they poured wonderful Rhine champagne, which I had not tasted before. They repeated for me that local saying that Mosel wine is like a girl sixteen, Rhine wine is like a girl twenty-one, and Rhine champagne is like a widow thirty-five. By midnight, they had me convinced. It is difficult to imagine a more beautiful scene than the Rhine on a moonlit evening seen from the windows of this mountain-top hotel. The next day, I returned to our youth hostel to find that once again, my life was to change.

Rhineberg

Chapter 24

Agi

June, 1945

Until Koblenz, my main duty had been to perform examinations. On June 10, I was ordered to supervise civilians crossing the bridge that had been constructed near Koblenz. All civilians crossing there were to be dusted with DDT powder to destroy lice. By this means, we hoped to keep typhus out of Western Europe, and possibly out of all Europe.

This assignment came while great changes were taking place in my unit. A number of my companions had accumulated many points from years of service and were being sent home. I had been in the Army for about a year and a half and had more medals than they, but still not enough points to get out. With the exodus of a number of companions, one of the sad things for me was that our poker game would be broken up. We all enjoyed it, and I kept myself in money from that game. I sent almost all of my pay home to be saved and invested there.

At this point, I received my duffel bag, which I had long since given up for lost. Surprisingly, its contents were in pretty good shape. The uniforms, shoes, and my 201 file, which held all my vital information, were all moldy, but surprisingly, some brushing and airing made them quite usable again. In combat, we were supplied with enlisted men's clothing, but now we were to wear officers' uniforms, and thanks to my duffel bag, I would have to buy very little. Most of the time, however, I continued to wear enlisted men's clothes with my medical and captain's insignia. From my time as battalion surgeon, I was the only one in our company entitled to wear the combat medic's decoration. All uniforms now had the wagon wheel insignia of my division.

One of my most successful accomplishments at this point was to play the piano for our men and officers in the evening. I had collected a lot of popular music sent by some Army service, along with batches of paperback books. I had saved all of it, and now was the time to put it all to use. I was never especially good as a pianist, but I could play well enough for the men to sing along. It got to be a regular thing after dinner. Adding a bit of wine made my music and the singing sound much better than it probably was. I spent more time at the piano then than I had in my entire life, but like my training in German, my music study paid off.

One of the big challenges for us as officers was to keep our troops entertained. There was a fairly good athletic program, but facilities were poor. Our area, for example, had no place to put a ball-field, so, our only sports were volley ball and horseshoes. We had occasional movies. One night the men waited patiently for two hours for a projector to show *Meet Me in St. Louis*. The film did not arrive. One night, after waiting a half hour, the boys were greeted by a film which started off quite well; though the sound was not too good. The generator broke down in the middle of the second reel. The next day that film was sent to another outfit.

Our men got a chance to go to Liege, a fairly interesting Belgian city, every week or two. To do so, they had to travel in Army trucks over bad roads for almost two hundred miles each way. They then had a twelve hour pass in the city and returned having spent many hours on the road. There were longer passes to Brussels, Paris, and the Riviera, but because these were in great demand, only a few of our men were able to get them. Even at this late date, many of our officers had not had more than a twelve-hour pass. The officers made sure that they took their chances with the enlisted men, and they did not pull rank. You saw these scruples in men who had been in combat much more than in the rear echelons.

In the Army when you were unhappy with a situation, you were often told to "tell it to the chaplain." The chaplain could never do anything but sympathize with your plight. My feeling was that most of the men did not want religion. They wanted women—women to dance with, women to talk with, and of course, to sleep with. The Army was not much help.

While awaiting my move to Koblenz, I decided to take one of those horrendous trips to Liege. I wanted to get out of Germany, to see some friendly people, and to be able to talk with civilians. The trip was rough, but worth the trouble. I rode with the truck driver. We went through Bonn, Cologne, Duren, and Aachen. By this time, I had grown used to seeing the extensive ruins. They had a sameness, like dead people.

It was a gloomy day, but Liege seemed to brighten it. The city had changed greatly since I was there last. It had been cleaned to a spotless state. Flags were flying everywhere in the continued celebration of V.E. Day. The streets were crowded with happy, good-natured people. Though prices were high, I had less of a sensation of being clipped than in Paris. All the cafes were open. There were chairs and tables on the sidewalks around all the squares. The larger stores were surprisingly well stocked, though the prices were high. Liege seemed much larger than when I had stopped there briefly while we were fighting in Belgium.

I arrived in town at about 10:30. My first move was to get $40 worth of Belgian money. That was about the least I could spend on a conservative day in such a city. I walked through the streets looking in shops, most of which had been closed on my previous visit. I had lunch in one of the leave hotels, where I could get a good meal for very much less than at the restaurants in the city. It included steak, French-fried potatoes and cauliflower—all rare in my part of the world. After lunch, I shopped around a bit and then went to a real movie in a proper theater. It was *Wilson*, which I thought very worthwhile.

After the movie, I got a shave and a haircut in the wonderful barbershop I had visited long before. The barber was an old and dignified man. The rooms were full of surprising things. The walls were completely covered with a collection of beautiful plates. These were some of the best I had ever seen, and I had been exposed to fine china. The only wall space not covered by plates was taken by oil paintings that were very good. The furnishings were lovely antiques, except for the barber's chairs. The shave was complete with fancy stuff on which I usually took a pass. This time, I wanted to try everything this shop had to offer.

I was just about to start the afternoon off with a drink at a sidewalk cafe, when I met up with a couple of armored infantry officers. They were veterans, and we had a good deal in common; so we had dinner together. After dinner in an officers' mess, we went back to touring cafes. We found a beautiful one which was upstairs off of one of the main streets. It was tastefully furnished, and it had the best liquor we had tasted in some time. There I met another officer from my company who had found a couple of nurses from one of the nearby hospitals. He was all but engaged to one of them, and I had known the other quite well, for she had been at U.C. in San Francisco. That was some coincidence. We had a fine time.

This cafe had been made into an officers' club and had previously been a nightclub. It had a nice dance floor and a good orchestra. We had two bottles of cognac and a bottle of champagne which, with our earlier drinks, had us in a relaxed mood for the long trip home. I had a chance to talk with women and to dance, but the time was too short. We got back at 6:30 in the morning, and I slept until 3:00 in the afternoon. When I awakened, I found my room spotless, in contrast to its previous condition. Before I had left, we were each looking after our own rooms, but the military government sent some German women ("furlines," the GIs called them) to clean up for us, and my room shone.

Though I knew I was to take charge of a river crossing north of Koblenz, before leaving for that assignment, I received orders to move some sick Russians from Daaden, north of Limburg, to Baumholde near the French border. We were gradually moving the

Russians to areas where their own people could take over. We used ambulances and a large truck for this trip of about four hundred miles over roads of varying quality, which made it unpleasant for me and, most of all, for my patients. It was a big job to move those sick people such a distance. I had to look after their various illnesses, their comfort, and their nutrition. I was exhausted.

In general, the Russians were appreciative of what we were doing. I finally got them to our destination at 1:00 in the morning. There I was greeted with a large hello, "Tovariche, Comrade Captain," etc. The people were quite emotional, as I found most Europeans to be, but the Russians, in spite of the hardships, were much more jolly than any other people I had seen. Of course, they had reason to be. They were liberated from forced labor in Germany, and the sick had expected to die knowing the Germans took little interest in their health. The U.S. Army did a remarkable job with displaced persons, especially, when you consider that there were more displaced persons in Europe than soldiers in the U.S. Army.

On that difficult journey, we saw some spectacular scenery. The trip took us through the Black Forest, which was like a park. It also took us along the lower Mosel which was very beautiful from an entirely different aspect than I had seen before. Here we traveled along the tops of the mountains bordering the river. We could look down on the Mosel as the sun set. It was the most beautiful sight I had seen in Germany. The river winds, and on the hillsides that run down to its banks are vineyards. We drove through numerous small towns untouched by the war. Like the others we had seen, these towns had little churches with steeples and the split timber, pitched roofed houses. It was beautiful country, but I did not think the Germans deserved it. When I returned from this journey, I rested most of the next day, knowing I was to move to my new job.

I went to Neuwegen, a very small town just north of Koblenz near the bridge that our engineers had constructed over the Rhine. My job included not only supervising the delousing of people who were about to cross the river, but also identifying those with major diseases. I immediately was happy with the assignment; because I was able to talk with civilians, and especially with Germans for the first time since my brief conversation with the Burgomeister on the Mosel. Here, also, for the first time, I felt like my own boss.

I did not have to be in any formations, which was luxury, and had quarters in a lovely, undamaged small hotel, the Zum Wilden Mann. Part of the hotel was used for dusting, and each of the six men I had brought with me had his own room, which was sheer luxury for them. My room was large, with a comfortable bed, a sink, a table, a chaise lounge and, closet, plus, of all things, I had room service and maid service. There was a large double window looking through trees to the Rhine and the bridge. There was a spotless swimming pool up the street. I was assigned to eat meals with some men with whom I had served as a battalion surgeon. It was wonderful to be with them and to find that they had survived. The mortality rates in infantry battalions were horrendous.

My staff included a female Russian doctor, two young German nurses, two maids (Anna and Hanna), my six aid men, and Agi Fritzen, the administrative secretary of the station. She had been imprisoned for giving food to French prisoners who were doing forced labor in the area and had been freed from prison when our troops arrived.

Agi was quite stylish, considering the shortage of materials. When I first saw her, she was wearing civilian clothes. She had a white blouse with puff sleeves, a dirndl skirt, and two-toned shoes. Shortly thereafter she changed into her work clothes, consisting of a simple white dress taken in at the waist. She wore no jewelry. She was almost my height, was brunette, and had lovely features. Her eyes were brown and pleasantly large. She had a ready smile. It was obvious from the start that she knew her job and kept everything running smoothly. Happily for me, I could converse with Agi and the other Germans.

A steady stream of people passed through the station on their way across the Rhine. Most of them were French, Belgians, Dutch, and Luxembourgers who had been either prisoners or slave laborers. There were some Russians as well. The doctor did a brief superficial examination of each one. The inside of their clothes was dusted liberally with DDT. Then, they were sent on their way. A few were kept to be further evaluated in a local hospital. I found that, although I really had little work to do, I stayed around a good deal. I was interested in Agi. On my second night there, I asked Agi if I could escort her home.

She agreed. She lived a little way north of the station. It was a beautiful night. We walked along the river and got to know each other a bit. She was amazed at my accent and at my ability to write in German script. I learned that she had grown up in Koblenz. Her father had died before the war, and she, an only child, lived with her mother. She had some business administrative background. Her curiosity about me was endless. I told her most about my life before the war and tried not to dwell on combat. She had been frightened by the bombing. She and her mother lived in an apartment that had a very deep cellar. They had spent most nights there. I was sorry when we reached her home. We said a rather formal good night.

The next day I had notice that I was to get a three day leave for rest and recuperation in Dinant, Belgium. I felt ambivalent about going because of my increased interest in Agi, but it was hard to turn down what was considered to be a plum. I walked Agi home again. We talked about our life plans. She wanted to be an administrator, and I hoped, if I survived the Pacific, to return to advanced medical training. We parted with a gentle kiss. She knew I was to leave for Dinant.

My destination in Dinant was the Chateau d'Ardenne, which had been a summer home of the king of Belgium. The route went through the city of Luxembourg, Arlon, Bastogne, and Rochefort. This was the general area of the great Ardennes battle. I had never been in any of these cities except Bastogne, of course, under very different circumstances.

The city of Luxembourg is really beautiful and, though relatively small, gives the impression of being larger than it is. It is built on high ground that is broken up by deep canyons bridged by high, graceful stone viaducts. The city, with its graceful, slim, and neat architecture, is on varied elevations, and is unique and lovely to see.

Bastogne was much different from my last stay there. The fields around it, which had been covered with snow broken by the debris of war, were now producing abundantly. Almost all signs of battle had been removed. There were no more battered trees lying by the road, no more miles of signal wire laid everywhere our army went, and very few vehicles, as there was a serious shortage of fuel. The city itself had been cleaned up considerably, but the evidence of a great battle was still present. As I drove along the wide road leading to the city, I remembered every landmark sharply, and my pulse quickened as some of my earlier fear returned. I had been down that road too many times before, always watching for a place that would give cover if necessary. Along that road, I had friends wounded and killed.

The rest of the Ardennes showed evidence of war: ruined towns, occasionally, a ruined vehicle. Yet, one would never know from the area as it was when I revisited it that one of the great battles of history was fought here with the loss of so many lives. A truly large number of Americans gave their lives for what they thought was right or, in many cases, because they had no choice. It had been a war of movement, so it will never be possible to have battlefields outlined as they had been in earlier history. I felt that it was just as well. We have too many monuments to the folly of mankind.

The Chateau d'Ardenne was huge. It had splendid grounds which were only fairly well maintained. There were beautiful nonfunctioning fountains, and lovely sculptures and vistas. The first night there, after dinner in a formal dining room, there was dancing with nurses also on leave to fairly good music.

Later, I went to a neighboring town for a celebration in honor of returning prisoners. There was street dancing, much drinking, and good will. My social success surprised me: many of the selections played for the street dancing were dedicated to me. Of course that always called for more dancing and back slapping. It took less to make the average European happy than it did most of us, perhaps because we have too much or because except for our time in combat, our pleasures had not been forcibly taken from us.

The next morning I played tennis with one of the other officers on leave. In the afternoon, we played golf on the Chateau's golf course. I played fairly good golf, but this course was tough because the grass was long. Apparently, they did not have proper equipment to cut it. Those sports were fun in view of the fact that I had played neither tennis nor golf for about two years. In the evening, there was more dancing with a fair number of civilians. I was a bit bored, so I joined a gay little party of performers who had given a show there, and again, felt somewhat removed. I thought a good deal about Agi. The next morning I played more golf, and that afternoon went swimming in the Chateau's pool and then boating with a ballet dancer from Brussels. In the evening, again, there was dancing. I was bored and left for a small town nearby to spend the evening with civilians. It was pleasant, as far as it went. Of course the beds and other comforts at the Chateau were superb, but I was happy to leave to get back to "dusting" and especially, to Agi.

I arrived at the station after dinner, having stopped along the way at an officers mess. I got into bed early and began to read. There was a gentle knock on the door. I climbed out of bed and opened the door. It was Agi.

Neither of us said a word, though by now my German was very good. We kissed. This was different from any kiss I had ever had. There was an intense feeling of passion. When we finally separated, she began unbuttoning her uniform, all the while looking at me with those lovely eyes and with a faint smile on her face. She stood before me naked, lit by the reading light near my bed.

Her body was splendid. She was slender with full but small breasts. In a moment, I had her on my bed, and I turned out the light. Starlight—or perhaps it was moonlight—came in through the windows. We embraced only briefly before we began the most passionate lovemaking I could imagine only in my dreams. She was at once tender and loving, then, almost violent. Finally, we had to get dressed because of the curfew for civilians and soldiers.

When I walked her home, I brought with me some gifts I had brought for her from Dinant. These included all kinds of makeup, which was difficult to get in Germany, and a silk scarf. For a long time, we kissed good night. I floated all the way home. I had never had an experience like that in my life, even with Ann.

There were major problems. There were still rules about fraternizing. To be with Agi during the day, I could use the excuse that I had to be sure that my station went well. In walking her home, I used the excuse that I was concerned for her safety and that she was important in my work. There was otherwise little excuse to be alone with her, day or night. We had to work out some sort of an M.O.

Essentially, we had the time between closing of the station and curfew. That varied, but usually it was about two hours. I would eat dinner early; Agi ate in a small dining room in the hotel with the other civilian workers. Some time after that, she would come to my room by the back service stairs. The brief visits in the evening were wonderful. In my lifetime, I had not had this much time alone with a woman, and this was a special woman.

She always brought something with her. On a couple of occasions, she brought books of German poetry from which she read favorites of hers. She brought examples of her painting, and I showed her some of my efforts. Before long, she would lead me to the bed. Sex, became better and better as we got to know each other.

My days were leisurely. All the literature ever written is always ready for someone with a little time, and that is what I had at this juncture. My life had been so full of formal training that I had missed a good deal of education. I was determined to fill the gap. I read everything I could lay my hands on. It was great fun. I also continued to paint with my box of seven colors. I also tried to figure out what was going on in the world by reading newspapers, including the German magazines and by talking to the Russian doctors, prisoners, and soldiers. I had conversations with all sorts of Germans, Belgians, Luxembourgers, French, and Americans who passed through the station. As had many before me, the more I learned, the more ignorant I felt. To my surprise, I came to the conclusion that Man is fundamentally a good guy.

The more I learned of Germany, the more confused I became. The country was regimented, yet the family still seemed to be a more important unit than in other countries. The Frau was respected and treated particularly well by her family. She was not the work animal that women often seemed in other countries. But the Germans also used male slave labor. I was not sure of morals, but my impression was that the Germans may have been a bit more strict than their neighbors.

The Germans were certainly more modern than other people I had visited in the sense that they showed industry and intelligence in dealing with the ruined great cities. They approached this problem in a reasonable fashion. First they cleaned up the debris and reestablished utilities, then immediately began rebuilding, usually attempting to retain the character of the area. In a short time, they had put up ingenious cranes that speeded up building. It was the first time that I had seen these tall machines in the center of a building so that they could work in all directions. With all their problems, I was impressed with the cleanliness of the Germans. They were only equaled by the Dutch. In these ways, they seemed rather like us. On the other hand, they had been able to modernize by looting their neighbors.

With all of the qualities of the Germans, I felt I would much rather live with the French, to whom the enjoyment of life was more important than order, modernization, or efficiency. There was one thing about which I was sure. Though I had lost a great deal by being involved in the war, I felt that I would enjoy the rest of my life more as a result of what I had experienced. That seemed to be a better than even exchange.

Suddenly, without much prior warning, in true Army fashion, I received orders to return to Brodenbach, get my unit organized, and move out immediately. We were moving to a camp in France to prepare to go to the Pacific. There was still a question as to whether we would get to stop over in the States. This meant, of course, that I had to leave Agi.

There is no question that I had grown closer to her than to any woman I had ever known. I had fantasies about marrying her.

I do believe she would have said yes, but the problems would have been monumental. I was not supposed to have anything to do with Germans beyond my duties. Suppose I could marry her. If lucky enough to survive the war in the Pacific, I planned to continue training. How could I support a wife? And how would my family and friends at home take such a marriage?

I drove back to the hotel to pick up my stuff. With the help of the maids, the room was cleared. It was just after noon. I went to find Agi. Of course, she had heard. I met her on the way down the stairs. Even though it was daytime, she came to my room without saying a word. The room was empty, but the afternoon sun poured in through the double windows, which were wide open.

Agi was crying, but she knew it was impossible for us to plan anything together. She gave me a silver ring with her name on it which she took from her finger, and I gave her a gold pin I had acquired on leave. We talked a bit. We spent the rest of the afternoon having sex. I lost count of the number of orgasms. My room had a screen at one end, behind which was a wash basin, and, of all things, a bidet. They came in handy. We knew that this would probably be the last time we would see each other. When I finally had to leave, she watched from the door with tears running down her face, but with that wonderful smile of hers. I will never forget her.

There are some interesting things about sexual activity to consider. From England on, I had lectured to the men on the prevention of venereal disease. The best protection was condoms. There was a huge supply. There was no easy treatment for venereal disease, and the Army knew that those diseases would disable fighting men. For me, my major worry was not of disease, but I did not want to get any woman pregnant. I felt very strongly about that and was very careful. Such a conception would have been a disaster.

When I got back to Brodenbach, I was told we were to move out the following morning. For men of my unit, sudden moves were no problem. Much to my surprise, everyone seemed to know about my relationship with Agi. A number came by to commiserate with me. The men I had taken with me to the dusting station particularly knew what a wonderful woman she was.

The new word was that we were to get a month home and then return to duty in the Pacific. I felt it would be a good time to strengthen my roots at home. I could hardly wait. Knowing this softened the blow of leaving Agi.

Agi

Chapter 25

Norfolk

July, 1945

Our convoy leaving Brodenbach was much different. The men had had time to clean all the vehicles and to repack equipment. We looked very "G.I." As we drove out of the valley toward France, we noted that everywhere people were repairing and reorganizing; particularly in the cities that had been bombed. Who I felt was typical of the Germans was a man that I noted near Coblentz. He was riding a bicycle. He wore a snappy business suit, a Homburg, and a good looking overcoat, and he carried a cane.

As we drove along the road, I had a great deal of time to think. What was all this with Agi? Was our intense feeling mainly because each of us had been deprived for so long? If times were different, would we have been able to make our relationship work for a long time? Instinctively, I knew it was impossible for us to plan anything together. I did not even take her address or give her mine. That may have been cruel, but in retrospect, I thought it was probably right. There was no point in encouraging thoughts of a future together when such ideas were essentially impossible. The whole thing reminded me of stories of the First World War, but it did not make the separation easier. I had a lot more to face now. Because I had served only eighteen months or a bit less, and even though I had been in combat for two hundred sixty four days, I was going to the Pacific for the invasion of mainland Japan. Though many of those in a situation like mine felt that the war would be over before we got there, I had learned not to be so sure. I had not expected to get to Europe in time for the invasion of France. Something else that I was aware of was that my experience would probably not get me to a better job. The Army liked keeping experienced units together. The only good word was that we were quite likely to go to the Pacific via the States, and that I would likely get some home leave. Leave, knowing that I would be heading for Japan, would not be joyous, but it would be good to visit with my family.

Progressing toward our destination to Camp Norfolk, I noted many changes from my previous trip along the same route, but in the opposite direction. The landscape had already changed. It had been churned up from vehicles and tanks. It had had shell holes everywhere, and the ground was almost covered with communication wires. Now the holes had been filled, the ruts had been smoothed, and the wire was gone. I suspected the wire had found its way to the black market. There were still ruined tanks and artillery pieces around, but even most of these had been cleared. Spring planting had been done; and the battlefields were now green.

There was another big change. That was in me. I had entered the service from an internship. In the academic hierarchy, interns are low, just above students. I had been intimidated by professors and to a degree by residents. I had been an excellent student, and I did my job well, but I was certainly not confident. I was busy learning my profession, often from nurses. Now, I had been in command of men whose lives were in danger. From the time I took over my battalion aid station, though I had had men wounded, I did not have one killed. That was quite unusual for men with the combat medics. I learned to place my aid stations in as safe a position as possible, and I taught my men how to protect themselves while helping the wounded. The same situation prevailed in my position in our collecting company. Consequently, I had garnered tremendous respect from my men. They either thought I had learned good military judgment or that I had brought luck with me. In any case, they ended up following me willingly.

Because of this relationship, I felt confident and stronger than I had been in my whole life. The strength seemed to come from my being able to cope with the variety of new problems, even with that generated by Agi. Also, I was in better physical condition than when I had spent most of my time in a hospital or classrooms. I had faced down a high ranking officer in the Ardennes when I knew I was right about frostbite. I did not worry about doing things by the book, I did what was best for my men and the wounded. These changes in me, were obviously going to stand me in good stead—if I survived.

Camp Norfolk was about forty-five miles from Rheims. it was in the middle of a dusty field. It consisted mainly of hundreds of pyramidal tents. There was a temporary airplane hanger a few hundred yards away. There was a large stage that was covered with a canopy, and it was faced by a crude amphitheater of wooden benches that would seat a large number of men. Our section of the camp had a huge sign that one of the men had made. It said, "110 MED BN." Under that was a picture of a medic crawling with a litter with bullets flying over his head. Beneath that in each corner was our division insignia, the wagon wheel. In the center was "35th Infantry Division."

I shared a tent with three other officers. There were showers not far away and a mess hall. However, this was a pretty dreary situation, and we all resolved to see as little of it as possible.

The first night there, I went to a movie. It was about Ernie Pyle, a famous war correspondent in Italy. A battle scene was shown and there was the sound on the screen of incoming mortar shells. Half of the audience dove under the benches. They were the men who had been in combat and one of the reasons they were alive was because of this reflex they demonstrated. I was under the bench right with them.

The next day, I went to see Rheims. Surprisingly, it was something of a disappointment. The cathedral was, of course, beautiful, but it suffered, because its famous windows had been removed for safety. The city of Rheims was rather nice, but to my surprise, was not nearly as beautiful or interesting as Nancy. The kings of France picked a poor place to be crowned, I thought. The city was depressing. The people were underfed. They seemed to have little drive. There was little of beauty in their city. There was little question in my mind that most of Germany, even in its badly damaged state, was more beautiful than the parts of France I had seen, with the exception of Paris. To this point, I had seen nothing that compared with the Mosel Valley, or the upper Rhine. Even in ruins, the Germans gave the impression of being cleaner. The German people living in completely ruined cities appeared to be more interested in being personally clean and in cleaning their environment than were the French in essentially undamaged cities. I felt that the people of Luxembourg combined the best qualities of the Germans, French, and Belgians.

We got little mail. We made a pleasant expedition to a private beach near Chalons where we could swim. I found that I was getting bored having read too much, played too much cards, and having completed all the work necessary for our big move to the Pacific. I really had to work only a half day each week doing sick call. I wanted to get to Paris.

I found David Roth and arranged for a truck to take us to Paris. It took us three hours to get there. The ride was not bad; the roads in this area were exceptionally good. We arrived about ten-thirty. We parked in a lot between Invalides and the Grand and Petite Palaces. Then we went to the Louvre. It was worth the trip. Of course, all the objects of art had not been returned, but most of the more famous ones were already back in place. At the head of the first stairway we ascended was the Winged Victory in its completely plain setting with daylight streaming upon it from a large window on the left. She was splendid. Across from the Victory were the picture galleries. As we walked through the first door we could see the Mona Lisa. It impressed me as being much more beautiful than any reproduction had led me to expect. The most impressive quality, so far as I was concerned, was the actual glow of the skin colors. Every picture on display was a famous one, and I recognized just about every one. There were beauties of Rembrandt (a self portrait), Franz Hals (including that wonderful Bohemian), Delacroix, Manet, Monet, Degas, Cezanne, Reubens, El Greco, Fra Angelico, Andrea del Sarto. It was wonderful. I especially liked the French school of the period of Cezanne. Apparently, these paintings had been hidden from the Germans, and the first to be brought out were the best to help restore the luster of the Louvre and Paris. We ate at a nice transient officers' mess. We spent most of the afternoon in the lovely Place Tertre in the Montmartre. I took Dave to the bar on the corner where I had played the piano when I was on my leave from Germany. They would not let Dave and me pay for drinks, which were quite expensive. The owner who had been so kind to me at my first visit was out of town visiting family, but I told the bartender that I would return. Then we wandered through many of the cafes which are always jammed on Sunday in France. We spent the evening mixing with the locals and eating some superb food. It was a fine day, but we ran out of gas on the way back. Gas was scarce, and we had not requisitioned enough. On the way back, I decided that I would return the next day and stay a while.

  I did return with extra clothes so that I could stay a few days. Just before I left Paris on the first day, I noted a Red Cross office where a worker kindly booked me for the next day at the Crillon. I had heard about it, and it was now a hotel that saved a certain number of rooms for officers on leave. One thing had become obvious to me: Paris was very expensive for us. The reason was simple. We got fifty francs for a dollar of pay. However, if I had a dollar American, I could get a hundred francs. I decided I would have to resort to barter and so should my men. Accordingly, when I returned, I had with me a fine bottle of cognac from our supply and a carton of cigarettes which were worth at least two hundred francs a pack. I also arranged that if any of my men went to Paris, they could take a bottle of cognac or a couple of bottles of wine that they could drink or sell. I sold enough to finance my stay. I proceeded to a bar in Pigalle, the part of Paris below Montmartre where soldiers congregated. I sat at a table in a busy bar and indicated to the owner that I had stuff to sell. The cognac got me the equivalent of a hundred dollars of pay, five thousand francs. I also did well selling part of my cigarettes and very well selling a one pound Hershey bar. I was now set up and ready to check into the Crillon across the city. The Metro was running, and I got off at the Place de la Concorde.

The Crillon is part of a group of buildings looking out on the square. These are colossal mansions, one on either side of the Rue Royale, which opens into the Place. The one on the left contains the Crillon Hotel and the American Embassy is of similar architecture and right next door. The buildings have colonnades like those of the Louvre, but more beautiful. Of course this is one of the most splendid areas in Paris. You can look up the Champs Élysées to the Arc de Triomphe. The view is framed by tremendous rearing horses. You can look into the square at the Obelisk from Egypt. Two beautiful fountains were the only ones I had seen flowing. The view is backed by a bridge leading to wonderful government buildings. The Eiffel Tower was visible in the distance. There are other horses with wings framing a view down the Tuilleries gardens to the left. At the end of the surprisingly well kept gardens was the Arc de Triomphe du Carrousel, mostly of pink marble. The square was awe inspiring as was the Crillon when I entered. I had never been in such an elegant hotel. I went to the desk and asked for the best single room, and I got it promptly. A bellman carried my small bag to the room. It had a high ceiling, gold woodwork, and French doors that opened to a small balcony overlooking the square. There was a large double bed with tall posts at each corner. The furniture was quite ornate, but in good repair. The bathroom was a dream after what I had been using at Norfolk. There was a huge tub with a hand spray. There was a separate small room for the toilet, and a bidet next to the sink. The sink had elegant gold hardware, and there was a good-sized mirror over it. There was a simple cabinet with glass doors in which to store bathroom supplies.

I still had the small vest pocket camera that I had carried since Normandy, and I was able to find some film. The film was old, but it was better than nothing, and I hoped it would work. I resolved to use it as part of my plan. Whatever the future, I decided to enjoy this wonderful city. I had learned more and more to enjoy life as it comes and worry about the future when such concern might do some good. I now was able to afford to buy gifts for the people at home; so I headed up the Champs Élysées toward the Arc de Triomphe. This seemed to be the most elegant shopping street. Later I was to find others. I stopped at Guerlain, knowing that my mother and sister loved their perfume. Perfume was in short supply, but I was able to buy two bottles. I believe they were left over from before the war, but at least they came from Paris. I enjoyed going through the stores. Some of the things for sale were very attractive, but the cheapest purse (suede) was seventy six dollars, a lot of money. I could not carry enough stuff to barter for such an item, and it would put a dent in my supply of francs. Whatever the faults in the pricing, the French showed excellent taste, not only in what they wear, but in their display and decoration. It was rare to find any display or furnishing that did not show a marked effort in arranging. In the course of my travels in this area, I went into Chanel which was quite elaborate and a little less welcoming to a soldier, even though I was wearing my dress "green" shirt and a tie along with a new overseas hat. I also wore my combat medics badge, but no decorations. Across the street from Chanel was Matchabelli. That was a name I recognized. The woman who managed the firm was there. She was born in America. Her husband was Matchabelli. I would have liked to buy my mother a hat because, both she and my sister loved them. The cheapest was sixty dollars, which was a lot. The best, as far as I was concerned, were semi-sailors with high crowns, veils, and occasional things stuck on. I stopped along the Champs at sidewalk cafes, but at meal time, I had the good sense to go to a nearby officers mess where I had a splendid meal for very little. It was called the Park Club near the Place de la Concorde. There was music with the meal, and there was dancing at night. The service was excellent, the setting quite Parisian. It had obviously been a major restaurant that looked out on a small park. It was large, cool, pleasant, and in excellent taste. It was painted in flat white with green trellises, white fixtures, and some red drapery. The huge windows looked out on park trees. There were plenty of colorful potted plants placed in excellent positions. I met one of my old friends from school there, Bob Holmes. He had been a medical officer with an artillery unit in our division, but I had not seen him in many months. We had a lot to talk about. I resolved to return to this club, which was even more attractive than the one in Brussels that I had visited so long before.

    After lunch, I returned to the Louvre, having arranged to send the two bottles of perfume home, one to my mother and one to my sister. Later I was able to get one bottle of good perfume at a store for combat soldiers. I sent that to Chris. After a pleasant revisit to the splendid works of the Louvre, I decided to go to the Montparnasse. It was a section of the city about which I had heard and read a great deal. I had never been there. Not only was it a pleasant residential district, but the area along the Boulevard Montparnasse had the nicest cafes, restaurants, and night clubs in Paris. I was very much surprised; because, I had heard so little about this part of town. There was hardly a soldier to be seen. The district of Pigalle and the Champs Élysées catered to soldiers, and it is there they could be found in large numbers. In the Montparnasse, were the nice people of Paris. The bars were pleasant, and in excellent taste. The night clubs were not noisy or too jammed, and there was air conditioning. I was intrigued by the fact that frequently people both male and female, told me their troubles even though my French was only fair. I began to feel that I had a motherly look. On the other hand, I had learned to be a good listener. At least I got to meet interesting people. Certainly, because the district was more proper, it did not appeal to most soldiers. For me, it was the most attractive area in Paris, and I vowed to return if possible.

Everywhere I looked there were attractive women. Even the shop girls looked good on the street. They carried scarfs used in different ways. They had carefully done hair. My problem was that I had yet to meet anyone. I was not interested in the Army women, but I found myself interested to get to know French women, though I often thought of Agi. That late afternoon, I went to a tea dance at the Crillon. The girls were of especially high class. The contrast with the average young woman that soldiers are likely to meet was tremendous. One girl was especially nice. She was the daughter of the French Minister to Eire. In the better classes, the families were much more strict with their daughters until they were married. After that, they could do almost anything without causing scandal. In this respect, the French were quite different from us. Knowing all of that, I made a date to take this young woman to dinner and dancing at the lovely officers club, the Park. She agreed but warned me that she would be accompanied by a chaperone. In the evening, I went to the Casino de Paris. It, of course, had an elaborate stage review like the Follies Bergere and very good. I went with Bob Holmes, and our seats were practically on the stage. At that time, it was located near the place de la Trinite which was not far from the Crillon. It was a variety show with singing and dancing by both male and female entertainers. There were huge production numbers which featured beautiful women in various degrees of undress with elaborate costumes. We enjoyed all of it, especially the gorgeous women. The whole scene was unreal for me. There was this tremendous change from combat, even the occupation, but more recently from the primitive conditions at Norfolk. I relaxed and enjoyed it and did not dwell on questions of the future.

While staying at the Crillon, I began to do more extensive touring. I thought I was being very touristy when I went up the Eiffel Tower, but the view was splendid on the clear day I chose.

From there, I went to Invalides to see that building and Napoleon's magnificent tomb. I went to the opera where I saw part of a performance. The best part was the entrance way which had a monumental stairway with a majestic colonnade of Corinthian columns with suitable frieze. There again was a row of French cavalry-men on each side of the stairs. They wore helmets with dramatic plumes and they all had bright shining silver breast plates. I saw La Madeleine, which is a church in a building that copied the Parthenon in Athens. The Place Vendome was impressive with its tall tower made from cannons captured by Napoleon, and there was a statue of him at its top. I guess that I enjoyed the Cité the most. Of course there was Notre Dame that I had visited long before, and nearby a major surprise, Sainte-Chapelle.

While exploring around the Cité, I went into a courtyard where I came upon a small but elegant church, Sainte-Chapelle. I had never heard of it. I decided to go in. I entered the lower chapel which was nice, but not remarkable, and I almost left; however, I noted a narrow staircase, and wanted to see where it went. It led me to the upper chapel and to one of the great sights of my life, the stained glass windows. These tall windows encouraged me to look up toward heaven. I later found that they were the oldest windows in Paris and essentially portray the entire Bible. The scene was breathtaking because the windows were on all sides and the colors were brilliant, especially the red and blue. I could not tear myself away, particularly when the afternoon sun poured through those radiant scenes. I wrote home of my discovery and resolved to return if ever possible.

I finished one day with a visit to the Pantheon. I was looking at the murals that were quite beautiful when an old caretaker came along and began rounding up all the people who were there. I thought it was closing time and joined the mob. We went out a door, and into an entrance to the tombs under the Pantheon where there were I think forty-two tombs mostly, it seemed of Napoleon's soldiers. The guide spoke French only. He talked about people most of whom interested me very little. I finally got out and walked through the Latin Quarter, an area of students mostly from the Sorbonne. It was very lively since it was Sunday. That evening, I took Elaine, the young woman whose father was the French representative in Eire, to dinner. She picked me up in a car with a driver. In the front seat was an older woman who was to be our chaperone. I was not sure what she would do in the course of the evening. We set a time for us to meet her. We had a fine dinner at the Park Club and then dancing. It was a pleasant evening. Elaine spoke some English. There were no sparks; so, I remained vague about future plans. The next day, I returned to Norfolk for fourteen hours of sick call.

I returned to Paris and took a room in the Montparnasse. It was on the top floor. Fortunately the small lift worked. I had a view over the city and it was quite charming. On my first day there, I went shopping in a neighborhood store where the salesgirl, Odile, was quite attractive and pleasant. Odile had a perky manner and blond good looks that appealed to me; so I invited her out to dinner. She picked a bistro close by. No one there spoke English. But, of course I had a guide. She picked a nice meal that was surprisingly inexpensive.

Odile lived in a suburb; so after dinner I walked her to the Metro, but we agreed to meet on the following day, a Sunday. She was right on time in the lobby of my hotel. She took us to a resort area out of Paris at Pecq. There was a beautiful large swimming pool surrounded by a beach. The pool was on the edge of a river. The river in this area was a center for sail boating which made a lovely background. On the other side of the river on a wooded hill stood the Chateau du St. Germain and its large park. Near the pool, there was a casino which was partly damaged by bombing, but the bar was functioning. There was a row of cabins to dress in. Odile had brought a two piece bathing suit, and I rented trunks. The brevity of the French bathing suit was surprising to me. The girls wore about a three inch width of cloth for bras and no more than a G-string for their lower anatomy in most cases. Men's shorts were equally brief. Actually, I thought this style took away some of the female allure, in that little was left to the imagination. Odile had brought lunch, which consisted of a long baguette of bread split to make a huge sandwich of ham and excellent cheese. I bought a bottle of vin ordinaire. It was a lovely day. We swam and lay in the sun and talked. We returned to Paris in the early evening and had a light dinner in another small bistro close to my hotel. Cautiously, after dinner, I asked her to my room. She said she would come briefly; for she had to return home or her mother would worry.

The man at the desk made no comment when I picked up my key and we both rode up in the little lift with its folding gate. She explored the room briefly, then, we kissed. I had never been kissed like this. The remarkable use of the tongue was something worth knowing. We were both undressed helping each other here and there. There was a little daylight left and we had not turned on lights in the room. Her body was quite lovely. She was slender but had rather full breasts with erect nipples. She led me to the bed where after some wonderful exploration of each other, she introduced me to something about which I knew nothing, oral sex. It was as surprising as first sex. It was wonderful, and I wondered why I had never learned about it before. It only emphasized how unsophisticated a young doctor was in those days. We then proceeded to have more usual types of sex. We were both having a splendid, if somewhat exhausting, time. Suddenly, she said she had to go or she would miss the last train. Reluctantly, I got dressed and went with her to the metro station. She did not seem afraid of going home alone. We agreed to meet again.

The next day, I went to her shop to find another young woman there. She said that Odile had to stay home for "a while" because her mother was very ill. I agreed to check from time to time. I was terribly disappointed.

There was every reason to continue to enjoy Paris. I went to the Luxembourg Gardens which were bright with beautiful flowers. At one end of the garden stood the beautiful Palace. Marie de Medici built it for herself when her husband Henry IV died. I did not know too much about architecture, and I did not recognize the Italian influence. This palace had had many uses after the death of the queen. I elected not to go in. I then wandered back to the vicinity of Notre Dame and took a number of pictures with my trusty vest pocket Kodak. The film was still questionable. In the evening, I went to the hit musical comedy of Paris, "Un Femme par Jour." Even though, I did not understand too much French, I enjoyed the evening very much. The songs, music, dancing, and comedy were very good, and I only missed some of what must have been very clever lines, according to the laughter of the audience. It was by far the nicest theater in which I had been. It was much nicer, larger and newer than the homes of the Follies, and the Casino de Paris. The next day, Odile had not returned, and I returned to camp to do my weekly stint in the dispensary. The camp was full of rumors, but there were no movement orders. I collected more cognac and cigarettes to fund my next trip to Paris. Surprisingly, our store of alcoholic beverages was holding up. That night, I played a bit of poker with my usual success. The camp was dreary after Paris.

 I returned to Paris, this time staying in a pleasant little residential hotel in the section called Villers, a lovely district not far from the Arc. This hotel had very special rates for U.S. Army officers. It was nice to eat in a pleasant place where there was music, clean table cloths, good food, and nice company. The Army newspaper, Stars and Stripes suggested that we would probably be leaving for Le Harve in a few days. I resolved to make the most of them. I remarked to my friend Dave who had come with me, that, at this point, I felt more at home in Paris than at any other city besides San Francisco. The next morning, I went back to Pigalle to sell my Cognac and some, but not all, of my cigarettes. I was now well-funded especially, because I had done fairly well in the last poker game at camp.

 The city was abuzz with major news. The Russians had entered the war against Japan. Most of us felt that they were hoping to gain a great deal by that. On the other hand, we still felt indebted to the Russians for their help in destroying the German Army. The big news was that the U.S. had dropped a big bomb on a major Japanese city. I was one of a few who understood what that big bomb represented. I had learned of the potential of an atom bomb. My fear was that there might be world-wide effects from the radiation generated by the explosion. Doctor Lawrence had put that fear into our minds. There were no reports of problems beyond the target, but I still was worried.

    I walked along the Rue de la Paix, not far from my hotel, to the Ritz, which is on the Place Vendome. I particularly liked this square. There were uniform arcades at ground level. The buildings were all topped with pitched roofs, and there was a continuous row of dormer windows. The Ritz Hotel was at one side of the square. During the war, like the Crillon, it had been taken over by high ranking officers, but now it was returning to its status as one of the great hotels of the world. Though the area's buildings were closely built, the Ritz, had lovely gardens and courts. It was quiet and restful, not bustling and rushed like the best known American hotels. I had the most expensive lunch of my life in one of the courtyards with beautiful flowers and elegant people, especially the women.

    After lunch, I wandered through the shops in the area. They were the most luxurious I had seen, and now were well-stocked. The rue de la Paix was especially elegant. There were beautiful handbags, leather goods, and novelties, but the prices were huge. A cute ceramic pin caught my eye. It was not too elaborate but it cost almost five hundred Francs which was over ten dollars for me. So, it would not be difficult to think how expensive were more important items. The only merchandise I bought and paid for was perfume, which seemed like a relatively good buy and something safe to ship home. I got to be a collector of perfumes and resolved to take some home with me. I would very much have liked to buy other things I admired, but the costs were just too high. Interestingly, I frequently ran into people I knew from home. A number of men of my sister's generation, about four or five years older than I, were able to get headquarters jobs in places like Paris or London. In a way, I resented their wearing army uniforms; for I felt we had earned ours. But they knew how to work the system better that I did.

That evening, we heard that a second bomb had been dropped. I, for the first time, became quite sure that the war would end before we could get to the Pacific. The remaining question was when would we get to go home?

The next morning, as usual, I stopped by the shop where Odile worked. She was there. Her mother was a bit better, but still ill. It sounded to me as though she had mild to moderate heart failure. In any event, I suggested to Odile that she get dressed up that evening after work, and I would take her out for dinner. I felt that my time in Paris was almost over; so I wanted to see some of my favorite places. I went to the Montmartre to the little bar where I had played the piano to have a last drink with the owner. Then I walked over to Sacre Coeur to look out at the city. I went to Notre Dame to admire the rose window. Sainte-Chapelle was a must stop. I had an expensive coffee at a sidewalk table at the Cafe de la Paix near the opera and saw a number of people I knew. I had lunch in a sidewalk cafe on the Champs Élysées. I walked from there to my hotel, took a long shower, and dressed in my dress shirt and best pants. For the first time, I put on my decorations which included the Combat Medical Badge, the Bronze star with an oak leaf cluster (in place of a second medal), the E.T.O. ribbon with five battle stars. I even put on a tie. I then went to pick up Odile. She looked great. She had borrowed a simple black dress that showed her off well, and she wore her Hermes scarf. Her hair which was relatively short had a pert French look.

We went to a nightclub that had been taken over for officers, the Amoral. Odile was impressed. I do not think she had ever been in a place so elegant with crystal chandeliers, freshly painted furniture, and luxurious place settings. I picked a small booth for dinner. There was a dance floor. In addition to soldiers, there were a good number of civilians. I guessed that they worked for various Army offices in the city. The feeling was festive. That was because everyone felt that the war in the Pacific was winding down; though V.J. Day had not yet been proclaimed. We had a superb meal, beautifully served. We had a good deal about which to talk. Odile was about twenty and had had the equivalent of a high school education. She knew more English than I knew French but we managed. She asked some about my war experiences, but soon found that was not a good subject. She was curious about my impressions of Paris. Then there was dancing to a remarkably good orchestra. I am sure that Odile had never had such a splendid evening. Her eyes sparkled, and she enjoyed every second. It was obvious that she liked being with me. At midnight, there was a big drumroll, and an announcement. V.J. Day had been proclaimed. The room exploded with cheers. The French were happy for us because they knew that many of us had been slated to go to the Pacific. The next announcement was a bit of a shock. All soldiers based at Camp Norfolk were to return there that evening. I took Odile to her Metro stop, and after a long parting kiss, again I left a woman with tears running down her face. I picked up my gear and went to the motor pool where I knew I could pick up a ride back to camp.

The stay at Norfolk had been quite wonderful because of my frequent visits to Paris and also because Odile was great fun to be with.

Chapter 26

Lucky Strike

August, 1945

Almost immediately after V.J. Day, we moved to Camp Lucky Strike, which had originally been set up as a staging area for us to go on leave to the United States and then on to the Pacific. We were no longer responsible for our vehicles. For me, the only responsibility was occasional sick call. One thing that was made clear to us was that going home did not mean that we were out of the Army.

The Army's plan was to discharge men according to the number of points they had accumulated. The first group out was to have eighty five points, and I, in spite of my decorations and five battle stars, only had fifty-nine. My time of service was only about a year and a half, whereas many of our officers had been in the Army for three or four years. On the other hand, I had no idea what they would do with me and others in my situation. The outlook was even worse for the enlisted men. No consideration was given to the combat infantrymen. They always were in the poorest location, were at the greatest risk, got the fewest comforts, and accumulated the fewest points. They did get an extra five points for the combat infantry badge, but none of us felt that was enough reward for what they had been through. We all thought that men with pull would get out before the true fighting men.

I was thankful that I made it safely to this point and that I no longer would have to face combat. I had also thought that they might delay my trip home on leave, but the plans for moving my division had been completed, so we were going to be among the first to go home. Actually, now that the war was over, I would have welcomed the chance to tour a bit more.

We got to Camp Lucky Strike by third class railroad. It was a twenty four hour ride. After a night's sleep, I was ready to look around. We did not know how long we would be there, and there was nothing to do in this camp. I visited the little town of St. Valery about thirty miles away. Fortunately, I could still obtain a jeep and driver. From about twenty miles inland, I began to smell the sea, and I could hardly wait to get a look at it. That had been the main reason for my trip. It was very pleasant once more to see the ocean. San Franciscans all have a fondness for the sea, and I was surprised at how much I had missed the ocean after being away from it for so long.

The town of St. Valery had sustained terrible damage, most of which was not yet repaired. It lay in a break in the very steep cliffs that form a natural fortress along the coast. It was here that the Scots landed on D-day. A murderous landing it must have been. The fortifications were terrific, and there was only one draw where an invading force could land. Because of the steep cliffs, the final victory of these brave men was truly amazing.

The fortifications were still intact. The obstructions in the water were still present. There were still masses of barbed wire along the tops of the cliffs, and all of the mines had not yet been removed from the beach. Our armies had met and overcome so much and so bravely. We had every reason to be proud. We felt that we had met the best the enemy had to offer, and we—amateurs at war, by German standards—had beat the hell out of them. Certainly, we made some terrible mistakes, but the surprising thing was that we did not make more. We had won, and there was no question about that. All of us hoped that this hard won peace would hold.

We were pleased to hear that our stay at Lucky Strike would be brief, only a couple of days. To our surprise, we were to have about two weeks in England, and then early in September, were to go home by ship. I hoped to be able to visit London and perhaps other parts of England. It rained most of the remaining time in France, and that reminded us of our time in Normandy just over a year before.

We played a lot of cards, and on the last night, I got into the highest stakes game of poker in my life. After midnight, I was quite far ahead and was ready to quit and go to bed. But, there was a major in the game who had lost quite a bit and insisted that we continue. Quite awhile later, he and I got into quite a hand.

We had both bet rather heavily. It was a hand that I probably should have dropped on, but I could afford to see it through. A number of other players stayed for the draw. I had four hearts—the two, three, four, and five—and an off card. I planned to draw to them to make a flush, or a straight. The major had two pairs, one of which was aces. We each drew one card. He drew a third ace, so he had one of the best hands in poker. I drew the six of hearts giving me a straight flush—an even better hand.

Our betting became intense, and with a number of raises. The other players had dropped out. The major bet all the money he had and even placed his watch as added security. Now, there was no point in raising, and I might not have done so anyhow. This was the best hand of my life. Of course, my hand won. I refused to take the major's watch. That still did not make him happy.

I now had about four hundred pounds, which was a fortune in those days. A pound was worth over four dollars. There was an Army rule that the largest bill we could have was a one pound note. It had something to do with trying to keep soldiers from selling their equipment on the black market. A bunch of one pound notes would be difficult to hide. In anticipation of our trip to England, we all had converted whatever money we had to pounds, and I now had a musette bag full of one pound notes. This was more money than I had ever had and represented more than a half year's salary. I was more than ready for England.

I found Dave Roth and he agreed to go to London with me. He had a wife and a child, so I said the trip would be on me. We went in assorted ships to Southampton. We were told that we were to sail on the Queen Mary in two weeks and could do whatever we wanted during that time. Our division of some 15,000 had housing allocated close by. Those who wished to travel were free to do so, and it was their responsibility to be back when the ship sailed. The powers were sure that no one would miss this boat.

Dave and I packed lightly and went to the train station where we bought tickets to London, first class this time. In London, we got a cab, and the driver had a wonderful cockney accent. I asked him what was a good hotel in London. He said, "The Savoy is a good hotel," so I asked him to take us there, and could he find us some Scotch whiskey on the way? Good Scotch was not easy to find, but cab drivers know how to find things. We bought a couple of bottles.

We arrived at the Savoy in our best combat clothes, which were certainly not elegant. Our dress uniforms had been sent ahead before we knew we were to stop in England. At the door, I asked the driver how much he made a day. It was not a large amount, so I asked him how would he like to be our driver while we were in England. He was more than pleased to do so and waited at the door while we went to ask about accommodations.

The man behind the desk in this imposing lobby was in formal dress. He said that, unfortunately, there were no rooms available. I said that was indeed unfortunate, because we had heard such good things about the Savoy. I thought that perhaps they did not want soldiers, particularly those dressed as we were, but this proved not to be the case. A manager overhearing our conversation said they did have a suite and that we could have it for the price of a room. That was great news.

We were escorted to the suite by a porter who carried our skimpy baggage, while I carried the musette bag. There was a large parlor looking over the Thames, a bedroom with two large beds, and the largest bathroom we had ever seen, with two sinks, a toilet, a bidet, and a huge tub with a spray that could be used as a shower. Luxury!

We cleaned up. The English love decorations, so Dave and I put ours on. Then, I converted some of my money to larger bills, and though I left most of it in the hotel safe, what I took with me in my pocket that day was more money than I had ever had in my pocket before.

Outside, in the cul de sac that led up to the Savoy, was our driver. We told him that we were ready for lunch. He knew just the place, which was a pub nearby. We had been in pubs before in Bodmin and Plymouth. This one was a bit more elegant. The dining room was upstairs, but we chose to eat in the bar where a pleasant barmaid was making sandwiches. We ordered, got large tankards of beer, and felt just marvelous.

People seemed happy to see us. During the war, the British often resented Yanks, because they were a bit noisy and had much more money than the British soldiers. But now, most of the Americans had already left London—the Headquarters types had the pull to get home fast—and already there was a bit of nostalgia. We were treated well. I probably tipped too much.

After lunch, I asked the cab driver if he could find me some film for my vest pocket camera, and he did. It was much better film than I had had for a long while. I then asked him to take us around London. I still have the photographs I took. We saw the Admiralty Arch, Pall Mall, Buckingham Palace, the Scotch Guard in bearskin helmets, and the great statue of Queen Victoria. We passed St. James Palace, a red brick affair with many chimneys and crenelated battlements and wandered about Piccadilly Circus for a bit. Our next stop was Trafalgar Square and Nelson's Monument in the center, guarded by four huge lions. I particularly liked the Christopher Wren church close by.

As we drove around we were appalled to see how much of the city was missing because of the damage caused by bombs. It was strange to see a huge area with no building standing, yet adjacent to it neoclassical buildings in surprisingly good shape, such as the pub where we had lunch. The vacant areas—which were everywhere—had been cleaned up. Bricks were piled neatly. But, no reconstruction had begun, probably because most of the workmen were still away in the various services and also because the war had been over only for a short time. I had not expected to see such devastation.

In the late afternoon, we returned to the hotel. I asked the hall porter what would be a good thing for us to do that evening, and he suggested that we might enjoy eating in the Grill and then going to a play at the theater next door. That sounded great to us.

We retired to our room for some Scotch, baths, and a rest. The Grill was quite elegant. We were glad that we had selected it; since the dining room was even more formal. We had our first fish since leaving the U.S. The waiter suggested Dover sole, and it was delicious, although quite expensive. We had some wine and felt regal. After dinner, we went next door to the Savoy Theater. The play was "The First Gentleman" with Robert Morley as Prince Regent in 1814 and Wendy Hiller as his daughter, Princess Charlotte. Morely was already famous, and Wendy Hiller, though young, was obviously very good. There was a large, good cast. We agreed that it was one of the best plays we had ever seen. Of course the circumstances made it even better.

After the theater, we returned to our splendid quarters and called the valet, a pleasant older gentleman. We gave him our uniforms, including Eisenhower jackets, and asked him to see if he could spruce them up. We also gave him our shoes and even our dirty clothes. We then hit those luxurious beds and slept wonderfully.

In the morning, we ordered English breakfast in our room. Despite shortages, it had everything: bacon, eggs, scones, jam, sausages, and a huge pot of poor coffee. While eating, we searched the newspaper that came with breakfast for things we might want to see or do. While all this was going on, the valet brought our clothes. We hardly recognized them. The trousers had razor creases. The jackets had not only been cleaned, but also the various insignia—division shoulder patch, cloth gold bars representing time overseas, Presidential Citation patch, and others had been sewn on in a much more professional manner than I had been able to do. Our jackets were worthy of General Eisenhower. We could see ourselves in the shine on our shoes. Wonderful!

We were ready to see more of the city. We arranged for tickets that evening at the Palladium near Oxford Circus. Then, we were met at the door by our driver.

Our first stop was St. Paul's Cathedral. To us, it was truly remarkable that this magnificent structure, with its huge dome, had not been seriously damaged, though it stood surrounded by devastation from the bombing. Because most of the raids had been at night, I could not believe that the Germans deliberately spared St. Paul's. The most impressive part of the interior was the vastness of the space. I believe that the windows had been covered or removed during the fighting, but now wonderful light poured in. The elegant wood carving throughout, which I had learned to appreciate long before, I found out had been done by the famous wood worker Grinling Gibbons.

We went from there to see the Tower of London and the Tower Bridge, both powerful symbols of London to us. I do not recall why we did not go inside the Tower. Perhaps we felt we had so much more to see and that day were trying to get a feel for the city as a whole. We drove to Westminster Abbey, where a great deal of work was being done to repair damage of the war. Again, it had miraculously survived, as had most of the Palace of Westminster, the seat of government. Big Ben was functioning.

We went to another pub in the area for lunch. It, too, had survived the bombing, though many buildings in the area had been demolished. Then, we spent the afternoon wandering about the stores. For the most part, there was a bit more merchandise for sale than we had expected. Most everything was expensive. Though I had plenty of money, I hesitated to buy anything of value, being uncertain of shipment. There were some very good buys in silver. The general mood of the people was elevated, though everyone seemed to have lost friends or relatives in the war.

For dinner, the hall porter at the hotel sent us to Rules, a restaurant nearby. It was probably the oldest restaurant in London and was in a district that had sustained some damage. It was a bit run down, but had a certain English charm. We drank Scotch and water—of course with no ice—and grouse served rare. We did not especially like it, but accepted it as part of the scene. The dessert was trifle. I liked that mixture of fruit, cream, and I do not know what else. After dinner, we went to the Palladium to see a musical, "Funfare, Happy and Glorious." It was a musical review with some comedy and a good deal of flag waving, mostly British and American. We enjoyed it.

Our days continued in a similar vein. We particularly enjoyed the theater, especially "Sweet and Low," starring the great British comedienne, Hermione Gingold. We laughed more that evening than we had in the entire time since we left home. Years later, I had the chance to see Hermione Gingold again and also Wendy Hiller, whom we had seen on our first night. We saw Daphne du Maurier's "The Years Between," Phyllis Dixley, England's most popular pin-up girl, in "Peek-a-Boo Again," a night club like show that went on most of the night. We took in a very English farce, "See How They Run," which had an extremely long run.

We decided that we should see some of the countryside and went to Oxford, which was a pleasant surprise. The hotels were full, so we stayed in a bed and breakfast in a very old building on Magpie Lane near the beautiful church of St. Mary-the-Virgin. We saw Christ Church, Oriel, Corpus Christi, Merton, and Magdalen. We thought Merton was particularly beautiful, with its lovely tower and spacious grounds. We ate in pubs.

Our breakfast at Oxford came as a big surprise after those we had at the Savoy. The main dish was kippers, that rather dry smoked fish, and to us neither exciting nor what we would think of as breakfast. However, that was what they had, and that is what we ate, along with bread and jam, and butter, which was still not easy to get.

We passed Blenheim Palace on the way back to London, and I guess it was the largest residence we had seen anywhere. It was a rainy day, so we did not stop on our way to the Savoy, where they had kept our room for us.

I asked the hall porter, who obviously knew everything, where we could get some non-professional female company. We just were not interested in the prostitutes, who swarmed in the Piccadilly area. He suggested a dance for service men to be held that evening in the hotel ballroom. After dinner in the Grill, we went. There was a good orchestra playing for a large number of service people and some civilians. Since most Americans had already left town, there was an excess of women. Dave and I danced with a number of them and finally, we each selected the one that we liked the most.

My choice was a WREN serving in the female branch of the Royal Navy. Her name was Rebecca, and she did not like to be called Becky. She had worked in Naval Headquarters through the war, had spent many nights in shelters, and had survived the horrendous bombing of the area in which she lived.

She had short-cropped light brown hair and interesting hazel eyes. We found it easy to talk with each other, and I did not have to worry about language difficulties. So that was a pleasure I had not had for over a year, except in the couple of instances when I was with American nurses. Dave had disappeared with his choice, and I took Rebecca home in our cab. Dave and I had plans for the next couple of nights, so I invited her out for the evening three nights later, which would be our last night in London.

We had heard that Bournemouth had a lovely beach and was a popular place for Londoners to go. The next day, still keeping our room at the Savoy, we left in our cab for the coast. The best part of the trip was a stop at a small town along the way, where we stopped at a small shop for something to eat and came out to find the cab surrounded by children. They had never seen a London cab, and we let them climb in and look around. I went back to the shop and bought a bunch of hard candies and gave them to the well mannered kids. Then, we drove off to Bournemouth amid cheers.

We got to town and the weather was miserable. It was cold and gloomy, and the large beach looked uninviting. Our driver took us to Compton Acres nearby, which had a number of different types of gardens—Japanese, English, and others—but they had had minimal care during the war. We returned to the hotel, which was reasonably nice, but dull, and then went to a movie. We went to bed early and decided to return to London. The only good part of the trip was the kids and the London cab.

That night, I picked up Rebecca and took her to a restaurant close to where she lived, Scott's on Piccadilly. It was a fine restaurant with polished wood and specialized in fish. I had eaten very little fish for over a year. I had liked the Dover sole at the Savoy, so I ordered it again, in spite of its high price. We had drinks before dinner. Mine was Scotch and water, and hers was sherry.

She was a very practical woman and was planning to go to University as soon as she got out of the WRENS. She had been very matter of act about the horrors of the bombing, and I was sure that she would rather forget it, as I wanted to forget the horrors of war. After dinner, we went to Noel Coward's "Sigh No More," a comedy of manners with the fine actor, Cyril Ritchard, and a very good actress Madge Elliott. We both enjoyed it.

On this night, Dave got our cab. London curtain times were early. Our performance began at 6:45. It was not far to Rebecca's apartment. She invited me in. One thing led to another and we ended up in bed together. We both knew nothing special could come of this. I was surprised at this development but, of course, welcomed it. We both enjoyed ourselves. She was obviously an experienced woman, and this was not a short evening. When I got home, I sent her as a gift a package containing coffee and other things hard to get in England at that time.

It was time to return to Southampton. Our bill at the Savoy was not as large as I had expected. Our cab driver took us to the railroad station, and I think he was sorry to see us Yanks go. I paid him and gave him a generous tip. I still had quite a lot of money left. The trip to London had been a great reward.

Shows we saw in London 1945

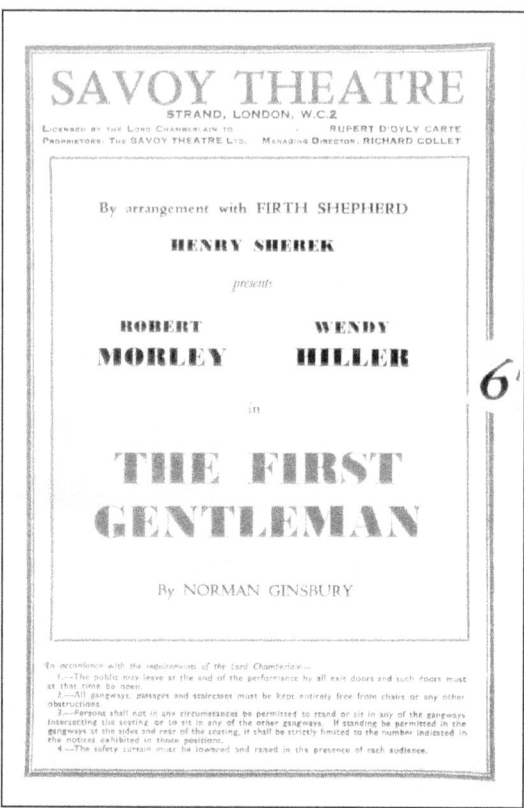

Shows we saw in London 1945

Lucky Strike 251

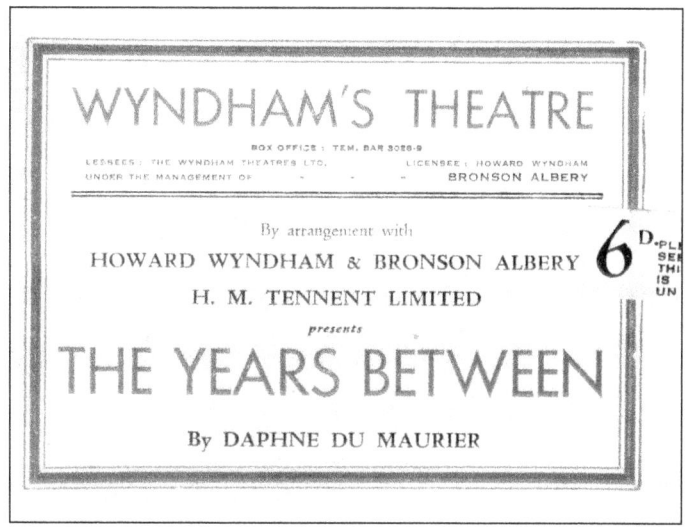

Shows we saw in London 1945

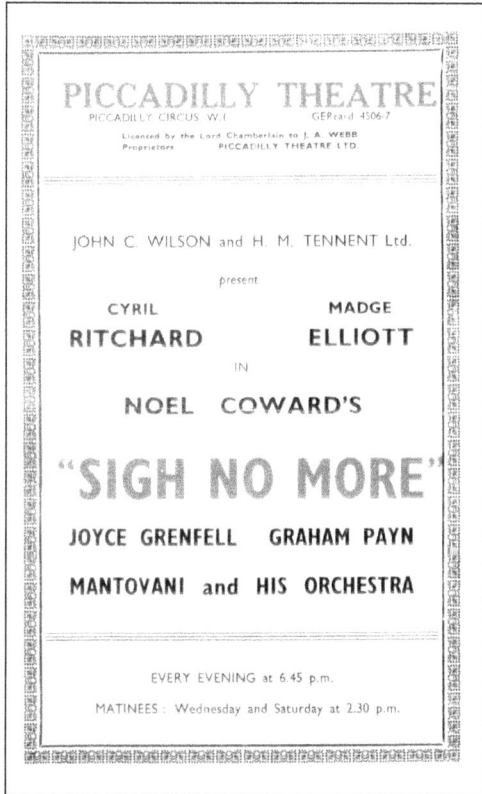

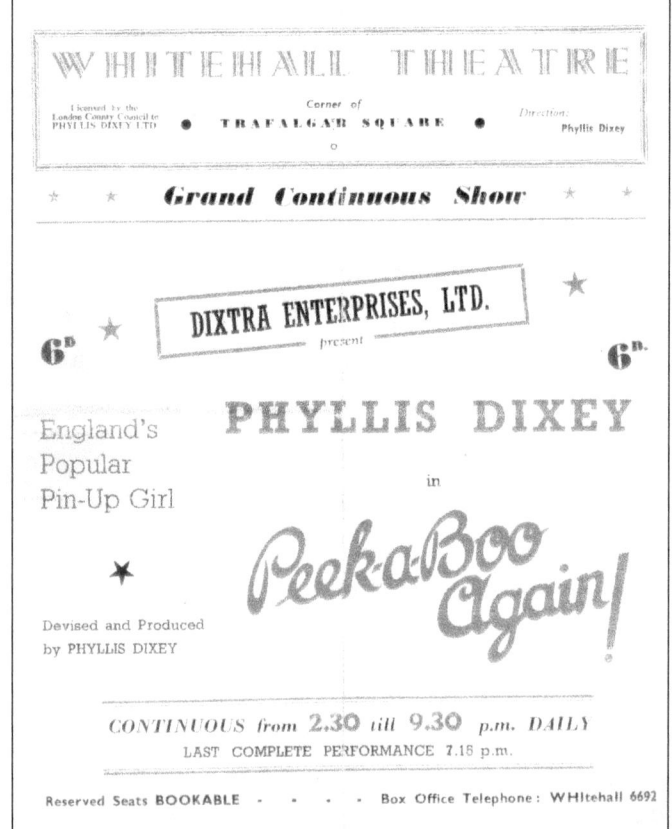

Chapter 27

Home

August–December 1945

The ship that took us home was the Queen Mary. It was a beautiful large ship set up to hold fifteen thousand men of our 35th Division. Half the men slept while the other half were on deck. Our cabin, designed to accommodate two, had layered bunks for six officers. We slept when we could. No one complained. We were going home.

The dining-room had been kept as it had been for passengers. It was large with a high ceiling, elegantly set tables, and was reached by a flight of broad stairs. The staff was well-trained, and the food was quite good. All of this was in dramatic contrast to the living quarters on board for officers and men.

We played a lot of cards, mostly poker, but some hearts and bridge. I did well in all of them, and my considerable funds gave me an advantage over most other players. On board ship, we were required to wear a tie and often an overseas cap. I wore only one decoration, my Combat Medical Badge, of which there were few. We sailed from Southampton September 5.

It was a quick trip home, since the Queen Mary was the fastest passenger ship afloat. Someone had made a huge map of the areas in which we had traveled and had it fastened along the side

Back in the U.S.A. waiting to fly home

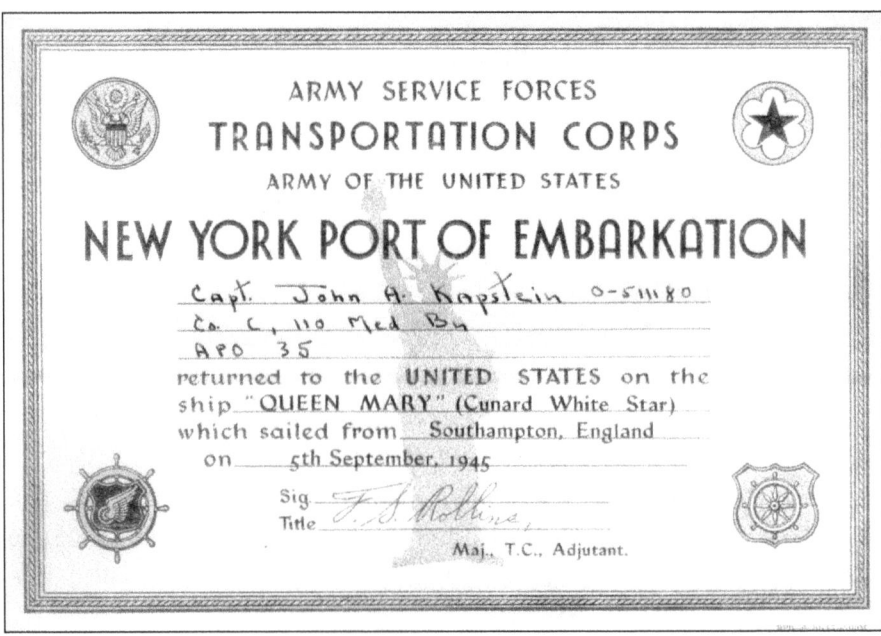

Embarcation pass

of the ship. The official count of those aboard was 14,943. Besides the 35th, there were 388 from the Navy, 197 WACs, 60 Army nurses, 25 Red Cross workers, and 63 civilians. It was quite a load. I did not talk with one woman all the way. We arrived in New York September 10.

Our general, Paul Baade, was quoted in various papers as saying, "If there are any soldiers better than these anywhere, I'd like to know it." He went on to say, "Every time they needed someone to block a hole, they threw us in. They are all good soldiers in our Army, but there are none better than mine." The division had had 25,000 casualties which was more than the total number of men in the division. We had had many replacements. Only a few of us at battalion level made it back: only 15% of those who landed were with us when we returned to New York.

Our division was the one in which President Truman had served in World War I. So he made special mention of what we had done. The *New York Times* devoted a major amount of space describing our return and our accomplishments. As we landed there were cheers from all aboard, and the huge horn of the Mary blew. There was an Army band. The decks were full, soldiers leaned out of portholes. It was great!

We were to get thirty days leave and then return to Camp Breckenridge. We were taken by train to Camp Kilmer in New Jersey to await transport home. By some good fortune, I was put on a plane. It was an old DC8. The door was held shut with bailing wire, and the seats were rough, but I did not care. The plane had flown a huge number of missions as a transport, and I felt it could make one more. This was my first time on a plane, so I did not have the sense to worry. Besides, I was going home.

My orders: "to reception station Camp Beale, Calif. Rept. to CO for purpose of being ordered to desired places of recuperation, rehabilitation and recovery for a period not to exceed thirty days, plus travel time, upon completion of which will return to Camp Breckenridge, KY." Beale was near Sacramento. I caught a truck that was going to the Presidio in San Francisco and was on my way.

O CHRONICLE, TUESDAY, SEPT. 11, 1945   PAGE 3

ETO Veterans

Queen Mary Brings Back 15,000; Gen. Baade Returns With the 35th

NEW YORK, Sept. 10 (AP)—The British liner Queen Mary, her sides decorated with so many banners she looked like a huge floating billboard, slid out of the fog into New York harbor today, jammed with nearly 15,000 veterans of the European war.

Yells, whistles and shouts of the soldiers, mostly Kansans, Missourians and Nebraskans from President Truman' old World War I Division, the 35th, heralded the ship's arrival as she ended her fifth westward crossing. The noise reached the dock long before the liner did.

Soldiers and the largest contingent of WACS to be returned to the United States from Europe covered every inch of space on the open decks.

They hung from ladders and thrust their heads through portholes. A huge may of Europe on the starboard side had heads where Paris and Berlin were located.

"OH, HAPPY DAY"

One sign, showing four happy soldiers singing and bearing the wagon wheel of the old Santa Fe Trail, the insignia of the 35th, read, "Oh, Happy Day!"

Another emblazoned in red, white and blue, said "Hello America—35th Division." Still another, fastened to the deck, declared "Dear Mom—Your Boy Has Returned," and was signed by three New Yorkers.

The ship carried the one millionth soldier to sail home from Le Havre since V-E Day. He was Corporal Almon N. Conger of Tacoma, Wash., Army officials said.

Returning with his troops was Major General Paul W. Baade, commanding general of the 35th. He led his men down the gangplank, and said "if there are any better soldiers anywhere, I would like to know it."

"Every time they needed somebody to block a hole," the general said, "they threw us in. They are all good soldiers in the Army, but none of them are better than mine."

The division suffered 15,800 casualties, he said, adding that of its original strength of 13,000 men, only 15 per cent remain.

BRITISH OFFICIALS

Although the men were ordered home for redeployment to the Pacific, General Baade said he did not think they would be sent. He said the division would be reassembled at Camp Breckenridge after the men had 30-day furloughs.

Also aboard were a number of British officials, including Admiral of the Fleet Sir James Somerville, head of the British military mission to Washington, and General Sir Hastings Ismay, personal military adviser to Prime Minister Attlee.

My parents had a small but nice apartment at 1101 Green Street on Russian Hill. The apartment was on one of the top floors with views of the Bay. On my way through town to the apartment, I saw that San Francisco had not really changed. It looked clean and bright. It was the first city I had seen in a while that had not in some way been damaged, with the possible exception of the center of Paris. People seemed to be going about business as usual. I was a bit surprised to see a number of young men in civilian clothes, and I wondered how they had avoided service.

When I got to the apartment, my parents were not home, but Eula was. She was a black woman who had worked for my parents and my sister for many years. She was like a member of the family and greeted me with a bear hug. She then held me at arm's length to get a view of me, and she liked what she saw. She said that my mother had gone to get my father from his store. Because the apartment had only one bedroom, they had set me up in a large closet, which was all right with me.

I was eating a piece of Eula's fried chicken when my folks walked in. They had expected me much later in the day, and they could not believe their eyes. My mom of course, got a little teary, but a hug and some kisses rapidly cleared that up. She was well-dressed, as always, in a black suit with a big bow at her neck. My dad also greeted me with a big hug and kiss. He and I had been in the habit of greeting and separating with a kiss. He, as always, was well-dressed in a gray double breasted suit, with a white handkerchief in his breast pocket, and a tie.

Questions poured out at me. They were impressed, that though I had gained weight, I looked in great condition. I do believe they expected to see a thin, beaten-down soldier. I found that all of the family were well, but I wanted to see the others. At the time, my brother was in the Navy stationed at Saipan. As soon as I finished more of Eula's wonderful chicken—which really convinced me I was home—we left for my sister's home in our family car, a black Cadillac Seville.

I had on the clothes I had worn in London, complete with a growing amount of "fruit salad" (decorations): the Combat Medical Badge, a Bronze Star ribbon with Oak Leaf Cluster representing a second Bronze Star, an ETO ribbon with five Battle Stars, a North Atlantic Ribbon for surviving the crossing going over, an Occupation Ribbon, and a Victory Ribbon. Most of the time, I wore only the most important ones, which were the Bronze Star, the Combat Medical Badge, and the ETO ribbon with five Battle Stars.

My sister, her husband, and their four children greeted me with enthusiasm, and everyone was impressed with how well I looked. We had drinks and dinner—my first home dinner in about twenty months—and tried to bring each other up to date. My Dad's store had been doing well, and he looked forward to my brother joining him. My brother planned to get an advanced degree at Stanford after the war. The Navy sent him to Harvard Business School. My mother had a growing business in interior design. My brother-in-law had been involved in supplying certain foods for the armed services. My sister had been a volunteer for the Red Cross. I was especially pleased to see my sister's children, and I told the girls how I had their names put on my command truck. The boy had not really known me. They were all interested in my uniform. Most of the evening was spent in bringing me up to date on San Francisco.

I returned to the apartment with my parents. We talked about my plans. I went to bed depressed. I could not understand it. I had been looking forward so much to getting home. But it was disturbing that everyone in San Francisco had been going about his business as usual. What should I have expected?

The next day, I made two calls. I found that Chris was away at school in Oregon. I had hoped that, knowing I was coming home, she would be in town. I called my professor, Doctor Traut, and told him that I expected to be out of the service by some time early next year. He was cordial and said there would be a spot for me whenever I got out, but to give him as much warning as possible. He told me that he was impressed by my military service, especially since he had served in World War I. I thanked him for that and for his reassuring letter. But that was all I was inclined to do. I was not up to calling friends, and anyway, most of them were still away in the service. I was not especially interested in dates.

My mother had bought me a large leather scrapbook with my name engraved on the cover. I had brought all the pictures that I had taken home with me and spent a couple of days putting them in the book, along with some special papers, like the citations for the medals. I was getting more depressed.

I did go out and walk around a bit. In her practical way, my mother suggested that I get out and make some dates. I called the most attractive young women I had known before the war and one or two suggested by my sister. I still had a great deal of money, and my father, as always, was generous in his offers to provide more if I needed it.

The dates, though with lovely young women, were boring. These girls had not done much in relation to the war effort. They had been in college, but did not seem smart to me. We usually went dancing. Some danced better than others. There was one, Meta, whom I did like, but she seemed to have been already taken. In general the young women were looking for husbands, not careers. They did not understand what war was about, and I was not about to try to tell them.

I went to see my friend Bill, who was in a hospital where they were trying to repair his wrist shattered by a bullet in eastern France. He kept his helmet, which had a bullet hole in it. The bullet had gashed his scalp, but fortunately did not enter his skull. I went to my club to see what was going on there. The men there were mostly of my brother-in-law's age. They had been deferred because of their families or some other reason. I left. I read a lot. Somehow or other I just could not get used to it all.

A couple of days before, I agreed to a blind date. A good friend of my parents "knew a girl who would be great for John to meet." My family knew her family, though not well. Her father was a busy lawyer. Her family lived in St. Francis Wood, a nice residential area across the city. I had resisted a number of blind dates, but for some reason, I thought I would give this young woman a try.

Gwen lived in a lovely Spanish-type home which was approached through a very nice patio with flowers growing around. She met me at the door, and I was struck by her good looks. She was about five feet two with long, light brown hair and blue eyes set in a lovely face. I met her mother who was pleasant and there was a bit of talk about mutual friends. We went dancing at the Mark Hopkins Hotel on Nob Hill. A wonderful thing for me was that in San Francisco, dress uniform was a dress "green" shirt and "pink" pants. No tie was required. The Mark accepted that policy, of course. I got a table near the dance floor. I ordered a Scotch and water; she ordered a soft drink. I suggested that she try Bourbon and soda or ginger ale. She did not usually drink except when her father made Old Fashions on special occasions, but she ordered a bourbon and soda, and seemed to like it.

She was a very bright woman and a Stanford Phi Beta Kappa. At that time, there were not many women who made that society. She danced like a dream. That was a special pleasure. Though I was only a fair dancer, I loved dancing. It had been years since I had danced with anyone who was really good. Gwen worked for the State in a secretarial job. That, too, was unusual; since none of the girls I had known in San Francisco worked, except for Chris. Gwen had grown up in San Francisco, as had her parents, but I had never heard of her before. Our paths just had not crossed. She had met a number of service men during the war, but I think I may have been the first she had known who had been in combat.

I felt at ease with her, and something told me that she could well be the girl for me. After all the women I had met at home and overseas and after all my experiences, this woman seemed to me to be the ideal companion—for life.

Suddenly, more of my friends began arriving home, and my mother decided that I should have a cocktail party before I returned to duty. When I took Gwen home, I invited her to the cocktail party at my parents' apartment a couple of days later. Fortunately, she could come. Her father brought her, and he said he would pick her up after a couple of hours. When she walked in, I looked at her and somehow felt a surge that meant something special had happened to me. A number of my friends and their dates were there, so I introduced her around. Some of the young men present asked who she was and why they had not met her. I told them she was mine, but I do not think they paid any attention to my claim. They knew I had just met her.

November 6, 1945, just when I was feeling that things were looking up, I received orders to report to Camp Breckenridge in Kentucky. The war was over, yet the doctors from my unit were ordered to that godforsaken spot, where there was a hospital, but little to do. It seemed that the commanding officer wanted people to command. Almost all of the patients in this small hospital were German prisoners of war. We were not near any major town, and all we wanted to do was to get out.

One United States senator appreciated the plight of soldiers being kept on active duty with nothing special to do. I got together a petition signed by all of the doctors who were with me and sent it to him. He wired me back that he would be happy to examine each case if I would send the number of points that each of us had accumulated. his wire stirred up our commanding officer. As punishment, November 20, he separated me from my friends and sent me off to Wakeman General Hospital in Camp Atterbury, Indiana.

This was an active hospital. When I reported there, the commanding officer said, "Captain, you have been in combat all this time. What would you like to do?" I asked him what was the best service in his hospital. He replied that his hospital was the plastic surgery center for the United States Army. I asked to be assigned there. The next day, I reported to Colonel Blocker, one of the world's leading plastic surgeons. (Later an institute was created for him in Texas.)

Dr. Blocker immediately put me to work. He was doing great work in reconstructing faces that had been partially blown away. To reconstruct, he often brought tissue from the abdominal wall. This was done in stages: first a tube was made of abdominal wall tissue, and it was attached to the chest. When adequate circulation was established, the end which had been attached to the abdomen was attached to part of the face, and when that developed blood supply, the lower end also was attached to the face. Then the tissue was molded to fit the defect. He also reconstructed ears and other parts of the body. To raise the morale of the men beginning the reconstruction process, Dr. Blocker would always place these men upon whom he intended to work in wards with men whose reconstruction was near completion. It was not unusual for reconstruction to take over a year.

The way we worked was quite wonderful. Dr. Blocker would outline for me what he wanted done. We worked in an operating room with two tables. He would be at one and I at the other. We each had assistants. We sat in comfortable chairs. He said, "I don't care how long it takes you, but do just as I tell you." So, I made careful incisions and learned to use multiple and very fine stitches, often of very fine wire. After that time, I was known for my beautiful scars, even though most were on the abdominal walls of my patients.

Though I was enjoying this work, I was restless. I wanted to get back to Gwen, get out of the Army, and get on with my life. Thanksgiving, a major event in my family, was miserable for me, as were Christmas and New Year's. I probably drank too much at the best officers club I had seen in the United States, which also had unusually good food. I had very little social life. But I worked hard and did learn.

One day, I went to headquarters to see what my chances were of getting out. I had enough points, but the Army bureaucracy moved slowly. The general trend was to get out in two to six months. I met a tech sergeant who worked in the office. He had once been stationed in San Francisco, so we had a lot to talk about. He said that he was working on some discharge orders and would add my name, since I was qualified, at least in his eyes. I said, "Great," not knowing whether or not he could swing it. Within a day or so, I received the orders. "WP his home at 1101 Green St., San Francisco, for relief from AD (active duty), not by reason of disability, w/TDY en route at Sep. C (separation center) Cp. Beale, Calf., as required for processing." I was to report there January 14, 1946.

Naturally, I was overjoyed. I took fond farewell of Colonel Blocker and traveled by train to Camp Beale near Sacramento, arriving on the 14th. I was offered promotion to Major if I signed up for the reserves, but I was not interested; I wanted out. That decision kept me out of Korea. I hitched a ride on a truck going to San Francisco and was home the next day, with six weeks of terminal leave with full pay and a chest full of various ribbons and my Combat Medical Badge.

Doctor Traut was true to his word. Only a few days later, he put me to work as a resident in the University of California Service at the San Francisco Hospital.

Gwen had written to me daily, and we found that my initial impression was right. We were secretly engaged in February and married June 16, 1946.

JOHN A KAPSTEIN

To you who answered the call of your country and served in its Armed Forces to bring about the total defeat of the enemy, I extend the heartfelt thanks of a grateful Nation. As one of the Nation's finest, you undertook the most severe task one can be called upon to perform. Because you demonstrated the fortitude, resourcefulness and calm judgment necessary to carry out that task, we now look to you for leadership and example in further exalting our country in peace.

Harry Truman

THE WHITE HOUSE

Afterthoughts

Looking back on World War II from the perspective of 2001, I have a number of lasting impressions. Most important: there is no excuse for wars and their horror. There is little glory in combat. My first days in combat are burned into my brain. The days were long, and I seem to recall graphically almost everything concerned with that period: the confusion, the terrain, the weather, even trivialities. I remember the terrible wounds. These memories were brought to light by the letters I had written, and that had been saved. I did not look at those letters until about three years ago. They reminded me of why I have supported anti-war movements. The acquisition of a field typewriter early after the invasion, left behind by a chaplain working with me, made it possible to write more then, and while writing of those times, to have more information.

In 1944, our army had widespread prejudices. African-American soldiers were not treated as equals. In almost all cases, they were in separate units commanded by white officers. Yet they did exemplary service. The *Red Ball Express*, a unit of black truckers who brought supplies to us as we advanced from the beach in Normandy, was one example. We worked with an excellent tank outfit in which the highest-ranking black officer was noncommissioned. Jews fared a little better, but there was widespread anti-semitism. I noted that Jewish officers rated as "superior" often were passed over when advancement in command was available. In most cases, the Army could not avoid promoting combat officers who put in their time; however, the best positions rarely went to Jews. That experience led me to change my name from Kapstein to Kerner when I married. I did not want my children to face that sort of prejudice. There has been a considerable change for the better when we see military leaders like Generals Colin Powell and Creighton Abrams.

We are so indebted to the World War II medics. Despite the enormous casualty rate during the invasion, ninety-nine percent of the wounded evacuated to England survived. In administering morphine and cigarettes, the medics often eased the way for the dying.

At that time, I felt that I was doing the right thing in trying to help stop the Nazis, and I still do. However, had our leaders acted earlier, with political wisdom and economic aid, I think they could have prevented that war and those that followed.

John Kerner, M.D.

For sales, editorial information, subsidiary rights information or a catalog, please write or phone or email:

iBooks
1230 Park Avenue, 9a
New York, NY 10128, US
Sales: 1-800-68-BRICK
Tel: 212-427-7139
www.BrickTowerPress.com
email: bricktower@aol.com

www.Ingram.com

www.ingramcontent.com/pod-product-compliance
Lightning Source LLC
Chambersburg PA
CBHW030639150426